The Kant Dictionary

BLOOMSBURY PHILOSOPHY DICTIONARIES

The *Bloomsbury Philosophy Dictionaries* offer clear and accessible guides to the work of some of the more challenging thinkers in the history of philosophy. A-Z entries provide clear definitions of key terminology, synopses of key works, and details of each thinker's major themes, ideas and philosophical influences. The *Dictionaries* are the ideal resource for anyone reading or studying these key philosophers.

Titles available in the series:

The Deleuze and Guattari Dictionary, Eugene B. Young with Gary Genosko and Janell Watson

The Derrida Dictionary, Simon Morgan Wortham

The Descartes Dictionary, Kurt Smith

The Gadamer Dictionary, Chris Lawn and Niall Keane

The Hegel Dictionary, Glenn Alexander Magee

The Heidegger Dictionary, Daniel O. Dahlstrom

The Husserl Dictionary, Dermot Moran and Joseph Cohen

The Marx Dictionary, Ian Fraser and Lawrence Wilde

The Merleau-Ponty Dictionary, Donald A. Landes

The Nietzsche Dictionary, Douglas Burnham

The Sartre Dictionary, Gary Cox

BLOOMSBURY PHILOSOPHY DICTIONARIES

The Kant Dictionary

LUCAS THORPE

BLOOMSBURY

LONDON • NEW DELHI • NEW YORK • SYDNEY

Bloomsbury Academic

An imprint of Bloomsbury Publishing Plc

50 Bedford Square	1385 Broadway
London	New York
WC1B 3DP	NY 10018
UK	USA

www.bloomsbury.com

Bloomsbury is a registered trade mark of Bloomsbury Publishing Plc

First published 2015

© Lucas Thorpe, 2015

Lucas Thorpe has asserted his right under the Copyright, Designs and Patents Act, 1988, to be identified as Author of this work.

Financial support for work on this project was provided by Boğaziçi Universitesi BAP project 5706: Realism from Kant and Reid to Sellars, Williamson and McDowell

British Library Cataloguing-in-Publication Data
A catalogue record for this book is available from the British Library.

ISBN: HB: 978-1-8470-6578-0
PB: 978-1-8470-6579-7
ePDF: 978-1-4411-4700-4
ePub: 978-1-4411-2248-3

Library of Congress Cataloging-in-Publication Data

Thorpe, Lucas.
The Kant dictionary/Lucas Thorpe.
p. cm. – (Bloomsbury philosophy dictionaries.)
Includes bibliographical references (p.) and index.
ISBN 978-1-84706-579-7 (pbk.) – ISBN 978-1-84706-578-0 (hardcover)
1. Kant, Immanuel, 1724-1804 – Dictionaries. I. Title.
B2751.T56 2014
193–dc23
2011037082

Typeset by Deanta Global Publishing Services, Chennai, India
Printed and bound in India

I would like to dedicate this book to my parents,
Michael and Jacky Thorpe.
To Polly, Ben, Theodore and Yolanda Moran.
And especially to Zübeyde Karadağ for all the support
she has given me through the writing of this book.

CONTENTS

Chronology of Kant's Life and Works

1792   *Religion within the Boundaries of Mere Reason*

1795   *Perpetual Peace*

1797   *Metaphysis of Morals*

1798   *Anthropology from a Pragmatic Point of View*

1804   Kant dies (12 February, 11 a.m.)

Kant's Life and Works

Kant was born in 1724 in Königsberg, and he spent his entire life living in, or very close to, the city. Königsberg is today the Russian city of Kaliningrad, but was at the time of Kant the capital of East Prussia and an important trading port, and so although Kant did not travel beyond the immediate vicinity of his home city, he was not cut off from the major currents of European thought. Kant was educated in a Pietist environment, and at the age of 16 he entered the University of Königsberg and spent most of his life either studying or teaching at this institution. Early in his career Kant worked as a *Privatdozent*, which meant that he was allowed to teach but was not paid by the university; instead he received payment from individual students who attended his lectures. Kant normally lectured for about 20 hours a week on topics as diverse as logic, metaphysics, physics, geography, ethics, pedagogy, natural right, and even the theory of fortifications.

Like most German universities of the time the University of Königsberg consisted of four faculties or schools: the 'higher' faculties of theology, law and medicine, and the 'lower' faculty of philosophy. The theology faculty was the most respected and influential, and the philosophy faculty was regarded by many as the handmaiden of theology. Although Kant does seem to have believed in God, he was critical of organized religion throughout his life and pushed for the autonomy of philosophy from theology. It should also be remembered that philosophy was a much broader discipline in the eighteenth century than it is today. It included what has today become the natural and social sciences. This is one reason why today the highest degree in subjects, apart from law, medicine and theology, is the doctor of philosophy, or PhD. Although students were exposed to a wide range of viewpoints, the philosophy of Leibniz and Wolff formed a core part of the philosophy curriculum, and much of Kant's early work was concerned with problems emerging from their philosophy. He was also extremely influenced by Newton. So, for example, his earliest work, the *True Estimation of Living Forces* (1744), attempted to mediate between a Newtonian and Leibnizian understanding of the nature of force.

Despite his heavy teaching schedule Kant published regularly. One of his first important works was the *General Natural History of the Heavens* (1775) in which he defends a version of what is now known as the nebular hypothesis, or the Kant–Laplace theory. He explains the emergence of the universe and planetary systems through the interaction of forces of attraction and repulsion over millions of years. He also argues that the Milky Way is probably a rotating disk of star systems, seen sideways on, held together by gravitational forces, and that the distant stars also probably have planetary systems around them and that some of them are homes of extraterrestrial life. Over the next 15 years Kant published a number of interesting works such as the *Physical Monadology* (1756) and *Dreams of a Spirit-Seer* (1766).

In 1770, at the age of 46, he was finally rewarded for his efforts and was appointed as professor of logic and metaphysics, for which he had to write an inaugural dissertation in Latin. This work, *On the Form and Principles of the Sensible and Intelligible Worlds* (1770), prefigures many of the themes of the *Critique of Pure Reason* (1781). For example, he rejects the Leibnizian claim that sensation is merely a confused form of understanding and proposes a radical distinction between the intellect and sensation. He also argues that space and time cannot be understood in purely conceptual terms and are merely the non-conceptual, subjective forms of sensibility, and not features of things as they are in themselves. These are claims he would develop in the *Critique of Pure Reason*. At this point in time, however, Kant still believed in the possibility of traditional metaphysics, arguing that the pure intellect can provide us with knowledge of the intelligible world and immaterial things, such as God and the Soul.

After his appointment as professor, Kant published almost nothing for nearly 11 years, a period often referred to as his 'silent decade'. Finally in 1781 he published, at the age of 57, his monumental *Critique of Pure Reason* (1781), which launched what is known as his critical period and soon established his international reputation. When Kant first wrote the *Critique of Pure Reason* he thought that it would serve as a basis for the whole of philosophy, and did not plan to write any other Critiques. But this soon changed and by the end of the decade he had produced two more Critiques: the *Critique of Practical Reason* (1788) and the *Critique of Judgment* (1790).

One of the most remarkable things about Kant the philosopher is that he covers a huge range of topics; as a consequence, his influence spread across a huge range of disciplines and areas. Rather than examining Kant's work in chronological order, it makes more sense to examine his work thematically. We will begin by examining the *Critique of Pure Reason* (1781) and his theoretical philosophy; we will then look at the *Critique of Practical Reason* (1788) and his practical philosophy; finally we will examine the *Critique of Judgment* (1790) and Kant's aesthetics.

In the *Critique of Pure Reason* (1781) Kant offers a middle ground between rationalism and empiricism. Kant argues that philosophy must start with an examination of our cognitive capacities and that our experience of the world involves the cooperation of two distinct faculties which he calls 'intuition' and 'understanding'. Intuition is the faculty through which objects are given to us, and he argues that space and time are subjective forms of our intuition rather than being features of things as they are in themselves. Understanding is the faculty of conceptual thought, and Kant argues that in addition to requiring that objects be given to us in intuition experience also requires the application of certain *a priori* logical concepts, which he calls the 'categories'. These categories include concepts such as cause, substance, unity and plurality. And he argues that there are certain *a priori* principles that govern the application of these concepts to objects of possible experience, such as the principle that every alteration must have a cause. In claiming that we can have such *a priori* knowledge of the spatio-temporal world Kant is disagreeing with empiricists such as David Hume. Now, although we can have synthetic *a priori* knowledge of the world as it appears to us (which he calls the phenomenal world), Kant argues that we can have no knowledge of things-in-themselves. In denying the possibility of knowledge of things-in-themselves, Kant denies the possibility of rationalist metaphysics. We can have no knowledge of objects, such as the soul or God, that cannot be possible objects of experience. One of Kant's main aims in the *Critique of Pure Reason* is to show that the proper task of theoretical philosophy is critique – an examination of the principles that govern our cognitive faculties and the limits of our knowledge. The *Critique of Pure Reason* immediately became the focus of intense philosophical attention and, Kant felt, widespread misinterpretation and so in 1787 he published a substantially revised second edition, which is referred to as the 'B' edition. In this edition many sections were totally rewritten. All recent English editions of the first *Critique* include both editions.

In addition to the *Critique of Pure Reason (1781/7)*, Kant's two other major critical works in theoretical philosophy are the *Prolegomena to Any Future Metaphysics* (1783) and *Metaphysical Foundations of Natural Science* (1786). The *Prolegomena* was intended to popularize the ideas of the *Critique of Pure Reason* and to respond to criticisms and what he took to be misreadings. He was particularly concerned to respond to accusations that he was advocating a form of subjective idealism akin to George Berkeley's (1685–1753). In the *Metaphysical Foundations of Natural Science*, Kant attempts to provide a bridge between the *a priori* principles introduced in the *Critique of Pure Reason* and natural science, particularly Newtonian physics.

At the heart of Kant's practical philosophy is the idea of freedom, for just as theoretical philosophy examines nature and the laws of nature, practical philosophy is an examination of freedom and the laws of freedom. Kant's most important works in practical philosophy are *Groundwork of the Metaphysics of Morals* (1785), *Critique of Practical Reason* (1788), *Religion within the Boundaries of Mere Reason* (1793) and the *Metaphysics of Morals* (1797).

In the *Groundwork* (1785), which is perhaps the most widely read of his works, Kant offers an account of what it is to have a good will, arguing that this has to do with the principle behind one's actions and not in the results that one achieves. A good person is someone who acts from duty and not from inclination, who obeys what Kant calls the categorical imperative. Kant argues that unlike hypothetical imperatives that are always conditional on the existence of particular contingent desires, the categorical imperative, the demand of morality, commands unconditionally and absolutely. And he presents three formulations of this imperative, which have become known as the formula of universalizability, the formula of humanity and the formula of the realm of ends. Kant also, famously claims that morality involves being free, or what he calls autonomous (*auto* = self, *nomos* = law), which is to be subject to a law one has made oneself.

In the *Critique of Practical Reason* (1788), which examines the *a priori* principles that govern rational willing, Kant offers a more systematic and developed account of the ideas introduced in the *Groundwork*. Originally, Kant had thought that the *Critique of Pure Reason* would provide a sufficient foundation for both a metaphysics of nature and a metaphysics of morals, and what became the *Critique of Practical Reason* was originally planned as an appendix to the Second Edition of the *Critique of Pure Reason* (1787). As he worked on his revisions of the *Critique of Pure Reason*, however, he decided to publish it as a separate work. Kant's first major aim in the *Critique of Practical Reason* is to show that pure reason can be practical. What Kant wants to explain is how reason can be the source of action, so this involves giving an account of what it is to have a rational will, and he argues that rational willing is connected to the idea of freedom, for to act rationally is to act under the idea of freedom. Kant argues that the actions of a rational being are determined by the law of reason, which Kant identifies with the moral law, rather than the laws of nature. This moral law is not an external constraint but pertains to the very nature of rational willing, and insofar as the will is determined by such a law, the will has determined itself, so Kant concludes that to be rational is to act autonomously. In this work, Kant also develops his account of the relationship between morality and happiness. Although it is easy to get the impression that Kant does not value happiness, this would be a mistake, for although the only unconditional good is a good will, he thinks that what he calls the highest good involves both morality and happiness. His point is not that happiness does not have value, but rather that the person who makes their own happiness their primary motivation does not deserve to be happy. And he argues that the good person, who is willing to sacrifice their own happiness when duty demands, deserves to be happy, and should be able to reasonably hope to be happy. However, he says that as there is no natural connection between virtue and happiness, such a connection needs to be grounded externally, and the only type of being that could do this would be a being that was omnipotent, omniscient and good. Thus, he argues that a commitment to morality requires a faith in the existence of God who has the power and will to proportion happiness to morality. Kant develops his account of the relationship between morality and religion in his *Religion within the Boundaries of Mere Reason* (1793) which is an account of the type of religion that morality requires. Although Kant is critical of much of traditional Christianity, in this work he offers an interpretation of much of traditional Christian doctrine, such as accounts of original sin and the role of the church, in terms of his rational morality.

Kant's last major work in practical philosophy was the *Metaphysics of Morals* (1797). In this work he attempts to provide an account of the whole system of human duties. The *Metaphysics of Morals* is divided into a Doctrine of Right and a Doctrine of Virtue. The Doctrine of Virtue contains his account of ethical duties. In the Doctrine of Right we find the most detailed account of Kant's political philosophy. Kant also discusses political issues in a number of his shorter works. The most influential of these are *What is Enlightenment?* (1784) and *Perpetual Peace* (1795).

In addition to groundbreaking work in both theoretical philosophy and practical philosophy, Kant also produced what has become probably the most influential work in modern aesthetics, the *Critique of Judgment* (1790) – even though only the first half of the book deals with questions on aesthetics (the second half deals with teleology and nature and our understanding of biological organisms). In this work Kant provides extremely influential accounts of the nature of beauty and the sublime, as well as important discussions on the nature of fine art, and the importance of genius for artistic creation.

As Kant really became famous only after the publication of the *Critique of Pure Reason* (1781), nearly all of the famous anecdotes that have come down to us about the regularity of his life date from this period of his life, when he was already quite old and set in his ways. It is worth remembering that Kant was extremely sociable and as a young man was considered quite a charmer and was fond of evenings playing billiards or cards; indeed, it seems that as a student he supplemented his meagre income with the money he made from his winnings. In the 1760s he seems to have become friends with a number of foreign merchants and in particular an English merchant called Joseph Green whom he seems to have visited many afternoons a week. Green loved Rousseau and Hume, and although Kant probably did not speak or read English well himself, he was kept up to date with the intellectual life of the English-speaking world through Green and his circle of friends. Green himself seems to have been quite an eccentric, who was known for ordering his life according to strict rules or maxims, and it seems that in his later life Kant himself adopted some of Green's habits for punctuality and having an extremely regular routine, for it was said that in his later years inhabitants of Königsberg could set their watches by the start of Kant's afternoon walk. Even in later life he visited his friends or entertained guests almost every day. He would teach and work in the morning and then in the early afternoon, normally from 1 p.m.; he would have guests over for dinner – and these dinners would often go on into the night – and Kant seemed to have particularly enjoyed gossiping and talking about politics, and was fond of a glass of wine, or two. In his anthropology lectures he regularly explained to students how to throw a good dinner party and discussed the harms and benefits of various sorts of narcotic substances. He thought that beer and opium made one heavy and dull, and hard spirits made one lose one's reason, and thus were to be avoided. He suggested, however, that drinking wine encouraged the virtue of sociability and was to be encouraged. Thus, although Kant travelled little and had the reputation for being dour, in reality he seemed to have enjoyed life and the world came to him.

A–Z Dictionary

aesthetic

Today 'Aesthetics' is the discipline that studies art and beauty, and other connected topics. The word 'aesthetic', which is derived from the Greek *aisthanomai*, meaning to perceive, feel or sense, had traditionally been used to mean having to do with sensation. Alexander Gottlieb Baumgarten (1714–62) was the first to use the word in the modern sense to mean having to do with judgements of taste and the feeling of the beautiful. Baumgarten argued that the experience of beauty involves judgements of taste, and he defined the faculty of taste as a capacity to judge according to the senses rather than the intellect, with judgements of taste being based upon our feelings of pleasure and displeasure. And he used the word 'aesthetics', for the first time, to name the science that examined judgements of taste and the experience of beauty. In the *Critique of Pure Reason* (1781/1787), however, Kant argued that a science of taste is impossible because there can be no *a priori* principles of the faculty of feeling, and he explained that he would use the word 'aesthetic' in the traditional sense to refer to the study of **sensibility** in general as opposed to **understanding**. Aesthetics in this sense has to do with the non-conceptual aspect of experience. In the **Transcendental Aesthetic** of the *Critique of Pure Reason* Kant examines what we can know about the non-conceptual aspect of experience *a priori*. His conclusion is that for human beings their sensible experience is necessarily spatio-temporal.

By the time he wrote the *Critique of Judgment* in 1790, however, Kant had changed his mind about the possibility of a science of taste, for in this work he argues that there can be *a priori* principles governing judgements of taste, and he adopts Baumgarten's usage of the word 'aesthetics' to denote a systematic examination of our capacity to make judgements of taste. See: **Transcendental Aesthetic**; *Critique of Judgment*; **beauty**; **sublime**.

Amphiboly of the Concepts of Reflection

Strictly speaking an amphiboly is an ambiguous sentence in which the ambiguity does not depend upon the equivocation of any particular term, but upon its grammatical structure. 'I shot the elephant wearing my pajamas' is an example of an amphiboly. The expression is, however, sometimes used merely to indicate an equivocation (using a word in more than one sense), and this is how Kant uses the term in the section of the *Critique of Pure Reason* (1781/1787) entitled the **Amphiboly of the Concepts of Reflection**. In this section Kant argues that Gottfried Wilhelm **Leibniz** (1646–1716) and his **rationalist** followers, such as Christian **Wolff** (1679–1754) and Alexander Gottlieb **Baumgarten** (1714–62), draw false conclusions because they fail to make a number of fundamental distinctions. Kant is particularly concerned with four pairs of concepts that we use in comparing representations which he calls the concepts of reflection. These concepts of reflection are: (1) identity and difference, (2) agreement and opposition, (3) the inner and the outer and (4) the determinable and the determination (matter and form). Kant's claim is that for each of these concept pairs Leibniz and his followers fail to distinguish between a real and logical use of the concept. So, for example, he argues that Leibniz fails to draw the distinction between the logical use of identity (numerical identity) and the real use of identity (qualitative identity) and this lies behind Leibniz' acceptance of the principle of the **identity of indiscernibles**. According to this principle, which is sometimes known as Leibniz' law, if two substances have all the same properties, then they are the same substance. Another way of thinking of this principle is in terms of the idea of the complete concept of an object. If we assume the possibility of a complete concept of an individual which lists all the properties that belong to the individual, then according to the principle of the identity of indiscernibles, there could only be one substance that corresponded to such a concept. In the Amphiboly, however, Kant argues that Leibniz is mistaken to take this logical principle, which can legitimately be applied to concepts, and assume that it also applies to objects. For, Kant argues, there are two uses of the concept of 'identity', one that applies to concepts and the other to objects, and Leibniz fails to distinguish between these two uses and this is why he is mistakenly committed to the principle of the identity of indiscernibles. Kant agrees with Leibniz that it is true that if two concepts contain all the same predicates, then they are the same concept, but our criterion for the identity of objects is different from our criterion for the identity of concepts. In the case of physical **phenomenal** objects we do have a criterion of identity which has to do with spatio temporal position, and Kant argues, in opposition to the principle of the identity of indiscernibles, that two points in space can be exactly the same in all of their properties but be in different places, hence making them distinct objects although they do not differ in any of their properties. When it comes to **things as they are in themselves**, however, Kant believes that we have no criteria for identity or difference and this is one of the reasons that he thinks that we can have no knowledge of things as they are in themselves. See: **Leibniz.**

Analogies of Experience

In this section of the *Critique of Pure Reason* (1781/1787) Kant is concerned with the applicability of the **categories** of **relation** – the concepts of **substance, causation** and **community.** Unlike the **Axioms of Intuition,** which examine the applicability of the categories of **quantity,** and the **Anticipations of Perception,** which examine the applicability of the categories of **quality,** where Kant examines all three concepts together in a single section and provides a single principle that governs the application of all three concepts, in the **Analogies of Experience** Kant provides a separate principle for each of the three categories of relation. The general principle of the Analogies is that experience of objects in space and time is only possible through the representation of the necessary connection of perceptions, and he argues that such a connection requires the applicability of the categories of relation to objects of experience.

In the Analogies, Kant is particularly concerned with explaining how it is possible for us to represent the temporality of experience, for he thinks it is clear that we do not perceive time itself, and so we need to give an account of how it is possible to experience the world temporally. He argues that there are three aspects of temporal experience involving the notions of persistence, succession and simultaneity, and so any account of the possibility of temporal experience has to explain how we are able to experience these three aspects of temporality. Although one moment follows another, time itself persists. And for any two events in time the first must be before, after or at the same time as the second. So the awareness of two events as being in time involves a capacity to distinguish between the events being successive or simultaneous, and Kant argues that the capacity to represent and distinguish between the persistence, succession and simultaneity of time and events in time requires the application of the three categories of relation. The category of substance is required for the representation of persistence, the category of causation is required for the representation of succession and the category of community (or mutual interaction) is required for the representation of simultaneity.

In the First Analogy Kant argues that the category of **substance** is necessary for the experience of persistence. Although we do not perceive time itself in order to represent temporal change, we represent time as something permanent, and represent change as the alteration of something that persists. Thus Kant argues that the representation of the permanence of the real in time is necessary for us to be able to represent the second aspect of temporality, namely temporal succession. That is he thinks that in order to represent appearances as successive, we have to represent them at the successive states of a permanent substance. It is important to note here the distinction between a permanent perception and the perception of something permanent. Kant's point is not that the experience of temporal change requires the existence of a subjective representation that we are continuously aware of; rather his point is that such experience requires the representation of some object that is represented as permanent, and he thinks that this requires the application of the category of substance. This permanent object is represented as the substratum of change.

In the Second Analogy Kant argues that the category of **causation** is necessary in order to represent temporal succession and to distinguish between states of an object being successive and simultaneous. There is some disagreement among Kant scholars over what exactly Kant is trying to prove in the Second Analogy. Some scholars believe that he is merely trying to prove that for every alteration there must be some cause, while others believe he is trying to prove that given the same type of cause there must be the same type of effect. Kant's statement of the principle of the Second

Analogy is that all alterations occur in accordance with the law of the connection of cause and effect, where an alteration is understood to be the change in the state of a substance. And he argues that the category of causation is necessary to distinguish between subjective and objective alteration. To explain this distinction he gives his famous examples of the ship and the house. Watching a ship sail downstream is an example of objective alteration. I can also look at a house, looking first at the door and then at the window. In both cases I am aware of various states of an object and in my subjective experience the states are represented as successive. In the case of watching the ship, however, I perceive that the states of the ship are objectively successive whereas in the case of the house, although my awareness of the window comes after my experience of the door I believe that the window and the door exist simultaneously and it is only my subjective experience of the door and the window that is successive. The difference in the two cases is that in the case of the ship there is a causal relationship between the two states of the ship. The ship, at least partially, is where it is now because of where it was the moment before. When an object is in motion there is a causal relationship between the positions of the object at each moment, and in his *Metaphysical Foundations of Natural Science* (1786) Kant argues that the Newtonian law of inertia is a more specific version of this principle restricted to motion. According to the law of inertia, an object with no forces acting upon it will continue in its state of motion or rest. According to this law, in the absence of any external forces acting upon an object, the present state of motion of the object is fully determined by its earlier states. It is important to stress that the principle of Second Analogy does not have to do with interaction between substances, and so in the Second Analogy Kant is not attempting to give an account of what happens when billiard balls hit one another. The causal principle of the Second Analogy has to do with alterations, and so it is concerned with the relation between the states of a particular object or substance. Kant's claim in the Second Analogy is that the state of a particular object must be causally dependent on the previous states of that object. Or more precisely: that in any alteration of a substance, the latter state of the substance is causally dependent upon the previous state of the substance (in a rule like way). Kant does not examine the principle that governs causal relations *between* objects until the Third Analogy.

In the Third Analogy Kant argues that the category of **community**, or interaction, is necessary in order to judge that two substances are simultaneous. Thus the principle he aims to defend in the Third Analogy is that 'all substances insofar as they are simultaneous stand in thoroughgoing community (i.e. interaction) with one another'. Kant's argument seems to be that for two substances, or perhaps the states of two substances, to be recognized as simultaneous we must recognize them as mutually related to one another, and the only way we are able to do this is through the use of some concept and the category of community just is the concept of such mutual relation. The problem is that even if Kant can persuade us that the recognition of simultaneity does require the application of some concept of mutual relation, the concept of community seems to involve far more than mere mutual relation, for Kant thinks that the concept of community is equivalent to the notion of mutual interaction, and it is not immediately obvious why our concept of mutual relation must involve the seemingly stronger notion of mutual interaction.

The three Analogies form the basis for what Kant calls the three laws of mechanics in the *Metaphysical Foundations of Natural Science* (1786). In this work, Kant attempts to provide a bridge between the *a priori* principles introduced in the Analogies and natural science, particularly Newtonian physics. Kant's three laws of mechanics are closely related to **Isaac Newton**'s (1643–1727) three laws of motion. The three laws that Kant identifies are: (1) the law of the conservation of the total quantity of matter in the world, (2) a version of the law of inertia, namely that every change of matter must have an external cause and (3) the law of the equality of action and reaction. These laws are presented as specifications of the three *a priori* principles introduced in the Analogies of Experience. The first law of mechanics is supposed to be a more specific version of the principle of the First Analogy, the second law is supposed to be a specification of the principle of the Second Analogy and the third law is supposed to be a specification of the principle of the Third Analogy.

analytic/synthetic

The distinction between analytic and synthetic judgements is essentially a semantic distinction having to do with what it is that makes a judgement true or false. Kant seems to offer three possibly distinct definitions of analyticity.

Kant most often explains that analytic judgements are judgements the truth of which depends merely upon the meaning of the terms involved and claims that in an analytic judgement the predicate concept is 'contained in' the subject concept. Kant calls a judgement of the form '*a* is *b*' a **categorical judgement**. In such a judgement *a* is the subject concept and *b* is the predicate concept, and so Kant's claim is that in an analytic categorical judgement *b* is contained in *a*. To understand what Kant means by this it is helpful to look at an example. In the judgement 'all bachelors are unmarried', 'bachelor' is the subject concept and 'unmarried' is the predicate concept, and this judgement is analytic because a bachelor is, by definition, an unmarried man, and so the concept 'bachelor' contains the concept 'unmarried'. Although Kant often explains what he means by an analytic judgement in terms of conceptual containment, it seems that this account of analyticity is too narrow, for it is not able to explain the way in which judgements that are not categorical judgements can be analytic. So, for example, the judgement 'something cannot be both a bachelor and unmarried' is not in subject-predicate form but would seem to be analytic, because if we know what the words mean, we know that it must be true.

Although Kant himself most often seems to define analytic judgements as those which are true in virtue of the meaning of the terms involved, he sometimes seems to identify analytic judgements with logical truths, and many contemporary readers of Kant prefer this account. On this account of analyticity an analytic judgement is one which is true in virtue of its logical form, or whose truth depends solely on logical laws and definitions. So, for example, many philosophers would argue that a judgement such as 'all bachelors are either happy or not happy' is a logical truth and so is analytic, but it is not clear that it is true merely in virtue of the meaning of the concepts involved. Some philosophers of logic would argue that it is true in virtue of its logical form, for, at least in classical logic, it is a law of logic that 'p or not p' is true. Other philosophers of logic, however, argue that what makes logical judgements true is the meaning of the logical constants, such as 'not' and 'or', involved in such judgements. If we take this second approach to logical truth, then the first account which explains analyticity in terms of the meaning of the terms involved in a judgement can be combined with the second that explains analyticity in terms of logical truth.

Kant's final account of what it is that makes a judgement analytic involves an appeal to the notion of contradiction. According to this account, if the denial or negation of a judgement is or implies a contradiction, then the judgement is analytic. Although this seems to be a good test or criterion for whether a judgement is analytic, it does not really seem to be a definition of analyticity for it does not explain what it is that makes analytic judgements analytic.

The easiest way to define synthetic judgements is in negative terms: a synthetic judgement is one that is not analytic. Kant himself, however, has a bit more to say about this. In an analytic judgement we do not need to look beyond the concepts involved to determine whether the statement is true. In a synthetic judgement, however, we have to go beyond the concepts involved and examine the objects picked out by the concepts. For example, to determine the truth of the judgement 'some bachelors are happy', we actually have to go and find some bachelors, and merely thinking about what the concept means will not help us here. In a synthetic **categorical judgement** the subject concept ('bachelor') picks out a set of objects, and the judgement claims that the objects picked out by the subject concept will also satisfy the predicate concept. To determine the truth of the judgement we have to know something not just about the concepts used but about the objects referred to.

One of Kant's most controversial claims is that mathematical truths and certain truths about the world are synthetic and *a priori*. And Kant sometimes suggests that the whole critical project can be understood as an attempt to explain the possibility of **synthetic *a priori*** knowledge. In terms of our knowledge of the world it would seem clear that this knowledge is synthetic and so the problem is to explain the way in which it can also be *a priori*. In the case of **mathematics** most philosophers agree that such knowledge is *a priori* but many would argue that such knowledge is analytic not synthetic. Kant, however, argues that judgements of arithmetic (such as $5+7=12$) and geometry (such as, the shortest distance between two points is a straight line) are synthetic. With the axiomatization of arithmetic and geometry at the end of the nineteenth century, however, many philosophers argued that mathematical judgements were analytic. See also: **synthetic *a priori*, mathematics**.

analytic method

Kant often distinguishes between what he calls the analytic or regressive method, on the one hand, and the synthetic or progressive method, on the other. He claims in the *Prolegomena to Any Future Metaphysics* (1783) and the first two chapters of the *Groundwork of the Metaphysics of Morals* (1785) to be pursuing the analytic method, whereas in the *Critique of Pure Reason* (1781/1787) and chapter three of the *Groundwork* he claims to be pursuing the synthetic method. The analytic method starts with something conditioned (such as a whole, or a consequence) and provides an analysis of the condition (such as the parts, or the ground). The synthetic method starts from the condition (such as parts, or something that is a ground) and proceeds to the conditioned (or the whole, or the consequence). So, for example, if we start by examining a whole and work out what sort of parts it is made of, we are following the analytic method. If, on the other hand, we start by examining a number of distinct things and work out how they can, and perhaps must, be put together, we are following the synthetic method.

In the *Critique of Pure Reason*, Kant claims that he pursues the synthetic method. In this work he is attempting to justify the claim that we can and do have **synthetic** *a priori* knowledge. He starts by examining the elements of human cognition, among which are the 12 **categories**, and attempts to show that the application of these categories to experience according to *a priori* principles is a necessary condition of experience. In this case the categories are the conditions and experience is the conditioned, and so, in the *Critique of Pure Reason*, Kant's argument moves from the conditions to the conditioned. In the *Prolegomena*, in contrast, Kant claims that he is following the analytic method. In this work Kant begins with the assumption that we have synthetic *a priori* knowledge and then gives an account of what must be the case for such knowledge to be possible. Similarly in the *Groundwork* Kant claims that in the first two chapters he follows the analytic method whereas in the final chapter he follows the synthetic method. Thus he starts by accepting the actuality of common-sense moral knowledge and in the first two chapters merely gives an analysis of what is involved in this knowledge. In the third chapter, however, he claims to be pursuing the synthetic method and rather than just offering an explanation of our common-sense moral judgements he attempts to offer a justification of them.

Answer to the Question: What is Enlightenment? (1784)

See: *What is Enlightenment?*

Anthropology from a Pragmatic Point of View (1798)

This text was the published version of Kant's popular Anthropology lectures, a topic he lectured on every year from 1772 to his retirement in 1796. Kant distinguished between what he calls physiological anthropology, which is a descriptive discipline which examines what nature makes of human beings, and pragmatic anthropology, which examines what man as a free, acting being makes of himself and what he can and should make of himself. Pragmatic anthropology is interested in human nature and human differences insofar as they are relevant for human practice, and as such pragmatic anthropology is the most empirical part of practical philosophy. Part of the goal of such a pragmatic anthropology is to provide us with empirical knowledge which can improve our capacity for practical judgement. The status of pragmatic anthropology within Kant's ethical system has been the subject of much recent debate, for Kant seems to be committed to the view that ethics is and should be a purely rational and non-empirical discipline, whereas anthropology is an empirical discipline. And so there has been much debate about the possibility of an empirical discipline that has to do with the empirical study of human freedom.

Anticipations of Perception

In this section of the *Critique of Pure Reason* (1781/1787) Kant is concerned with the applicability of the categories of **quality** (reality, negation and limitation) to the world. He argues for the **synthetic** *a priori* **principle** that 'in all appearances the real, which is an object of sensation, has intensive magnitude (or degree)'. Here it is useful to compare the notion of an intensive magnitude with that of an extensive magnitude. An *extensive magnitude*, the topic of the **Axioms of Intuition**, is a totality, and as such it is an aggregate of a plurality of units; an extensive magnitude, then, is a whole made up of parts. An *intensive magnitude* is, in contrast, one that can be represented only as a unity and 'in which multiplicity can be represented by approximation to negation = 0'. Examples of intensive magnitudes would be things such as colour, speed and mass. The colour of an object can be more or less red, but we do not think of the degree of redness as being an aggregate of units of redness. Similarly, the speed of a moving object can be more or less, but speed is not an extensive magnitude, it is not an aggregate of units of speed. The notion of a degree involves the categories of quality because the notion of a degree involves a certain limited amount of reality, and Kant thinks that the concept of limitation involves the concept of negation, and so judgements about intensive magnitudes involve the application of all three categories of **quality**. In claiming that in sensation the object is necessarily experienced as having a degree of reality, Kant is claiming that the material spatio-temporal world is not homogeneous, but different parts of the material world differ in quality. In claiming this, Kant is disagreeing with **Descartes** (1596–1650). Descartes had thought of the material world as a homogeneous fluid and thought of individual material substances as whirlpools, or vortices, in this fluid, differing from the fluid around them only in terms of their motion. Like **Leibniz** (1646–1716), Kant rejects this Cartesian view of matter, believing that individual bodies are to be thought of as centres of active forces and so differ in terms of quality, for example in having different degrees of mass. In suggesting that force and mass are, in a sense, qualitative notions, Kant is not suggesting that they are things that cannot be measured. Instead, he merely means that they come in degrees, and are thus intensive rather than extensive magnitudes. Kant's claim, then, in the Anticipations of Perception is that in experience we represent material bodies as centres of force that can act upon us and one another, and doing this requires the application of the three categories of quality to the world because forces are intensive magnitudes and these three categories are necessary to represent something as an intensive magnitude.

Kant is a bit clearer about this in the *Metaphysical Foundations of Natural Science* (1786). In this work Kant defends a dynamic theory of matter according to which physical objects fill space, and thus have properties such as solidity, hardness and impenetrability, as a result of their repulsive and attractive forces, with these forces understood as being intensive magnitudes because they come in degrees. The attractive force of objects penetrates all space and if attractive force was the only force, an object would occupy the whole of space, for there would be nothing to resist the sphere of its force. The repulsive force of objects, however, limits the space that particular objects fill and explains their solidity and impenetrability. This account of the nature of matter, however, necessarily involves the categories of quality because forces are intensive magnitudes. If this account of matter as we experience it is correct, it explains the necessity of the application of the categories of quality to objects of experience, for according to the dynamic theory of matter, these concepts are necessary to explain the basic properties of material objects such as solidity, hardness and impenetrability.

Antinomy of Pure Reason

An antinomy is a contradiction. The word is derived from Greek and literally means against (*anti*) law, (*nomos*). The section of the *Critique of Pure Reason* (1781/1787) called the Antinomy of Pure Reason is the second main chapter in the **Transcendental Dialectic**. In this section Kant examines our **idea** of the phenomenal world as a totality and argues that insofar as we try to think of the idea of the phenomenal world as a whole, we cannot avoid falling into contradiction. And he believes that reason naturally falls into such a contradiction because reason strives to think the unconditioned.

To understand what Kant means by the claim that reason strives to think the unconditioned, we should remember that Kant believes reason is the faculty of syllogisms. A **syllogism** is an argument with two premises and a conclusion. A good argument is one in which the premises imply the conclusion. But the fact that the premises of an argument imply the conclusion is not enough to prove the truth of the conclusion, for we must also know that the premises are true.

The most we can say without this is that 'if the premises are true then the conclusion is true', as such a syllogism only supplies us with a conditional (if . . . then) justification. To get something more than a conditional justification of a conclusion, we need another argument, showing that the premises are true. But this will lead to a new set of premises that are in turn in need of justification, and so on *ad infinitum*. An unconditionally justified conclusion would be one in which there are no premises in need of justification, and Kant believes that this idea of unconditional justification is the ideal that reason strives for. This is not to say that such an ideal can ever be satisfied, it is just that reason is never satisfied with an argument that has premises that are unjustified. Reason is, in this sense, restless and perpetually unsatisfied, always seeking firm ground to serve as the foundation of its thought and arguments. And when firm ground is not found, reason always demands that we dig deeper. Now, the fact that we should continue digging until we find firm ground does not imply that such firm ground is to be found and that we will not go on digging forever. It might be the case that conditional justification is the most we can ever achieve and the absence of unconditional absolute justification does not, Kant believes, undermine the importance or value of conditional justification. The fact that reason can never be fully satisfied does not mean that we should give up reasoning.

Now, Kant believes that when we think about the phenomenal world, the world as we experience it, reason seeks some type of completeness or totality, and we mistake what reason desires for something that could actually exist, and it is this that leads to the contradictions that Kant calls the antinomies. Kant himself identifies four antinomies, all of which have the same structure. He shows that when thinking about the world as we experience it, there are good arguments to support contradictory conclusions, which he calls the thesis and antithesis. The first antinomy has to do with whether or not the world is infinite in extent; the second is about whether material substances are infinitely divisible or whether they consist of simple parts; the third is about whether everything that happens is causally determined or whether there is a free cause, that is a cause that is not itself an effect; and the fourth antinomy has got to do with whether or not everything that exists is contingent or whether there is some necessary being. With the first two antinomies, which he calls the mathematical antinomies because they concern the magnitude of the phenomenal world, Kant argues that both the thesis and antithesis are false. With the second two antinomies, which he calls the dynamical antinomies, Kant argues that both the thesis and antithesis are true, but in different senses; in both cases Kant argues that the thesis is true of the **intelligible** world, whereas the antithesis is true of the **phenomenal**.

In the first antinomy Kant's *thesis* is that the phenomenal world has a beginning in time and is enclosed by boundaries and his *antithesis* is that the world is infinite with regard to space and time. In the second antinomy the *thesis* is that there are simple, indivisible, material substances, and the *antithesis* is that there are no such simple indivisible substances. Both of these antinomies have to do with the infinite, for the first antinomy asks whether the phenomenal world as a whole is infinite or finite in extent, and the second asks whether or not matter is infinitely divisible. Kant's conclusion is that in both cases both the thesis and antithesis are false. This may seem to be a strange conclusion to reach, for one might think that if the world is not finite it must be infinite, so either the thesis or antithesis must be true. Kant's response is that there is no such thing as the phenomenal world as a whole, for the idea of the phenomenal world as a whole is incoherent, and so both claims can be false. His argument here, then, is that both claims can be false in the same way that some philosophers think that because there is no present king of France, both the statements 'the present king of France is bald' and 'the present king of France is not bald' are false. Similarly, if there is no world as a whole, then both the claims 'the world as a whole is infinite' and 'the world as a whole is finite' will be false. To understand why Kant thinks that the idea of the **phenomenal world** as a whole is incoherent, it is necessary to recall Kant's claim in the **Transcendental Aesthetic** that space and time are our forms of **intuition**. What he means by this is that we can only experience objects as in space and time, and the world as we can experience it, or what Kant calls **the phenomenal world**, is necessarily spatio-temporal. One consequence of this is that human experience is necessarily partial and limited, for to experience something as in space and time always involves an awareness that there is some space and time that is not experienced. For an object to exist in space and time presupposes that there is space and time around or beyond the object, otherwise the object experienced would not be *in* space and time. To experience something as 'now', as temporally present, involves an awareness that there is some past that is not experienced, and to experience something as 'here' necessarily involves the awareness of some 'there' that is not 'here'. Another way of putting this is that the whole of space and time is not the sort of thing that could exist in space and time. Now, if existing in space and time is a condition of the possibility of experience, then the whole of space and time is not a possible object of experience, and so all we can possibly experience is a part of the phenomenal world, not the phenomenal world as a whole. The phenomenal world as a whole, then, cannot be a possible object of experience. Although we can only experience a part of the world, reason assumes that the idea of the phenomenal world as a whole is coherent. To be phenomenal is to be experienced as partial. Reason, however, assumes that whenever we can think of something as a part, there must be some whole of which it is a part, and which is not itself a part. Thus Kant concludes that we only have the world-whole in concept but not in intuition, and his thought is that the first two antinomies are the result of confusing the fact that we have the concept of wholeness with the existence of an object. The world cannot be given or experienced as a whole, and so questions about the magnitude of the world are badly formed. Kant offers a similar argument in the second antinomy about whether matter is infinitely divisible or not.

The third antinomy has to do with **freedom** and **determinism**. The thesis argues for the existence of freedom, whereas the antithesis argues that everything in the world happens in accordance with the laws of nature. By freedom, in this context, Kant means the idea of an uncaused cause, or a cause that is not itself an effect, and so the question he is primarily concerned with here has to do with the possibility of a first cause, for a first cause is the idea of a free cause, for it is the idea of a cause that is not itself an effect. In the Second **Analogy of Experience** Kant has argued that everything that happens in the phenomenal world must be subject to the laws of nature. And so he is committed to the position that each event must have some previous event or set of events as its cause. It is this argument that supports the antithesis, the claim that every cause must be an effect of some prior cause. On the other hand, if we think of the whole series of causes, reason demands that we think of this series as having a beginning, and hence implies the existence of a first, or free, cause. Both the thesis and antithesis seem to be true. Kant's solution is to argue that both the thesis and antithesis are true. However, a first or free cause cannot be thought of as something existing in time, for anything existing in time must be subject to the deterministic natural laws, and so any event in time must be caused and so cannot be an uncaused cause. So, Kant concludes that the idea of a free cause is of something **intelligible** rather than **phenomenal**. A free cause cannot exist in space and time, and so a free cause must be an intelligible rather than a phenomenal cause. If we think of time as involving a series of events, then Kant's thought is that the causality of a free, intelligible cause must be something outside the temporal series, because any cause that is a part of such a temporal series must also be an effect caused by earlier members of the series. Although the causality of an intelligible cause must be outside the temporal series, there is no contradiction in thinking of the effects of such a cause being encountered in the series. Thus, Kant argues, if we distinguish between the phenomenal and intelligible realm, between the realm of nature and the realm of freedom, we can accept both the thesis and antithesis. The antithesis is true because there can be no free causes *within* the phenomenal realm, but the thesis is consistent with this because there is no contradiction in thinking of an uncaused cause existing *outside* the phenomenal realm. Now, although Kant believes we have no theoretical justification for believing in the existence of any free (and hence intelligible rather than phenomenal) cause, he will argue that we have moral reasons for believing in the existence of such causes, for practical reason demands that we think of ourselves as such causes insofar as we regard ourselves as bound by the moral law.

In the fourth antinomy, the thesis is that there exists a necessary being, the antithesis is that everything that exists is contingent. Once again Kant argues that although the antithesis is true of all phenomenal objects, this is not inconsistent with the thesis, for this claim leaves room for the possibility of the existence of a non-phenomenal, or intelligible, necessary being. Once again, however, Kant argues that, from the theoretical perspective, we have no good reason to believe in the existence of such a being. He will argue, however, that we do have moral reasons for believing in the existence of such a being, for our idea of God, as traditionally understood, is of just such a necessary being, and Kant thinks that we have moral reasons for believing in the existence of God. See also: **freedom; reason**; Transcendental Dialectic.

apodictic

An apodictic judgement is one that has the force of a logical demonstration; in other words such a judgement is one that is represented as necessarily true. In his table of judgements Kant lists the three different modalities that a judgement can have. Judgements can either be **problematic**, assertoric or apodictic. Problematic judgements are judgements that are represented as **possibly** true, assertoric judgements are judgements that are presented as actually true and apodictic judgements are those that are represented as necessarily true. See also: **necessity.**

appearances

Kant famously distinguishes between appearances, or **phenomena**, and **things-in-themselves** and argues that we can only have knowledge of appearances and not of things as they are in themselves. Appearances are objects of possible experience. Kant argues that because our form of intuition is spatio-temporal, such objects necessarily exist in space and time, and he famously argues that there are certain *a priori* **principles** that govern the application of the categories to appearances. When talking of appearances, Kant is talking about the physical world around us and it is important to remember, however, that by terming such objects appearances he does not regard them in any way illusory or subjective. Appearances, then, are for Kant physical objects existing external to the mind in space and time. See: **phenomena; things-in-themselves, transcendental idealism.**

apperception

Gottfried Wilhelm **Leibniz** (1646–1716) uses the word 'apperception' to refer to the capacity to engage in reflective thought, and Kant uses the word in a similar sense. Apperception, then, is the capacity for thought to reflect on itself and so involves a certain type of self-consciousness. This capacity to make our own thoughts and actions the object of our thought is what distinguishes rational human beings from non-rational animals and is essentially the activity of reason. Non-rational animals have the capacity to categorize and distinguish objects in the world, but they lack the capacity to make their 'concepts' the objects of their thoughts. It would seem that many animals possess 'concepts' in the sense of possessing a capacity to categorize objects in the world. Most animals seem to lack the capacity for meta-cognition, that is the capacity to make their own 'concepts' the objects of their thought. That is to say, animals lack the capacity of apperception. Because they lack this capacity, some philosophers claim that although animals are able to categorize objects in the world around them, strictly speaking animals do not really possess concepts. As human beings, on the other hand, we have the capacity to take our own concepts as the object of our thought and so we cannot just make judgements about objects in the world, but can also make judgements about our concepts, and it is this capacity to make judgements about our own concepts that is the subject matter of logic. And it is our capacity to engage in apperception that makes human **reason** possible, for reason is the capacity to make inferences and through these inferences it strives to unify and systematize our conceptual scheme. In order to engage in this activity, reason must represent our conceptual scheme as unified and it does this through the representation of a unified 'I'. Kant calls this representation of the unified 'I', which is thought of as having the functional role of unifying our thought, the **Transcendental Unity of Apperception**. Kant argues in the **Paralogisms of Pure Reason** that **rationalist** metaphysicians mistake this purely formal representation of 'I', which has no content, but is merely understood in terms of what its function is, namely its function of unifying thought, for the intuition of a simple substance that persists through time. That is, he argues that these rationalist metaphysicians mistake a simple (because contentless) representation for the representation of something simple, namely a simple substance. That is, the rationalist metaphysicians mistake a property of the representation for a property of the thing represented. This is akin to thinking that because Istanbul is represented by a dot on a map that Istanbul itself must be tiny.

a priori/a posteriori

The distinction between *a priori* and *a posteriori* is essentially an epistemological one, having to do with knowledge. *A priori* knowledge is knowledge that is prior to or independent of experience, whereas as *a posteriori* knowledge is empirical knowledge that is posterior to or dependent upon experience. It is important to distinguish between *a priori* and innate knowledge. The word innate is derived from the Latin *natus* (birth), so innate knowledge or ideas are those that we are born with. Kant does not identify *a priori* knowledge with innate knowledge. Thus, for example, mathematical knowledge is *a priori* but not innate. We are not born knowing that $7+5=12$ as we have to learn how to count first, so such knowledge is not innate. Such knowledge is, however, *a priori* because once we have learnt basic arithmetic we know that such judgements are true independently of any experience. Kant argues that there are two marks or criteria of *a priori* knowledge: (1) necessity and (2) universality. (1) If something is true *a priori*, we do not just know that it happens to be true but we know that it *must* be so. I do not just know that it happens to be the case that $7+5=12$, but I also know that it could not be otherwise. Not even God could create a universe in which $7+5=13$. This is not the case with *a posteriori*, empirical knowledge. Maybe all dogs have less than six legs, but perhaps God could have created a dog with eight legs. (2) Kant thinks that experience can never provide evidence for strict universality, but only for generality, and so, if we know something is true in a strictly universal sense, then we know that we do not know it on the basis of experience. A judgement has strict universality if we know that it admits of no exceptions. This is the case, Kant argues, with our mathematical, logical and metaphysical knowledge. For example, we do not think that $7+5=12$ is just true most of the time but that it is true without exception. Empirical knowledge is different. The evidence for the empirical judgement 'all swans are white', which was a favourite example in early modern logic textbooks, is based upon induction. When we make such judgements, we are not claiming that exceptions to the rule are impossible but merely that as far as we have perceived, there have been no exceptions to this rule. Indeed, black swans are to be found in Australia, so it turns out that the claim 'all swans are white' is false. *A priori* knowledge cannot be falsified in this way. See also: **synthetic** *a priori*.

art

Although in the *Critique of Judgment* (1790) Kant is primarily concerned with the **beauty** of nature, he is also interested in fine art. (The German for 'fine art' is '*schöne kunst*', which literally means 'beautiful art').

Kant claims that fine art, in order to be judged as beautiful, must look to us like nature, appearing free and unstudied. Now, beautiful objects must be rule-governed in some way, but if the artist consciously and mechanically follows rules in the production of an object, the resulting object will not look natural, and so in order to create an object that looks beautiful, the artist must possess a capacity to produce objects in a rule-governed way without being conscious of the rule. Kant calls this capacity **genius**, which he defines as a capacity by which nature gives the rule to art. What Kant means by this is that the artist must be able to create in a rule-governed way without consciously following a rule and so it is as if nature is working through the artist to provide the rule to the object. Kant's discussion of genius was aimed at the neoclassicism of his time, which tended to stress the importance of following rules in the production of art, and Kant's claim that the production of beautiful art requires genius had a strong influence on the development of romanticism.

Kant has been influential both among art critics and artists. He is often presented as advocating a strong form of formalism according to which the aesthetic qualities of objects have to do exclusively with formal features such as structure, harmony and proportion. Kant does argue that in judgements of beauty we do respond to the form of the object rather than its matter; so, for example, he argues that in a beautiful painting the source of the pleasure is the arrangement of colours, and in beautiful music it is the arrangement of the notes that gives us pleasure; a single colour or a single tone is not the sort of thing we could derive aesthetic pleasure from.

However, this aspect of his aesthetic theory, although perhaps the one that is most attributed to him by artists and art critics, is not central to his aesthetic theory.

autonomy

The idea of autonomy lies at the heart of Kant's ethics because he identifies having a good will with being autonomous. The word autonomy comes from Greek. In Greek *'autos'* means 'self', and *'nomos'* means 'law', and so to be autonomous means to be a law to oneself. A major influence on Kant in the development of his idea of autonomy was Jean-Jacques **Rousseau** (1712–78), who had argued in his *On the Social Contract* (1762) that in an ideal republic one gives up one's natural freedom to do what one wants, but gains something far more valuable – being subject to laws one has made oneself, which he names moral freedom. Many readers of Kant stress that autonomy involves self-rule and self-determination and a form of independence, and suggest that this is what Kant really values about autonomy. It is true that Kant does believe in the value of self-determination and independence, arguing in *What is Enlightenment?* (1784), for example, that to be enlightened is to think for oneself, and arguing in the *Groundwork of the Metaphysics of Morals* (1785) that the opposite of autonomy is heteronomy, which means to be determined by something external. It would be a mistake, however, to identify the notion of autonomy with independence or self-determination, because, for Kant, autonomy involves more than the idea of self-determination and independence. For, central to the idea of autonomy is the notion of giving law, and Kant thinks that to be autonomous does not just involve ruling oneself, but involves giving law for a possible **community** or **realm of ends**, which involves the idea than in autonomous law-giving, one is giving law both for oneself and for others. The obvious model here is Rousseau's conception of citizens in a republic, each of whom shares the same general will and who are (collectively) both sovereign and subject to the laws they have jointly given. Thus in the *Groundwork of the Metaphysics of Morals* (1785) Kant presents the third formulation of the **categorical imperative** both in terms of being autonomous and in terms of being a member of a possible realm of ends, and this close, perhaps analytic, connection between the ideas of autonomy and the idea of being a member of a realm of ends should not be forgotten. See also: *Groundwork of the Metaphysics of Morals.*

Axioms of Intuition

This section of the *Critique of Pure Reason* (1781/1787) is concerned with the applicability of the **categories** of **quantity** (unity, plurality and totality) to objects of experience. Kant defends the **synthetic** *a priori* principle that 'all intuitions are extensive magnitudes'. An extensive magnitude is one where the representations of the parts make possible the representation of the whole. That is, an extensive magnitude is one that consists of a multitude of parts that are aggregated to form a whole, and Kant argues that all objects of experience, because they are experienced as extended in space and time, are magnitudes of this sort. If something is an extensive magnitude, then the categories of **quantity** must be applied to it because such a magnitude is a totality made up of a plurality of parts, and each of these parts must be thought of as a unity. Thus, judging something to be an extensive magnitude requires the application of the three categories of quantity. One should note that although spaces (and the bodies that occupy them) are extensive magnitudes, and hence are totalities consisting of a plurality of units, he does not think that these units are extensionless points. Instead he believes that space is indefinitely divisible, and so each of these units will itself be an extensive magnitude and hence each part of a space will itself be a space and so will itself be a unity made of parts. In other words, Kant thinks that the parts of a line are themselves lines, and that, strictly speaking, points are not parts of a line, but are merely limits of a line, and so a line is not made up of points. See also: **Anticipations of Perception.**

Baumgarten, Alexander Gottlieb (1714–62)

Baumgarten was a German rationalist philosopher and a follower of Gottfried Wilhelm **Leibniz** (1646–1716) and Christian **Wolff**

(1679–1754). Kant regularly lectured on metaphysics, and he used Baumgarten's *Metaphysics* (1739) as the textbook for his lectures. The organizational structure of the *Critique of Pure Reason* (1781/1787) is based upon that of Baumgarten's *Metaphysics*. In his *Aesthetics* (1750) Baumgarten was the first person to use the word 'aesthetics' in the modern sense to name the discipline that examines judgements of taste and the experience of beauty. In this work, which had an influence on the development of Kant's *Critique of Judgment* (1790), Baumgarten argues that the experience of beauty involves judgements of taste, and he defined the faculty of taste as a capacity to judge according to the senses rather than the intellect, with judgements of taste being based upon our feelings of pleasure and displeasure. See also: **rationalists.**

beauty

Kant's most important discussion of beauty is found in the *Critique of Judgment* (1790). In this work he provides an analysis of what is involved in judging an object to be beautiful. Beautiful objects produce a **feeling** of **pleasure,** but we do not regard all things that produce pleasure in us as beautiful, for there are many things that we regard as agreeable but not beautiful. For example, I enjoy chocolate, but this does not mean that I find chocolate beautiful. So, Kant thinks that experiencing something as beautiful involves both a feeling and a **judgement,** and Kant attempts to provide us with an analysis of what is involved in this judgement. Now, when introducing the **table of judgements** in the *Critique of Pure Reason* (1781/1787), Kant had argued that all judgements involve some (a) **quality,** (b) **quantity,** (c) relation and (d) **modality,** and in his analysis of judgements of beauty, he structures his discussion in terms of this fourfold distinction between aspects of any judgement. In the course of this discussion, Kant is careful to distinguish between what is involved in judging something to be beautiful and judging an object to be agreeable and judging an object to be good.

In terms of **quality,** Kant argues that the pleasure we have in the experience of something as beautiful must be *disinterested*. In saying this, one thing Kant wants to draw our attention to is the distinction between being beautiful and being useful. The picture on a banknote might actually be quite beautiful, but when someone gives me £100 note, the pleasure I get from seeing the note normally has to do with what I imagine doing with the money. Such pleasure is clearly not disinterested. So part of what it is for a pleasure to be disinterested is for the pleasure not to involve imagining how one can use a particular object. However, this is not at the heart of what Kant means by disinterested pleasure, for he explains that interest has to do with a representation of the existence of the object; so what is central to a pleasure being disinterested is that one does not care about the existence of the object. What Kant means by this is that disinterested pleasure does not depend on the existence of the object but on the experience of the appearance of the object. For example, imagine that one is enjoying looking at a £100 note but finds out that what one is looking at is not really a £100 note but merely a very good painting of the same. If my pleasures were merely interested, for example, I was enjoying thinking about how I would spend it, finding out that it was merely a painting would destroy the pleasure. If what I was enjoying was the object's beauty, however, then it would not matter whether the object really existed or not. However, when I am enjoying the beauty of an object, what I get pleasure from is the representation of the object and what I want is that the experience should continue, and I am not concerned with whether the object itself actually exists.

In terms of **quantity**, Kant argues that something that is beautiful pleases **universally** but without a **concept**. The first point Kant wishes to make here has to do with the distinction between something being agreeable and something being beautiful. Just because we find something agreeable, we do not expect other people to agree with us. I might like sushi, but I do not expect others to agree with me in this, for I recognize that everyone has their own taste. When it comes to beauty, however, we expect the same response from everyone. When I judge something to be beautiful, I do not just judge for myself but for everyone. For example, if I watch the sun set over the Bosporus and find it beautiful, I think that anyone who was in the same position should find it beautiful too. This is not to say that I believe that in actual fact any particular person standing here would actually find it beautiful; a property developer may look at the same scene and all that he can think about is the opportunity to build new hotels along its shores. In claiming that judgements of beauty are universal, Kant means that when we make such a judgement, we demand that others agree, and we may rebuke others if they do not agree with our judgement, thinking that their capacity to recognize beauty is somehow impaired.

Now, although judgements of beauty are universal in this sense, Kant believes that such judgements do not involve the application of concepts and this makes it difficult to understand how such judgements could be universal. When it comes to judgements that involve the application of concepts, it is easy to see how universal agreement can be required. For example, suppose one understands the concept 'cat', and one recognizes a particular animal as a cat. In such a case we expect others to agree with our judgement, and we think that someone who does not agree with our judgement either does not really understand the concept or has something wrong with his or her perceptual capacities. For, Kant thinks that concepts are rules, and understanding a concept involves understanding what something has to be to fall under that concept. But Kant thinks that judgements of beauty do not work in such a way. There is no objective rule that tells us what it is for an object to be beautiful in the same way as there is such a rule that tells us what it is to be a cat. Instead a beautiful object is one that affects us subjectively in a certain way, and Kant believes that we can explain how judgements of beauty can be universal by providing an account of how beautiful objects cause pleasure in us. Kant argues that the pleasure we get from experiencing a beautiful object is the result of what he calls the **free play** of our faculties, and in particular the faculties of **imagination** and **understanding**. The imagination is our faculty of having images, whereas the faculty of understanding is the faculty of conceptual thinking. Kant's thought here is that a beautiful object is one that allows a free play between these two faculties, and he thinks that the faculty of judgement mediates between the faculties of understanding and imagination. Kant distinguishes between two types of judgement which he calls determining and reflecting judgement. In a **determining judgement** one applies a particular concept to intuition. In a **reflecting judgement** one creates a new empirical concept to capture common features of different intuitions. In the experience of beauty which involves the free play of the imagination, however, one neither applies nor creates new concepts to determine judgements, but merely thinks over the object. An object is beautiful if it allows for such free play, and such judgements are universal because understanding and imagination are faculties that we all share, and so objects that allow a free play of these faculties for one should do so for all.

In terms of relation, Kant argues that a judgement of beauty involves judging the object to be purposeful, but without the representation of an objective end or purpose. That is, in such a judgement we judge the object to be purposeful without purpose. The notion of purposefulness without purpose is paradoxical. It is easy to understand how we can get interested pleasure in an object that we recognize as having a purpose. In such a case we are interested in what we can do with the object. I might love a chair because it is great to sit on and may enjoy looking at the chair because I imagine falling into it and sitting down. In such a case I regard the object as something that has a purpose, and I may get pleasure from seeing the chair if I desire to sit down and recognize that the chair would be good for sitting on. I may, however, see a chair that is a work of art and just enjoy looking at it. In such a case I do not care about its function or purpose. But this is not to say that I do not see it as purposeful; in fact I see it as something that should be looked at and enjoyed. Similarly, Kant thinks, when I watch a beautiful sunset, I do not think that the sunset has an objective purpose, but insofar as I find it beautiful I cannot help but think that the sunset is happening for a reason, but that purpose is subjective rather than objective. In the experience of beauty I regard the purpose of the sunset to be looked at and enjoyed. I think that what is happening is happing so that I can have the experience I am having. Thus in claiming that in a judgement of beauty the object is represented as purposive without purpose, Kant means that the object is regarded as objectively without purpose, but it is regarded as subjectively purposeful, with the purpose of the object being the pleasure I am getting. Kant's claim that in the judgement of beauty the object is represented as purposeful is important because he thinks that this means when we experience a natural object as beautiful, we must regard it as an artefact, that is, as something that is produced for a purpose. When we regard an artefact as beautiful, we already recognize it as purposeful merely because it is an artefact; but in order to judge an artefact as beautiful, we must also regard it as natural, and we must think of nature acting through the artist to create the artefact. This plays an important role in Kant's account of the importance of **genius** in the creation of beautiful **art,** for he defines genius as a capacity to create in a natural way, and so artefacts created by a genius will appear natural even though we recognize that, as artefacts, they were created with a purpose. Such works of art appear purposeful without objective purpose, for their only purpose is to be looked at and enjoyed.

Finally, in terms of **modality**, Kant argues that when we judge something to be beautiful, we regard the pleasure it produces in us as **necessary**. The necessity of such judgements is related to the universality of such judgements, for in his account of *a priori* judgements in general Kant has argued that **necessity** and **universality** are two features of any *a priori* judgement. One conclusion he draws from the necessity and universality of the pleasure in judgements of taste is that this presupposes the existence of a common sense. What Kant means by this is that when we make a judgement that something is beautiful, we assume that human beings are constituted in a similar way and that we all have similar capacities of understanding and imagination so that we are capable of experiencing the free play of these faculties in a similar way. It is only on this assumption that we can explain the possibility and communicability of judgements of taste. See also: *Critique of Judgment*; art.

beauty, free

In the *Critique of Judgment* (1790) Kant distinguishes between what he calls free **beauty** on the one hand and adherent or dependent beauty on the other. The distinction has got to do with whether our experience involves a specific concept of the beautiful object. For example, one can look at a flower and find it beautiful without knowing what flowers are or even thinking of it as a flower. This would be an example of free beauty. We can, however, find objects beautiful because they are perfect of their kind, and in order to find objects beautiful in this way requires a concept of the object. A watchmaker, for example, may find a particular watch beautiful *as a* watch because it fulfils its purpose so elegantly. In such cases the experience of the beauty of the object presupposes the concept of an object, and Kant calls such beauty adherent or dependent beauty. See also: *Critique of Judgment*.

beauty, ideal of

Kant's discussion of what he calls the **ideal** of **beauty** in the *Critique of Judgment* (1790) brings together his aesthetics and his moral theory. The ideal of beauty must be both exemplary and the paradigm of beauty and Kant argues that the perceivable human figure, and perhaps he is thinking of the human face in particular, serves as such an ideal, for the human figure can serve as a visible expression of moral ideas. In such a case, Kant suggests, there will be a harmony between the perceptible form of a human being and our moral ideal, which allows for a particularly rich free play between the faculties of imagination and understanding. See: *Critique of Judgment.*

benevolence

See: beneficence

beneficence

In the *Metaphysics of Morals* (1797) Kant argues that there are two principal duties of virtue. On the one hand, we have a duty towards ourselves, to strive for our own perfection. On the other hand, we have a duty to promote the happiness of others. What this duty demands is that we make the happiness of others our end. Beneficence is the virtue of acting so as to promote the happiness of others, and it is our primary duty of virtue towards others. When speaking carefully, Kant distinguishes between beneficence, which he claims is a **duty** involving the maxim of making others' happiness one's end and involves *acting* towards others in a way that promotes their happiness, and **benevolence,** which is the feeling of being satisfied or pleased by the happiness of others. Although we have a duty to be beneficent, Kant argues that we cannot have a duty to have benevolent feelings towards others, as feelings cannot be produced at will. A good person will be beneficent and help others in need even if they are not benevolent and do not get pleasure from the happiness they produce in others. This is not to say that Kant does not think that benevolence is a good thing, for he believes that we should try, insofar as it is in our power, to cultivate our feelings of benevolence.

Kant is often seen as too much of a rigorist in his ethics. His views on beneficence, however, are far less rigoristic than those of the **utilitarians**. For Kant argues that beneficence is a wide or imperfect duty. It does not specify when or how we should promote the happiness of another or who in particular we should help. Unlike the utilitarians, who believe that we should maximize the total happiness in society, Kant does not advocate the view that the duty to be beneficent requires that we aim to maximize happiness. We have a duty to care about the happiness of others, but how we do this is up to our free choice. So Kant thinks that there is nothing immoral in choosing to help one person in need rather than five, or with focusing our beneficence on those close to us. See also: *Metaphysics of Morals*.

Berkeley, George (1685–1753)

Berkeley was a British empiricist whose two best known works are the *Treatise concerning the Principles of Human Knowledge* (1710) and the *Three Dialogues between Hylas and Philonous* (1713). Berkeley is famous for denying the existence of material objects and advocating a form of subjective **idealism**. He argues that all that exist are thinkers and ideas, claiming that *esse est percipi (aut percipere)* – to be is to be perceived (or to perceive). For Berkeley, physical objects are merely ideas or collections of ideas. After the publication of the first edition of the *Critique of Pure Reason* in 1781, a number of critics accused Kant of advocating a form of subjective idealism like Berkeley's and in the second edition of the *Critique* (1787) one of his concerns was to respond to this accusation. This concern is particularly evident in a section he added to the second edition of the *Critique of Pure Reason* called the **Refutation of Idealism**. See: **formal idealism; Refutation of Idealism**.

canon

The distinction between a canon and an organon, which can be traced back to Epicurus (341–271), plays an important role in a number of Kant's *Critiques*. Whereas an organon is understood to be a set of rules for obtaining demonstrative knowledge and which can extend our cognition, a canon is merely a set of principles for discriminating between true and false judgements. One of Kant's central claims in the *Critique of Pure Reason* (1781/1787) is that **general logic** is not an organon but merely a canon. What he means by this is that we cannot extend our cognition by means of logic principles such as the **principle of non-contradiction**. This claim signals his rejection of rationalist metaphysics, for **rationalist** metaphysicians, such as Gottfried Wilhelm **Leibniz** (1646–1716) and Christian **Wolff** (1679–1754), had thought that logical analysis could extend our knowledge of the world. Thus Wolff, for example, had argued that the metaphysical principle of sufficient reason could be derived from the logical principle of non-contradiction. In claiming this Wolff was, to use Kant's language, illegitimately using general logic as an organon and not merely as a canon. See also: **logic.**

categorical imperative

Kant famously argues in the *Groundwork of the Metaphysics of Morals* (1785) that for human beings morality is a matter of obligation, for often the demands of morality conflict with our needs and desires. As such, morality is a matter of constraint, and this is why Kant argues that for human beings morality is a matter of imperatives or commands. Now Kant distinguishes between what he calls **hypothetical imperatives**, which tell us that if we will a certain end, we should also will the necessary means to the end, and what he calls the categorical imperative, which commands absolutely and unconditionally. Kant provides three formulations of the categorical imperatives. The first is the **formula of universalizability**, which he states in the following terms: 'Act only on that maxim by which you can at the same time will that it should become a universal law.' The second is the **formula of humanity**, which he states in the following terms: 'Act in such a way that you treat humanity, whether in your own person or in any other person, always at the same time as an end never merely as a means.' The third is the formula of the realm (or in some translations 'kingdom') of ends, which he states in the following terms: 'All maxims as proceeding from our own lawmaking ought to harmonize with a possible realm of ends as a realm of nature.' See also: *Groundwork of the Metaphysics of Morals*; universalizability, formula of; humanity, formula of; realm of ends, formula of; hypothetical imperative; unconditional value.

categorical judgement

In the **table of judgements** in the *Critique of Pure Reason* (1781/1787) the categorical form of judgement is introduced as the first of the three relations possible in a judgement, the other two being the **hypothetical judgement** and the **disjunctive judgement**. The categorical judgements are the basic building blocks of all judgements because the other two types of judgement relate judgements, and so require some categorical judgements to provide their content. A categorical judgement is a subject-predicate judgement, such as a judgement of the form '*a* is *b*'. In such a judgement *a* is the subject concept and *b* is the predicate concept. So, for example, in the categorical judgement 'Zübeyde is angry', 'Zübeyde' is the subject concept and 'angry' is the predicate concept. Categorical judgements can differ in their **quantity** and **quality**, so, for example, the judgements 'some students are happy' and 'not all students are happy' are also categorical judgements. Kant derives the **category** of substance (and properties) from the categorical form of judgement for a substance is a subject in which properties inhere, and the relationship between a substance and its properties is derived from the relationship between subject and predicate in a categorical judgement. See also: **hypothetical judgement; disjunctive judgement; substance; judgements, table of.**

categories, table of

Kant's table of categories, which is derived from his table of **judgements**, plays a central organizing role in his philosophy, with the structure of many of his works being derived from the structure of this table. Although Kant does not clearly explain the relationship between the table of judgements and the table of categories, he seems to think that the categories are concepts that are necessary for the application of the logical functions of judgement to objects. Kant divides the table into four classes and lists three categories under each class, and argues that the third category in each class involves the combination of the previous two. The categories of **quantity** are unity, plurality and totality; the categories of **quality** are reality, negation and limitation; the categories of relation are **substance, causation** and **community** (or interaction); and the categories of modality are **possibility, existence** and **necessity**.

For Kant the categories are *a priori* logical concepts that structure all of our thought. He also argues in the *Critique of Pure Reason* (1781/1787), for *a priori* **principles** that govern the application of the categories to objects of experience. For example, he argues in the Second **Analogy** for the principle that in experience, all alteration of substances must take place in accordance with the law of the connection of cause and effect. He argues against rationalist metaphysicians, however, that these principles are only principles that govern objects insofar as they can be experienced, and so denies that we can know that these principles apply to objects in general, which leaves open the possibility that the categories are not applicable to things as they are in themselves. See also: **judgements, table of.**

causation

Kant famously claimed that it was his reading of David **Hume** (1711–76) that woke him from his dogmatic slumbers, and many commentators in the English-speaking world read the *Critique of Pure Reason* (1781/1787) as primarily concerned with offering a response to Hume's skepticism about causation. Unlike the **empiricist** Hume, who argued that all our ideas, including our idea of causation, must be derived from sensations (which he called impressions), Kant argues that our concept of causation is an *a priori* logical concept that has its roots in our capacity to make hypothetical ('if . . . then') judgements. Thus he introduces the category of causation as the second category of relation in the table of **categories** presented in the *Critique of Pure Reason* (1781/1787). Kant argues that these categories are *a priori* logical concepts that are part of the logical structure of judgement. In a purely **logical** sense, the notion of causation is to be thought of as the ground-consequence relation. In a real sense, however, the notion of causation involves more than the notion of being a logical ground, for causation involves a temporal relation between cause and effect. So, in the Schematism of the Pure Concepts of the Understanding, Kant argues that a cause is something such that if it occurs something else, its effect, necessarily follows in a rule like way. Thus he claims that causation consists in the succession of the manifold insofar as it is subject to a rule.

In addition to giving an account of the *a priori* nature and content of our concept of causation, in the Second **Analogy** Kant famously tries to justify the **principle** that all alteration of substance must be subject to the law of the connection of cause and effect. Here Kant argues that the material world (the **phenomenal** world) is subject to strict **determinism**. There is some disagreement, however, as exactly how to interpret this principle, but at the very least it implies that any alteration of a substance must be the effect of some prior cause. Many commentators regard the Second Analogy as Kant's attempt to offer a reply to Hume, but it should be noted that in the Second Analogy Kant is primarily concerned with establishing a necessary, causal, relationship between the states of a particular substance and is not at this point arguing that there must be a causal relationship between individual substance. He will only argue for a necessary relationship between substances in the Third Analogy in which he defends a principle for the application of the category of **community** (or interaction) to objects of experience. Although Kant believes that this causal principle necessary applies to objects of possible experience, or phenomena, he does not believe that it necessarily applies to objects in general, and so he thinks that we do not know if **things-in-themselves** are subject to this principle. This leaves room for the possibility of a **free** cause, that is a cause that is not also an effect, and this possibility plays a central role in his ethics, for he argues that from the perspective of morality we must regard ourselves as free in this sense. In claiming that things-in-themselves might be free, Kant rejects the rationalist **principle of sufficient reason** as a general metaphysical principle that necessarily applies to objects in general. See: **Analogies of Experience; categories, table of; hypothetical form of judgement;** *a priori*.

character

Although Kant's ethics is often presented as being primarily concerned with the rightness or wrongness of individual actions, he is in fact primarily concerned with the character of agents, for having a **good will** is to have a particular type of character. In particular, to have a good will is to be **autonomous**, and Kant has a problem in explaining how it is possible for human beings to have such a character, for insofar as we regard ourselves as **phenomenal** objects, we must regard ourselves and our actions as subject to deterministic natural laws, and hence as unfree. In order to solve this problem Kant argues that although human beings, as phenomena, are unfree and hence not autonomous, this still leaves room for the possibility that we are or can be autonomous as we are in ourselves. In order to make sense of this account, Kant, in the **Antinomies of Pure Reason**, suggests that we can consider a moral agent as a cause, but can distinguish between what he calls the empirical character of the cause, through which its actions, as appearances, stand in connection with other appearances in accordance with constant natural laws, and the intelligible character of the cause, according to which it is regarded as the cause of the actions as appearances but is not itself regarded as an appearance; therefore, it is not itself subject to and determined by the natural laws that govern appearances and so can be thought of as free and potentially autonomous. Although it is difficult to make sense of the idea that as moral agents individuals are causes that have both an intelligible and empirical character, perhaps this does not matter. For perhaps all morality requires is that it is not contradictory to think of ourselves in this way even though we are unable to understand how it is really **possible** for us to be free. Kant himself, however, attempted throughout his career to make this idea comprehensible, although in his later ethical and religions writings, talk of an agent's intelligible character is replaced with talk of the agent's disposition. See: **freedom; transcendental idealism.**

cognition

The German word '*Erkentnis*' can either be translated as 'knowledge' or 'cognition', and in some English translations it is translated as 'knowledge'. There are, however, other words in German that can also be translated as knowledge, such as *Wissen*, which generally implies scientific knowledge, and *Kenntnis*, and so to preserve the distinction between these terms in English, translators today generally translate '*Erkentnis*' as 'cognition' and '*Wissen*' as knowledge. Cognition can be defined as our knowledge of objects by means of concepts and involves the cooperation of **sensibility** and **understanding**. For, as Kant famously claims, without sensibility no object would be given to us and without understanding no object would be thought and thoughts without content are empty and intuitions without concepts are blind. Cognition is intimately connected with the notion of truth, for Kant argues that truth, in the strict sense, involves the agreement of an idea with its object. Pure **analytic judgements**, then, do not provide us with cognition and hence are not, strictly speaking, true, for it is always possible that the concepts being compared in an analytic judgement do not refer to any objects and so the thought in such cases will be empty.

The human capacity for cognition, the topic of the *Critique of Pure Reason* (1781/1787), involves the cooperation of three faculties which Kant calls **sensibility, understanding** and **reason**. Sensibility is the faculty through which objects are given to us through **intuition**, understanding is the faculty by means of which objects are thought and subsumed under concepts and reason is the faulty of making **syllogistic** inferences based on **principles** and which attempts to unify our thought by organizing and systematizing the conceptual scheme of concepts. See: *Critique of Pure Reason.*

community, category of

In the *Critique of Pure Reason* (1781/1787), Kant introduces the **category** of community as the third category of **relation**. It is important to be aware that Kant identifies the category of community with that of mutual interaction, and often uses the words 'community' and 'interaction' interchangeably. The structure of the table of categories is derived from the table of judgements, and this table is divided into four classes: judgements of **quantity**, of **quality**, of **relation** and of **modality**. According to Kant there are three types of relational judgements: **categorical judgements** (*a* is *b*), **hypothetical judgements** (if p then q) and **disjunctive judgements** (p or q or r). The categories of **substance** and accident are derived from the categorical form of judgement, the categories of **cause** and effect from the hypothetical form of judgement and the category of community or interaction from the disjunctive form of judgement.

A **disjunctive judgement** is a judgement in which a number of judgements somehow restrict one another and fill up a logical space. So, for example, in the disjunctive judgement 'knowledge is either *a priori* or *a posteriori*'; the whole sphere is knowledge, and this sphere is divided into two exclusive parts which exhaust the possibilities. The assertion of the judgement that some piece of knowledge is *a priori* rationally excludes the assertion of the judgement that it is *a posteriori*. This is important for Kant's understanding of the way in which the disjunctive form of judgement is related to the category of community or mutual interaction. His thought here seems to be that the notion of mutual interaction involves the notion of exclusion and resistance, for one material substance fills space through its repulsive force by resisting the penetration of the force of other substances. It is this mutual interplay of forces which lies behind the mutual interaction of physical substances, and his thought is that we can understand this notion of exclusion *a priori* in terms of the way in which in a disjunctive judgement the assertion of one of the disjuncts excludes the assertion of all the others.

It is important to note that Kant believes that the concept of interaction is to be sharply distinguished from that of mutual causation, for the categories of community and causation are derived from different forms of judgement. We understand the importance of this claim by considering an alternative way of conceptualizing interaction. Defenders of such an alternative conception of interaction would argue that we can fully capture what is involved in interaction in the following terms: when two entities, say x and y, interact, x has a causal relation to y and y has a causal relation to x. Kant does not deny that this partially captures what is involved in the relation of interaction, but he does not believe that it is the full story, for he believes that when a number of entities interact, they must (a) constitute a whole and (b) mutually exclude one another. These two factors are essential to the relation of interaction and cannot be captured by appealing to the ideas of ground and consequence or to the hypothetical form of judgement. Thus, in his commentary to the table of categories in the *Critique of Pure Reason* Kant compares the causal relation to the relation of interaction/community and points out that in the case of simple causation the relation is one of subordination, whereas in the case of interaction the relation is one of coordination. What he means by this is that in a causal relation the consequence is subordinated to the ground. For this reason the ground-consequence relation is the principle of the **series**, for the relation of ground and consequence can provide us with a well-ordered chain of causes and effects. The relation of community, however, cannot be understood in terms of the idea of subordination, for when a number of entities are members of a community, they are not subordinated to one another but are coordinated with one another. The concept of coordination cannot be understood in terms of mutual subordination. When entities are coordinated with one another, they are parts of a whole and mutually exclude one another.

In his commentary on the **table of categories**, Kant explains that the categories he has listed do not provide a complete list of the *a priori* concepts of the understanding, for there are also derivative concepts, which Kant calls 'predicables', which can be derived from the categories. Under the category of community Kant lists two derivative concepts or 'predicables': presence and resistance. Kant's thought here seems to be that the reason why resistance is a predicable of the category of community is because our concept of resistance is to be understood in terms of exclusion, and we understand the notion of exclusion *a priori* through our grasp of the disjunctive form of judgement. What we mean if we claim that one thing resists another is that if (or, insofar as) the thing is posited, all the rest are excluded. The category of community, then, allows us to understand the notion of a number of impenetrable individuals (concepts) filling a conceptual space (another concept) and excluding other individuals (concepts) from their part of the conceptual space, without any appeal to the space of intuition. This is why Kant often equates the concept of community with that of interaction.

In the Third **Analogy** of the *Critique of Pure Reason* Kant argues that the application of the category of community to experience is necessary for us to make judgements of simultaneity arguing that things are simultaneous if in empirical intuition the perception of one can follow the perception of the other reciprocally. Indeed, the notion of simultaneity is so closely connected to the category of community that Kant changed the title of the Third Analogy from 'The Principle of Community' in the first edition to 'The Principle of Simultaneity, According to the Law of Interaction, or Community'

(B256) in the second. See: **categories, table of; disjunctive judgement; Analogies of Experience.**

concept

In the *Critique of Pure Reason* (1781/1787) Kant distinguishes between the faculties of **sensibility, understanding** and **reason,** all of which play a role in human **cognition.** Sensibility is the faculty through which objects are given to us through **intuition.** Understanding is the faculty by means of which objects are thought and subsumed under concepts. Reason is the faculty of syllogistic reasoning based on principles. Thus this threefold distinction between faculties corresponds to a threefold distinction between (a) objects, (b) concepts, and (c) principles. Kant characterizes what it is to be a concept in many ways, four of which will be examined here. Thus, Kant claims that concepts are (1) predicates of a possible judgement, that they (2) have the function of supplying unity, that they (3) are rules and that they are (4) always general.

First, Kant claims that concepts are predicates of possible judgements and as such refer to some presentation of an as yet undetermined object. A subject-predicate judgement (or to use Kant's technical language a **categorical judgement**) is a judgement of the form '*a* is *b*'. For example, 'The cat is hungry' is a subject-predicate judgement. In this judgement 'the cat' is the subject. It is not clear, however, what we should regard as the predicate. Logicians have offered three distinct accounts of what part of the sentence is the predicate. The predicate is either to be thought of as: 'hungry' 'is hungry' or '[ ] is hungry', where the square brackets are meant to indicate that the predicate is in a sense gappy and has a hole in it that needs to be filled with another concept or the **intuition** of an object in order to form a complete thought or judgement. This view of predicates (and hence concepts) as gappy, incomplete judgements is probably the most plausible way of reading Kant here. Although concepts are gappy in this sense in that they always purport to refer to objects and purport to have some domain of reference they can be applied to, we can abstract from this aspect of concepts, and this is what we do when making analytic judgements, for in such judgements we do not care about this aspect of concepts or to whether or not they actually refer.

Second, Kant argues that judgements have the function of supplying unity among our representations, and it is our possession of concepts that allows us to do this. In this sense Kant is thinking of concepts as universals which have the function of representing many as one. Thus, for example, the concept 'cat' allows me to represent a multitude of distinct objects as one. When I think of the concept 'cat', I am only thinking one concept, but this concept allows me to think of a multitude of distinct objects simultaneously. If we think of concepts as gappy, then thinking a concept is a way of picking out all the possible objects that could fill the gap.

Third, Kant often claims that concepts are rules. What he seems to have in mind here is that a concept is a rule for potentially dividing a set of objects into two classes: those that fall under the concept and those that do not. Concepts, then, function as rules for categorizing objects. The fact that understanding is the faculty of rules is one of the things that distinguishes it from **reason**, which Kant claims is the faculty of **principles**.

Finally, Kant believes that concepts are essentially general. To understand the significance of this claim, we must examine his account of the distinction between the faculties of understanding and sensibility, for the main thing that distinguishes the understanding from the faculty of sensibility is that concepts are essentially general whereas the objects of sensibility are particular and singular. In claiming that concepts are essentially general, Kant means that any concept can be further specified, and as such any concept is indeterminate in regard to what is not included in the concept. For example, the concept 'bachelor' includes neither the concept 'happy' nor the concept 'non-happy', and so neither the judgement 'all bachelors are happy' nor the judgement 'all bachelors are non-happy' are analytically true. This fact means that the concept 'bachelor' can be specified into the concepts 'happy bachelor' and 'non-happy bachelor' and these two more specific concepts are themselves general and so can be divided into more specific concepts. In claiming that all concepts are general Kant is denying the possibility of what Gottfried Wilhelm **Leibniz** (1646–1716) called the 'complete concept' of an individual, for Kant thinks that no concept can be complete in Leibniz' sense. In claiming this, Kant is denying the possibility of a lowest concept, that is, a concept that is completely specific and does not, in principle, allow of further specification. In this sense, concepts are radically different from objects, which are subject to what Kant calls 'the principle of thoroughgoing determination'. According to this principle, for any arbitrary concept any object will either fall under the concept or fall under the opposite of the concept. This means that for any concept there will be a determinate answer as to whether or not the concept can be applied to the object. Kant argues, however, that this is a principle that applies to objects, but not to concepts, for concepts are not fully determinate in this sense. And Kant thought that rationalist metaphysicians, and especially Leibniz, failed to make this essential distinction between the nature of concepts and the nature of objects. Now, although Kant thinks that all concepts are, in principle, general because any arbitrary concept can be further specified or determined, this does not imply that such concepts cannot be used to think of particular singular objects, for it is often the case that a concept is specific enough to pick out a single object in the world. So although all concepts are general, they can be used to make **singular judgements**. See: **reason; sensibility; intuition.**

Conjectural Beginning of Human History (1786)

This short essay was written as a response to his former student Johann Gottfried Herder's (1744–1803) *Ideas for a Philosophy of the History of Humanity* (1784). In this work, which is strongly influenced by Kant's reading of Jean-Jacques **Rousseau** (1712–78), Kant offers a speculative naturalistic account of the emergence of rationality and reason in the human species. Particularly interesting is Kant's naturalistic reinterpretation of the Adam and Eve myth in Genesis as offering an account of the emergence of reason and freedom in human beings. Originally, Kant claims, human beings, like all other animals, were guided purely by instinct, and this was a perfectly good guide for securing their **happiness**. For example, instinct represented certain objects in the world as edible and some as inedible. With the development of reason, which led to an expansion of our conceptual capacities, however, we came to classify things as edible that were either relevantly similar to the things instinct regarded as edible or to things that we saw other animals eating, even if our instinct represented the object as inedible. Reason then led to the expansion of our desires beyond those given to us by our instincts, and even towards things contrary to our instincts, and because of this, Kant argues, human beings were forced, for the first time, to make free choices as to whether to listen to their instincts or to their reason. Kant suggests that the story of Adam and Eve eating the forbidden apple is supposed to illustrate the development. Kant supposes that human beings were born with an instinct that told them that apples were inedible, but over time they came to recognize that apples were relevantly similar to other things that were edible, or perhaps they saw other animals eating apples, and so came to apply the concept 'edible' to apples. But this left them facing a choice because instinct forbade eating the apple, whereas reason and its concepts told them to eat it. What is particularly interesting, and radical, about this story is that Kant interprets the desire to eat the apple as coming from reason, and replaces what was the voice of **God** in the biblical story, which forbade eating, with the call of instinct. It is also worth noting that Kant presents reason as a faculty that expands desire beyond our natural instincts, which has the downside of leading to much unhappiness, but also leads to the possibility of free will and autonomy. See: **Rousseau.**

consequentialism

Consequentialism is the name of the moral doctrine that claims that the moral worth of an action is determined by its consequences or intended consequences. The most influential form of consequentialism is **utilitarianism**. Utilitarians argue that pleasure is the only good and pain the only bad, and that a good action is one that maximizes total net pleasure (pleasure minus pain) in society. Kant rejects consequentialist ethics, arguing that the value of an action is not determined by its consequences but by the principle behind the action.

constitutive principle

In the *Critique of Pure Reason* (1781/1787) Kant distinguished between constitutive principles and regulative principles. Constitutive principles are *a priori* principles for the application of concepts to objects, and as such allow us to extend our cognition. Kant argues that the principles of the **Anticipations of Perception** and the **Axioms of Intuition** are constitutive in this sense. Regulative principles, however, do not allow us to extend our cognition but merely tell us how we ought to think and organize our thought. So, for example, in the **Dialectic** Kant argues that reason demands that we seek unity in our conceptual scheme by always seeking greater **systematicity** and specification of our concepts, but this does not imply that complete unity can ever be achieved. Regulative principles demand that we seek something – but they do not guarantee that what we are looking for can be found.

constructivism

Moral constructivism is an extremely influential view in recent Kantian ethics defended by **John Rawls** (1921–2002) and his followers, many of whom interpret Kant as a moral constructivist. At the heart of the moral constructivist position is the belief that 'the right is prior to the good'. This slogan has become the rallying cry of Rawls' followers. To understand what this slogan means, we can contrast the constructivist position with that of the **utilitarian**, who believes, in contrast to the Rawlsian, that the 'good is prior to the right'. The utilitarian starts with a conception of the good (the greatest happiness) and defines the right (and the reasonable) in terms of this, for a utilitarian believes that an action is right if and only if it promotes the good, that is the greatest happiness. A moral constructivist, in contrast, starts with a conception of the right or the reasonable and defines the good in terms of this: a state of affairs is good if it was or at least could have been chosen in the right way. Rawls' claim about the priority of the right over the good can be understood as a claim about practical reason. The utilitarian will define reasonableness in terms of the good, whereas the constructivist will define the good in terms of the reasonable. Imagine a group of individuals who wish to share a cake. The utilitarian will argue that the procedure we use to determine how to divide up the cake is reasonable if it is intended or likely to produce the best decision, that is, a decision that maximizes total happiness.

The constructivist, in contrast, will argue that a decision is good if the procedure that is used to make the decision is a reasonable one; any outcome that is the result of a fair procedure will be good. In this approach, what it is to be reasonable must be defined independently of, and prior to, any conception of the good or the desirable. A moral constructivist, then, believes that the morally desirable must be defined in terms of the reasonably willable. A constructivist ethics, then, must start by providing an account of the reasonably willable, and this is precisely what Rawls believes Kant is trying to do when he introduces the first formulation of the **Categorical Imperative** in the *Groundwork of the Metaphysics of Morals* (1785), for Rawls argues that the first formulation of the categorical imperative, the formula of **universalizability**, should be understood as introducing a procedure to test the reasonableness of maxims. According to Rawls, then, the first formulation of the categorical imperative is an attempt to give an account of what it is to be reasonable that makes no reference to the good or the morally desirable. The first formulation of the categorical imperative, then, specifies a procedure to test the reasonableness of our maxims. According to this interpretation the second and third formulations (the formula of **humanity** and the formula of the **realm of ends**) do not specify the procedure a reasonable person should use to test the reasonableness of her maxims, but specify the objects that such a reasonable person will value. A reasonable person will value the humanity of herself and others, and will value the idea of being a member of a realm of ends. The notions of 'humanity' and 'a realm of ends' are concepts of the good, and as a moral constructivist, Rawls is committed to the position that these two ideas must be defined in terms of the procedure he believes is introduced in the first formulation. In other words, he believes that the second and third formulations of the categorical imperative are dependent for their content upon the first formulation. See: **Rawls, John; categorical imperative; universalizability, formula of.**

conversion

There is a tension in Kant's ethics between thinking of goodness of will as something that comes in degrees and thinking of it as a binary either-or matter. On the one hand, a good will would seem to be something that one either has or does not have. On the other hand, **virtue**, understood as strength of character seems to be something that comes in degrees, for we can be more or less virtuous. Now although Kant believes that we should strive to be perfectly virtuous, all we can reasonably hope for is a gradual but constant improvement in our character over time, and, given our nature, at any moment in time we will be less than perfectly virtuous. Kant also thinks, however, that morality requires some sort of moral conversion or rebirth, and this would seem to be an either-or matter. And it is not clear how these two views can be combined. The two views can perhaps be reconciled if we think of this either-or moment of rebirth as a firm resolution to start on the path of gradual moral improvement. This importance of a sudden moment of rebirth played a central role in the theory and practice of eighteenth-century Prussian **Pietism**. Kant himself received a Pietist education at the *Collegium Fridericianum*, where the encouragement of such a conversion experience was considered to be the primary aim of education. Students who had not yet experienced a breakthrough were expected to exhibit a repentant attitude and demonstrate that they were preparing to be 'born again', and a huge emphasis was placed upon breaking the child's natural will in the hope of provoking such a rebirth experience. And professing such a rebirth experience helped one to get ahead in the Prussian state bureaucracy and educational institutions. And it is clear that Kant was disgusted by this hypocrisy and the insincere effusions of emotionality this led to. Having said this, although Kant was opposed to much Pietist practice concerning a change of heart, he himself does argue, most notably in *Anthropology from a Pragmatic Point of View* (1798) and *Religion within the Boundaries of Mere Reason* (1793), that morality requires some sort of conversion or revolution of character. Kant conceives of such a revolution, or what he sometimes calls the establishment of character, as a firm resolution to strive for perfection and begin on the long path of gradual but constant moral improvement. He stresses, however, that this change of heart has to be freely chosen and so cannot be imposed on children by trying to break their wills and is more likely to occur later in life when one has reached maturity. Kant also found the Pietist practice of treating the rebirth experience of others as models to follow morally objectionable as it undermined what he took to be the purity of ethical demands. One of the dominant forms of Pietist literature at Kant's time was the conversion narrative, and these narratives were used as models to be emulated. But Kant thinks trying to imitate the behaviour of others undermines the purity morality demands. Given human weakness, taking the experience of another person, however virtuous she may be, is to take something less than perfect as our model, and this makes it much easier for us to give excuses to ourselves. Conversion, Kant believes, is something that we can experience personally, by choosing sincerely and resolutely to strive for moral perfection and to take the first step on the long path to this goal, but it is not something to be imitated. For Kant, we should try and be perfect, not try to be someone who is trying to be perfect. Although the Pietist notion of a change of heart plays an important role in Kant's ethics, he secularizes this ideal. For the Pietists this breakthrough involved subordinating one's natural inclinations to the divine will, whereas, for Kant, it involves subordinating them to the moral law. See: **Pietism**; religion; *Anthropology from a Pragmatic Point of View*; *Religion within the Boundaries of Mere Reason*.

Copernican Revolution

In the Preface to the second edition of the *Critique of Pure Reason* (1787) Kant famously compares his revolution in philosophy to that of Copernicus in astronomy. Previous astronomers had assumed that the sun circled the earth and Copernicus' revolution was to assume that the earth circles the sun. Kant argues that his philosophy provides an analogous revolution. Previous philosophers had assumed that physical objects exist independently of the knowing mind and that the mind is passive in experience. According to this view, knowledge consists in our representation of the object corresponding to the object. If we think of our ideas as like paintings we could say that knowledge consists of our mental pictures being accurate depictions of objects in the world. The problem with such a view is that it naturally leads to a type of skepticism about our capacity to know the world, for if our ideas are like pictures and all that we are immediately aware of are our pictures of objects, then we have no way of knowing whether these pictures are accurate representations of reality or not. In order to know whether our representations are accurate depictions of reality, we would have to have immediate access to both the idea and reality, to the picture and the object pictured. However, according to this model, we are only immediately aware of our ideas and not of the objects represented by these ideas, and so we can have no way of knowing whether these ideas correspond to the object or not. Hence, such a view ultimately forces us to a skeptical conclusion.

Kant's *Copernican revolution* is to suggest that instead of our representations corresponding to objects, we should assume that in knowledge the objects must conform to our representations. According to this position the mind is essentially active in cognition. Kant's thought here is that in order for something to be a possible object of experience, it must conform to certain constraints. Now, as these constraints on possible objects of cognition have to do with the way our minds work, we can learn what these constraints are, not by examining the world but by examining our cognitive faculties. Thus Kant's Copernican revolution suggests a new method for philosophy. Instead of starting, as traditional **metaphysics** did, with an examination of the mind-independent world, philosophy should begin with a **critique** of our cognitive faculties. The aim of such a critique is to discover the *a priori* principles that govern and limit our cognitive capacities. Kant names his style of philosophy, which begins with an examination of our cognitive capacities, **transcendental** philosophy. See: *Critique of Pure Reason*.

cosmological argument

The cosmological argument for the existence of God is the argument that the world requires a first cause, and such a cause must be God. Kant has a number of objections to this argument. First, it presupposes a commitment to the **principle of sufficient reason** (the principle that everything must have a cause). Now, in the second **Analogy of Experience**, Kant argues that this principle does apply to possible objects of experience (phenomena), for every alteration that can be experienced must have a cause. However, he believes that we have no justification for believing that the principle applies to things-in-themselves. So, given that the cosmological argument rests on the assumption that the principle of sufficient reason is a general principle that applies to everything, including things-in-themselves, Kant rejects the argument as resting on an unjustified, **dogmatic** assumption. Second, even if the universe must have a first cause there is no good reason to identify this first cause with God as traditionally conceived, for even if it could be proved that there must be a first cause there would be no good reason to assume that such a cause must be wise, omnipotent, omniscient and good. Kant discusses the cosmological argument in the Ideal of Pure Reason and the third **Antinomy of Pure Reason** in the *Critique of Pure Reason* (1781/1787). See: **principle of sufficient reason; Critique of Pure Reason.**

critical Kant

Kant radically changed many of his philosophical positions when he wrote the *Critique of Pure Reason* (1781), and so scholars generally refer to Kant's position from the time of writing the first Critique onwards as that of the critical Kant and refer to his earlier position as his **pre-critical** position.

critique

Kant aims to steer a middle course between **dogmatism** and **skepticism**. The **rationalist**s had assumed that human **reason** was capable *of a priori* knowledge of **things as they are in themselves,** and they thought that the task of metaphysics was to provide such knowledge, and Kant believed that such rationalist metaphysics was dogmatic. The skeptics had argued that all *a priori* knowledge was impossible. Kant argues against the dogmatist that we cannot have *a priori* knowledge of things as they are in themselves, but argues against the skeptic that we can have *a priori* knowledge of appearances, and we can secure such knowledge through a critical examination of our cognitive faculties. Kant believes that each of our capacities is structured by certain *a priori* principles, and a critique is a critical examination of a cognitive faculty that attempts to discover the *a priori* principles that govern the faculty and examines the scope and limitations of these *a priori* principles. Kant believes that there are three basic cognate faculties: our faculty of theoretical knowledge, our faculty of desire or will and our faculty of feeling pleasure and pain. The *Critique of Pure Reason* examines the scope and limits of our capacity of theoretical knowledge and concludes that although we can have no knowledge of things as they are in themselves, we can have *a priori* knowledge of objects as they appear to us. The *Critique of Practical Reason* examines the **faculty of desire** or the **will** and argues that to be rational, action must be constrained by the **moral law**. The topic of the *Critique of Judgment* is less clear. On the one hand, the topic of the *Critique of Judgment* seems to be the faculty of judgement. And Kant himself claims that this *Critique* is meant to offer a critique of the faculty of **judgement** and the book is divided into two sections: a Critique of **Aesthetic** Judgment, which might also have been called a critique of **taste**, and the Critique of Teleological Judgment. On the other hand, there are reasons to think that the *Critique of Judgment* started as a critique of our faculty of **feeling**, which is our capacity to feel pleasure and pain and one of the aims of the third *Critique* is to argue that that the faculty for feeling is governed by certain *a priori* principles.

The relationship between the three Critiques is the topic of much scholarly debate. Although Kant wrote the three *Critiques*, and they can be thought of a constituting one overall system, when Kant first began his critical project, he did not plan to write three Critiques. When he wrote the first edition of the **Critique of Pure Reason,** which was published in 1781, he did not plan to write a **Critique of Practical Reason** (1788). Indeed what became the *Critique of Practical Reason* was originally planned to be an appendix to the second edition of the *Critique of Pure Reason*, which was published in 1787. Similarly, the first evidence that Kant intended to write a critique of taste, which evolved into the **Critique of Judgment** (1790), is also dated to 1787. Indeed, when he first wrote the **Critique of Pure Reason,** there are reasons to think that he thought the project of the third *Critique* was not possible, as in 1781 he thought that there could be no *a priori* principles of taste, and so thought that a critique of this capacity was in principle impossible.

Kant sometimes explains that the relationship between the three Critiques is that the first Critique examines the realm of nature (natural science), the second Critique examines the realm of freedom (morality) and the third Critique examines our capacity for judgement, which, Kant suggests, is supposed to provide a bridge between these two realms. It is not clear, however, how judgement is supposed to play this bridging role, and the evidence suggests that Kant was not thinking of judgement in these terms when he first published the *Critique of Pure Reason*. See: **Critique of Pure Reason**; **Critique of Practical Reason**; **Critique of Judgment**.

Critique of Judgment (1790)

The *Critique of Judgment*, was Kant's third and final Critique, and is often referred to as the third Critique. When Kant started his critical project with the **Critique of Pure Reason** (1781/1787), he did not plan to write a second or third Critique. Indeed he thought that a critique of taste was impossible as he thought that there were and could be no *a priori* **principles** of the faculty of feeling. He seems to have started work on what became the *Critique of Judgment* in 1786, and originally his plan was to write a work entitled the Critique of Taste.

Kant wrote two introductions to the *Critique of Judgment*. The first, and longer, version of the Introduction was not published in the first edition of the *Critique of Judgment*, but was published separately. It is now, however, routinely included in modern editions and translations in addition to the published introduction. In both versions of the Introduction Kant explains the way in which the third Critique fits into his overall system. He argues that there are three main faculties of the human mind: the faculty of **cognition**, which was dealt with in the **Critique of Pure Reason** (1781/1787); the faculty of **desire**, or the will, which was the topic of the **Critique of Practical Reason** (1788); and the faculty of **feeling** pleasure and displeasure, which he suggests will be the topic of the *Critique of Judgment* (1790). Now in addition to this tripartite division Kant suggests that there is also a tripartite division of the intellectual powers of the mind into three capacities which he calls **reason**, **judgement** and **understanding**. Understanding is the faculty of **concepts**, and is the source of our *a priori* principles of cognition. It is understanding that provides the concepts and **principles** that govern the realm of nature. Reason is the faculty of **ideas**, and is the source of the *a priori* principles that govern the faculty of desire, for reason is the source of the moral law. It is reason, with its ideas and laws, that governs the realm of freedom. This leaves the faculty of judgement which, Kant suggests, somehow mediates between reason and understanding, and in so doing can somehow provide a bridge between the realm of freedom (the moral/intelligible world) and the realm of nature (the phenomenal world). Kant also suggests as a hypothesis that it is the faculty of judgement that is the source of the *a priori* principles of the faculty of feeling pleasure and displeasure.

Now, Kant distinguishes between two forms of judgement: **reflecting judgement** and **determining judgement**. When he talks of the faculty of judgement, it is the reflecting use of judgement that is, strictly speaking, called the faculty of judgement and is the topic of the *Critique of Judgment*. In the determining use of judgement we start with a given universal (which can be a rule, principle, law or concept), and the task is to find a particular that falls under the universal. So, for example, one may already possess the concept 'cat' and when one sees a particular cat, one may judge: 'this is a cat'. This would be an example of the determining use of judgement. The reflecting use of judgement begins with the awareness of a particular object or objects and the task is to find or create a universal under which to subsume the particular object or objects. Kant suggests that there are three main types of reflecting judgement which he names the logical, the **aesthetic** and the teleological use of the power of judgement, although in the body of the *Critique of Judgment* he only discusses the second and third of these uses of reflecting judgement. First, the logical use of the power of (reflecting) judgement involves the search for empirical concepts and laws that mediate between the categories and *a priori* principles and particular natural objects. In the *Critique of Pure Reason* Kant had provided arguments for the claim that very general concepts and principles must govern the natural world. However in order to apply these principles, they need to be made more specific and given empirical content, and Kant argues that it is the logical use of reflecting judgement that supplies this specification. So, for example, Kant argued in the Second **Analogy** for the very general law that every event must have a cause; however, the concept of a cause here is very abstract and general, and in order to apply this general concept, we need more concrete and specific conceptions of causation. For example, a fully developed science needs more specific causal notion such as the concepts of crystallization, gravitational force and electromagnetic force, and it is the task of the logical use of reflecting judgement to construct these concepts. And Kant believes there are *a priori* principles that govern the construction of such concepts, and in particular the idea of **systematicity**, for when we develop such concepts we must try and make them fit into our overall conceptual structure. The second use of reflecting judgement occurs in **aesthetic** judgements. Kant argues that in such judgements we do not attempt to subsume the object under a determinate universal concept, and that the only universal we can find is the idea of interpersonal agreement. So aesthetic judgements are judgements that do not involve the finding a particular concept under which the particular object being experienced can be subsumed. The third use of reflecting judgement is in teleological judgement, which involves recognizing both the teleology involved in the internal organization of living organisms and the purposiveness of nature as a whole. The second and third forms of reflective judgement are the main topics of the *Critique of Judgment*, for the book is divided into two main parts, the Critique of Aesthetic Judgment and the Critique of Teleological Judgment.

The Critique of Aesthetic Judgment is mainly concerned with offering an analysis of the **Beautiful** and the **Sublime**. The feelings of Beauty and the Sublime are two distinct types of aesthetic experience. Each involves both judgement and a feeling of pleasure, and Kant argues that in both cases the judgements have their own *a priori* principles.

The judgement involved in the experience of beauty has four aspects. First, the pleasure involved must be a **disinterested** one. In claiming this Kant is distinguishing between finding something useful and finding it Beautiful. When we experience something as beautiful, we are not interested in what we can do with the object or how it is to be used. Second, Kant argues that something is beautiful which pleases **universally** but without a **concept**. The first point Kant wishes to make here has to do with the distinction between something being agreeable and something being beautiful. Just because we find something agreeable, we do not expect other people to agree with us. Now, although judgements of beauty are universal in this sense, Kant believes, however, that such judgements do not involve the application of concepts, and this makes it difficult to understand how such judgements could be universal. Kant believes that we can explain how judgements of beauty can be universal by providing an account of how beautiful objects cause pleasure in us. Kant argues that the pleasure we get from beautiful objects is the result of what he calls the free play of our faculties, and in particular the faculties of **imagination** and **understanding**. Third, Kant argues that the judgement of beauty involves judging the object to be purposeful, without the representation of an end. This notion of an object being regarded as purposive but without purpose is paradoxical. In the experience of beauty I regard the purpose of the sunset to be looked at and enjoyed. I think that what is happening is happing so that I can have the experience I am having. Thus in claiming that in a judgement of beauty the object is represented as purposive without purpose, Kant means that the object is regarded as objectively without purpose, but it is regarded as subjectively purposeful, with the purpose of the object being the pleasure I am getting. Finally, in terms of modality, Kant argues that when we judge something to be beautiful, we regard the pleasure it produces in us as **necessary**. One conclusion he draws from the necessity and universality of the pleasure in judgements of taste is that this presupposes the existence of a common sense. What Kant means by this is that when we make a judgement that something is beautiful, we assume that human beings are constituted in a similar way and that we all have similar capacities of understanding and imagination so that we are capable of experiencing the free play of these faculties in a similar way. It is only on this assumption that we can explain the possibility of the agreement between individuals in their aesthetic responses and the communicability of judgements of taste.

In the experience of the **sublime** we take pleasure in things that are in a sense also the source of painful or displeasurable feelings. Kant distinguishes between two types of sublime, which he names the mathematically sublime and the dynamically sublime. The mathematically sublime is Kant's name for the aesthetic experience we have when we experience something huge or great, such as the experience one has when observing the pyramids or entering St Peter's Basilica in Rome. Kant believes that this feeling is produced when we experience objects that we are unable to fully grasp in our imagination. In such experiences although we recognize the object as a totality consisting of a plurality of parts, there are so many parts that we are unable to see how the object as a whole is constituted by these parts. The **quantity** of parts is just too great for our capacities of understanding and imagination to grasp and so even though there are a finite and determinate number of parts, there are too many for us to grasp them all simultaneously. And this feeling is, Kant argues, pleasurable. Now this feeling of infinity is really a recognition of the incapacity of our imagination, and one might think that recognition of an inability would be painful not pleasurable. Normally when we recognize that we cannot do something, the feeling we experience is one of frustration, not one of pleasure. Kant thinks, however, that this recognition of the incapacity of imagination gives us the feeling that there is more than the world of sense, for in a way such experiences transport us, at least in terms of feeling, into the intelligible realm. The second type of sublime experience is what Kant calls the dynamically sublime, which involves experiencing the power and terrifying force of nature, while recognizing that this power has no dominion over us. In such cases we recognize the destructive power of nature but feel safe. Some of Kant's own examples are the pleasure we get from experiencing overhanging and as it were threatening cliffs, or a powerful storm. Kant's account of the dynamically sublime might help to explain the pleasure we get from watching tragedies and horror films. Kant argues that the dynamically sublime involves the feeling of fear and normally fear is not pleasurable, and so Kant needs to explain how something that is normally the source of displeasure can be the source of pleasure. Kant's response is that we get pleasure if we recognize something as fearful but are not afraid. Such experiences allow us to feel our moral **freedom** in the face of nature, for they make us feel that however threatening nature may be to us, it is always possible for us to resist this power and this feeling of our moral freedom is, Kant believes, immensely pleasurable.

Although Kant is primarily concerned with the beauty and sublimity of natural object, he also has some interesting things to say about art, and he assumes that our appreciation of art involves the same aesthetic feelings as our experience of natural beauty and sublimity. In addition to being interested in the question of the experience of art, he is also concerned with the question of artistic creation, and argues that the creation of art requires **genius**. In saying this he does not mean to suggest that artists are a strange breed different from other human beings, for genius is a capacity that we all have, being the capacity to act in rule-governed ways without consciously following rules. Kant believes that such a capacity is necessary for the creation of beautiful objects, and so necessary for artistic creation, because a beautiful object must appear artificial, as the experience of beauty requires that the object be experienced simultaneously as both purposeful and natural. If an object is recognized as an artefact, then as such it will be recognized as being something that was consciously made and hence purposeful, and so the trick is for the artist to also make the object appear natural. Now, if the artist or artisan is merely mechanically following rules for the production of an object, the object will appear unnatural and clumsy. So Kant believes that the production of beautiful objects is only possible if the artist is not consciously applying rules and this capacity to produce an object that is rule-governed but without consciously applying or following rules is what Kant calls genius.

In the Critique of Teleological Judgment Kant examines the role of teleological judgements in our experience of the world. The word 'teleology' comes from the Greek '*telos*' meaning end or purpose, so teleology has to do with things that have ends or purposes. Kant argues that the experience of organic, living nature naturally leads to the idea of a designer and a purpose beyond nature. Kant distinguishes between what he calls relative purposiveness and internal purposiveness. We think of something as exhibiting relative purposiveness when we think that it exists for the sake of some other thing. Kant, however, is more interested in internal purposiveness. An individual exhibits internal purposiveness when certain of its parts exist for the sake of others, and the parts are both the cause and effects of the whole, and Kant thinks that all living organisms, or what Kant calls organic beings, exhibit internal purposiveness in this sense. For the parts of an organism are organs, and the organism cannot survive without its organs, so the parts are, in this sense, the cause of the existence of the whole. The organs, however, cannot exist as organs unless they are part of a whole, for what it is to be an organ is to play a certain functional role. So the heart, for example, cannot exist as a heart unless it is in a body pumping blood. So in an organism the whole is in this sense the cause of the existence of the parts. The idea of a whole in which the parts are causes of the whole but where the whole is the cause of the parts is, however, difficult for us to comprehend, and the only way we can think of a whole in this way is by analogy with a human-made artefact. In the case of a human-made artefact the *concept* of the whole, the design in the mind of the designer, is prior to the parts, and so in this sense in an artefact the whole (or at least the representation of the whole in the mind of the creator) is prior to the parts. But the whole artefact is made from the pre-existing parts and so in this sense the parts are prior to the whole. Thus, Kant suggests, our attempt to comprehend the internal purposiveness of organisms naturally and inevitably leads us to think of such beings as analogous to human-made artefacts, and this leads naturally to the idea of an intelligent designer or author of the organisms in nature and of nature as a whole. Thus, our attempt to understand internal purposiveness or organisms naturally leads to the idea of their relative purposiveness. Now, Kant's argument here has similarities to the traditional argument from design, or what Kant calls the **physico-theological argument,** for the existence of **God.** It is important to note, however, that Kant is not attempting to offer a theoretically valid argument for the existence of God. He is instead merely explaining why such a belief is natural and perhaps inevitable and his explanation is based upon the fact that we are unable to fully comprehend the nature of organisms without appealing to the notion of a designer. Our need to do this, though, may merely be due to the limited nature of our capacity to understand the natural world, and the fact that we are naturally led to think in this way does not imply that our thoughts here are true. See: **beauty; sublime; critique.**

Critique of Practical Reason (1788)

Kant's second Critique, which examines the *a priori* principles that govern rational willing, was originally planned to be an appendix of the second edition of the *Critique of Pure Reason* (1787). Originally Kant had thought that the *Critique of Pure Reason* would provide a sufficient foundation for both a metaphysics of nature and a metaphysics of morals. As he worked on his revisions of the *Critique of Pure Reason*, however, he decided to publish it as a separate work. Like the first Critique, the *Critique of Practical Reason* is divided into a Doctrine of Elements and a Doctrine of Method. The doctrine of Elements is in turn divided into an Analytic and a Dialectic.

The main aim of the Analytic is to show that pure reason can be practical. What Kant wants to explain is how **reason** can be the source of action, so the Analytic can be thought of as offering an account of what it is to have a rational will. He argues that rational willing is connected to the idea of **freedom,** for to act rationally is to act under the idea of freedom. Kant argues that the actions of a rational being are determined by the law of reason, which Kant identifies with the **moral law,** rather than the laws of nature. This moral law is not an external constraint but pertains to the very nature of rational willing, and insofar as the will is determined by such a law, the will has determined itself, so Kant concludes that to be rational is to act autonomously. Kant distinguishes between being subject to the laws of nature, which he identifies with being heteronomous, and being subject to the moral law, which is to be **autonomous.** Now, insofar as human beings are members of the **sensible world,** we must regard our actions as part of the natural order and as a consequence recognize our actions as subject to the laws of causality. Thus, insofar as we regard ourselves merely as members of the natural world, we must conclude that reason cannot be practical, for insofar as our actions are determined by natural causes, we cannot regard them as free. In order to regard ourselves as free, and hence in order to think of reason as practical, we must think of ourselves as members of what Kant calls the **intelligible world.**

The Analytic is divided into three chapters. In the first, and longest, chapter Kant argues that freedom and the moral law reciprocally imply each other. What Kant means by this is that to be free is to be subject to the moral law and *vice versa.* This claim is often referred to as Kant's reciprocity thesis. Kant's arguments for this claim are difficult and there is much controversy as to how Kant's argument is supposed to work. Kant himself introduces his argument for this distinction by making a distinction between material and formal practical principles. A material practical principle is one which requires some object to be the ground of action, and Kant argues that all material principles come under the general principle of self-love, and involve the desire for **happiness.** His idea here is that happiness always involves the desire for some object, and so insofar as we are motivated by self-love, it is the expectation of the feeling of pleasure from the reality of an object that determines our faculty of desire. Now, as freedom involves being self-determined, self-love, which for Kant means being motivated by a material practical principle, always involves the will being determined by some external object rather than being self-determined, and so insofar as we are motivated by self-love, we are not free. To be free or self-determined, then, implies that the fundamental principle of motivation is not a material principle, and Kant names such a principle a formal principle, and he argues that the only candidate for such a principle is what he calls the moral law or the fundamental law of pure practical reason. Kant's argument here is very similar to the argument he gives explaining the possibility of the **categorical imperative** in chapter two of the *Groundwork of the Metaphysics of Morals* (1785). His thought is that if self-determination involves being determined by the idea of law rather than by anything external to the will, then any particular law with specific external content will imply being determined by something other than the will, so the only candidate for such a source of determination is the bare concept of law itself. So Kant concludes that to be self-determined, or free, means that we are determined by the idea of law. Thus he concludes that self-determination requires that one's will is determined by the idea of lawfulness and so the fundamental principle or law of pure practical reason is: so act that the **maxim** of your will could always hold at the same time as a principle of giving universal law.

In chapter two of the Analytic, Kant examines the relationship between the concept of the good and the concept of the moral law, and argues that the concept of the moral law is prior to that of the good. This chapter has been central for recent **constructivist** interpretations of Kant's ethics by John **Rawls** (1921–2002) and his followers. According to the constructivists, one of Kant's central ideas is that the *right* is prior to the *good*. To understand what they mean by this it is helpful to compare Kant's position with a **consequentialist** doctrine such as **utilitarianism**. According to consequentialists the right action is the one that has the best consequences, and so according to consequentialists we have to know which outcome would be best in order to judge which action is right, and in order to know this, we need an account of what makes an outcome good or bad. The consequentialist, then, believe that the concept of the good is prior to that of the right because we need an account of what counts as a good outcome in order to understand how we should act. According to Rawls, one of the central aspects of Kant's moral theory is that the right is prior to the good, with a good outcome being one that is the result of right action. According to this view what makes an action right cannot be explained in terms of either its intended or actual consequences. The following example is helpful for understanding the difference between these two positions. Imagine one has to share a cake between two people, and one wonders what procedure for making the division would be morally right. The consequentialist will argue that we must first understand which outcome would be best and that the best or morally right procedure will be the one which is most likely to produce this outcome. The constructivist, in contrast, argues that we must first give an account of what it is that makes a decision procedure right and fair and claims that a good outcome is one that is the result of an action that has been decided upon by the right type of decision procedure. So, for example, Rawls argues that what is important is that the procedure is fair and so a good outcome is one that is fair. According to the constructivist, then, the right is prior to the good because we define a good outcome as one that is the result of the right, fair, procedure. According to Rawls, Kant is trying to make a similar point in his discussion of the relationship between the concepts of the good and the moral law in chapter two of the Analytic, for Kant's point is that what makes an action right is not to be understood in terms of a prior understanding of what it is that makes the object of an action good or desirable, but in terms of whether or not the **maxim** of the action is law-like (universalizable) or not.

Chapter three of the Analytic discusses the role of **feeling** in moral action. Kant argues that a good action is a rational action, and that in such an action the moral law, or reason, determines the will immediately. This may make it sound like acting morally and acting on feeling are opposed to each other, and many critics of Kant assume that acting on feeling and being determined by the moral law are incompatible ways of acting. In this chapter, however, Kant argues that moral action requires the existence of a certain feeling, which Kant calls the feeling of **respect** for the moral law, and he argues that this feeling must be caused by our consciousness of what morality demands.

In the Dialectic Kant examines the conflict between morality and the desire for **happiness**. Kant is often regarded as an enemy of happiness believing that to be moral involves not caring at all about happiness. But Kant's actual position is more sophisticated than this. Kant believes that we should subordinate our desire for happiness to the demands of morality, but he thinks that the good person is worthy or deserving of happiness, and he believes that insofar as we are moral, we can reasonably hope for happiness. But Kant rejects any account that identifies goodness with happiness. Such a view was very common among ancient philosophers. The **Epicureans**, for example, had argued that to be happy is to be virtuous, so a person who rationally promotes their long-term happiness in an intelligent way will behave virtuously towards others. They believed that truly enlightened self-interest would lead to virtuous behaviour. The Stoics, in contrast, had argued that consciousness of one's own virtue is sufficient for one's own happiness, and so believed that a truly virtuous and wise individual would be happy even if they were being tortured or sold into slavery. Kant rejects both of these positions. He argues that being good and being happy are two quite distinct things. Good people can be very unhappy; they can be wrongfully imprisoned, tortured or sold into slavery, and consciousness of one's virtue may make these things bearable, but this is not sufficient for happiness, for happiness involves the satisfaction of our desires. Now although Kant does not identify goodness and happiness, he does not think that happiness is without value but merely that its value is conditioned by morality. The happiness of a wicked person does not have value, but the good person deserves to be happy, and there is something wrong in a world in which good people are unhappy.

Kant, then, although he believes that having a good will is the only thing that is *unconditionally* good, does not think being moral is the only thing that is intrinsically good or desirable for its own sake. It is a bad thing if a good person is unhappy and a good thing if such a person is happy. Thus, although Kant believes that morality is the only thing that is unconditionally good, he does not think that possession a good will is the *Summum Bonum* or **highest good**. The highest good requires not just having a good will, but also the existence of a necessary proportionality between morality and happiness. Although a good person is one who is willing to sacrifice their happiness for what morality requires Kant believes that a good person can and should rationally hope for happiness. Happiness and morality, then, are two, quite distinct, elements in the notion of the **highest good** and a good person should both strive to realize and hope to obtain the highest good.

Based on considerations concerning the highest good, Kant argues for what he calls the priority of practical reason over speculative reason, for he thinks that morality demands commitments to certain beliefs that cannot be justified theoretically. There are certain things that we have and could have absolutely no theoretical evidence for, but which, Kant believes, we have moral reasons for believing, for if they were not true morality would be an empty fantasy. In particular he believes that morality demand that we believe in the immortality of the soul and the **existence** of **God**, and he calls these two beliefs postulates of practical reason. For morality demands that we believe in the possibility of the highest good, that is a necessary connection between happiness and virtue in the world. And he argues that as the moral law commands that we promote the highest good and given the fact that ought implies can, if we thought that the highest good were impossible to achieve, then we would have to conclude that morality and the moral law was an illusion directed towards impossible and imaginary ends. As a result of this Kant concludes that a commitment to morality requires that we believe in the immortality of the soul because morality demands that we strive for our own moral perfection. We are, however, not capable at any moment of achieving such perfection, but the most we can hope for is an endless progress in which we can slowly come to approximate this ideal. Insofar as the highest good involves the idea that we must have a good will, but all we can do at any moment is to slowly improve our character, morality demands that we think of the future as endless so we can think that slowly over time our character can slowly converge on and approximate this ideal. This is why Kant thinks that morality requires that we believe in the immortality of the soul. Kant's second postulate of practical reason is a moral argument for the belief in God. For, in addition to demanding that we strive to have a good will, morality demands a proportionality between goodness and happiness, and this implies that we should believe that the universe is ultimately just. Our moral commitments, then, mean that we should hope that both the good and the wicked will get what they deserve, and that, at the very least that this hope should not be unreasonable. Now, Kant thinks that it is only possible to believe in a just world if we believe in the existence of a necessary connection between virtue and happiness and given the fact that neither nature nor human beings can secure such a necessary connection, Kant argues that such a necessary connection is only possible if we believe in the existence of God – a wise, omnipotent, omniscient and just being who rules the world. Thus, Kant argues, our commitment to morality requires that we think of the universe as ruled by a wise and just ruler who proportions happiness to virtue, and this, Kant argues, is our moral conception of God. For insofar as we can rationally hope that good deeds will be rewarded, we need to believe in a just ruler of the universe. This is Kant's moral argument for the existence of **God**. It is important to note, however, that this argument is not supposed to be a theoretical argument for the existence of God; Kant believes that such an argument is impossible; rather it is meant to be a moral argument purporting to show that a commitment to the demands of morality commit us to believing in the existence of a wise and just ruler of the universe. See: *Groundwork of the Metaphysics of Morals*; *Metaphysics of Morals*; freedom; reason; autonomy.

Critique of Pure Reason (1781/1787)

After defending his **Inaugural Dissertation** in 1770, Kant published almost nothing for over 10 years, and this period of his life is sometimes referred to as his **silent decade**. During these 10 years he slowly worked out the ideas that would appear in his monumental first *Critique*. The first edition of the *Critique of Pure Reason* was published in 1781, and this edition is referred to as the 'A' edition. Although he had been working on this work for over 10 years, he claims to have written the text hastily in 4 or 5 months. It immediately became the focus of intense philosophical attention and, Kant felt, widespread misinterpretation. Although Kant stood by the content of the first edition, he felt that some of this misinterpretation was due to his lack of care in the way he expressed his ideas, and so in 1787 he published a substantially revised second edition, which is referred to as the 'B' edition. All recent English editions of the first Critique include both editions and the first and second edition page numbers can be found on the side of the page. When referring to the *Critique of Pure Reason*, it is standard practice to list the page number of both editions. So, for example, A81/B107 means that the text is found on page 81 of the first edition and page 107 of the second edition. The reason this system is used is so that regardless of what translation is being used, we can all refer to the same passages.

German philosophy in the eighteenth century was dominated by rationalist metaphysicians such as **Leibniz, Wolff** and **Baumgarten,** and the structure of the *Critique* is based upon that of an eighteenth-century German **metaphysics** textbook. These textbooks divided metaphysics into general metaphysics (ontology) and special metaphysics. Special metaphysics was in turn divided into three special sciences: rational psychology, which dealt with our *a priori* knowledge of the soul; rational cosmology, which dealt with our *a priori* knowledge of the world; and rational theology, which dealt with our *a priori* knowledge of God. Rationalist metaphysicians claimed to provide knowledge of things beyond our experience.

Rationalist ontology (general metaphysics) was understood to be the science of the properties of all things in general, and aimed at providing an understanding of the basic **categories** that structure reality. These metaphysicians also believed that there are a number of **principles** that can be applied to every type of being. For example, rationalist metaphysicians believed that everything that exists must have a cause and this was understood to be a general principle that is supposed to apply to all possible beings. It was known as the **principle of sufficient reason. Descartes,** the grandfather of modern rationalist metaphysics, for example, appeals to this principle in his first attempted proof of the existence of God in the *Third Meditation*, as his argument begins with the claim that everything that exists, including our ideas, must have a cause. Rationalist special metaphysics was based upon the assumption that we could, through our reason, acquire knowledge about three objects that were not possible objects of empirical experience: the soul, the world as it is in itself, and **God.** So, for example, rationalist metaphysicians argued that we know that the soul is a simple **substance.** Rationalist metaphysicians thought that such *a priori* knowledge is something that we can discover through our pure **reason.** Kant rejects this claim and his project involves establishing the limits of human reason. This is why his book is called the *Critique of Pure Reason.* He will argue that we can know (or 'cognize') nothing *a priori* about the mind, the world as it is in itself and God. We do not even know that the soul, the world as a whole and God even exist. Now, the claim that we lack such *a priori* knowledge does not mean that Kant does not believe in the existence of the soul and God. But, for him, it is important to be clear that such beliefs are not, and cannot be, justified theoretically. Although Kant denies that we can have any *a priori* knowledge about the soul, the world as a whole and God, he does believe that we can have some *a priori* knowledge about possible objects of experience. Kant calls objects that we can experience **phenomenal** objects. The soul, the world as a whole and God, are not things that we can possibly experience. When we think about God for example, all we have access to and can think about is merely our idea of God, and we do not have any access to any **transcendent** object corresponding to this idea; we can discover certain facts about our ideas, but however hard we look at an idea we are never going to establish whether there is any object corresponding to the idea or not. This is why Kant rejects, for example, Descartes' **ontological argument** for the existence of God. Kant calls things that we can think of but not experience, **Intelligible** or **Noumenal** objects and argues that we can have absolutely no knowledge of such objects. We do not even know if such things can exist. So if Kant calls something 'Intelligible' or 'Noumenal', this means that we possess an idea that purports to refer to something, but that we have no knowledge of the purported referent of the idea. So, for example, Kant thinks that the idea of God is not obviously contradictory, and so the idea of God is *thinkable*. However, Kant thinks that God is not a possible object of experience, we cannot meet him on the street, and so God is *not knowable*. In Kant's terminology, the idea of God is intelligible or noumenal. We can have no knowledge about God. We cannot even *know* that god exists. Despite arguing that we cannot know whether God exists or not, Kant claims that he is denying knowledge in order to make room for faith, and he will argue in the *Critique of Practical Reason* (1788) that we have good moral reasons for *believing* in the existence of God.

Kant rejects the possibility of *a priori* knowledge of reality as it is in itself and of objects beyond any possible experience. He argues, however, that we can and do have informative knowledge of necessary and universally true principles about our *experience*. In the Introduction to the *Critique* he calls such knowledge **synthetic *a priori*** knowledge, and he argues that the task of theoretical philosophy is to explain how such knowledge is possible. Kant's claim, then, is that we do have some *a priori* knowledge of **phenomena**. That is, we can have some *a priori* knowledge about objects that we can experience. Thus, for example, Kant thinks that it is a fact that everything we can experience is in space and time, and thus he believes that we know *a priori* that all phenomenal objects are spatio-temporal. Similarly, he believes that everything that exists in space-time is subject to causal laws. So he believes that the **principle of sufficient reason** is true and justified, but only for possible objects of experience (e.g. to what he calls phenomenal objects). That is, he thinks we can know *a priori* that everything that we can experience must have a cause. But he does **not** think that the fact that (1) Everything we can experience must have a cause implies that (2) Everything has a cause. Kant thinks that traditional Rationalist metaphysicians have illegitimately assumed that (2) follows from (1). In so doing they have taken a principle (1) that is perfectly valid for things that we can experience and have tried to apply it beyond experience, to things in general, including things as they are in themselves.

Although Kant rejects the main claims of rationalist metaphysics, the structure of the *Critique of Pure Reason* is based upon that of the traditional metaphysics text books. The first two major sections of the *Critique* are the **Transcendental Aesthetic** and the Transcendental Analytic, which correspond to the material covered in traditional rationalist ontology (general metaphysics). In the **Transcendental Aesthetic** Kant argues that space and time are necessary conditions of the possibility of experience. The Transcendental Analytic is divided into two main sections, the Analytic of Concepts and the Analytic of Principles. In Analytic of Concepts he introduces his table of categories, which include basic concepts of thought such as substance, cause, unity, plurality, existence, reality and limitation. He argues, against the **empiricists** such as **Hume**, that these concepts are not empirical but *a priori* logical concepts. They could not have been abstracted from experience but are derived from our capacity to make logical judgements. For example, our concept of **causation** involves the ground-consequence relation. Although here, one should be careful to note that Kant thinks that the notion of real causation involves more than the logical ground-consequence relation. Now, Kant argues, our understanding of the ground-consequence relationship is based on our capacity to make 'if . . . then' judgements or what Kant calls **hypothetical judgements**. Now, the ground-consequence relationship is basically a logical relationship that holds between judgements or thoughts, but Kant holds that it can also be applied to the physical world, for when we regard one event as the cause of another we think of the first event as the ground and the second as its consequence. But it is not clear what justifies our application of logical concepts to the world. Why should the structure of physical reality have any relation to the structure of thinking? This is the question that Kant addresses in the **Transcendental Deduction**, which is the section of the *Critique of Pure Reason* that Kant had most difficulty writing, and in the second edition of the *Critique* he completely rewrote this section. His argument is that the application of these logical concepts to experience is a necessary condition for the possibility of experience and this is what justifies the application of logical concepts to the world of experience. In the Analytic of Principles he examines each of the categories and argues for the existence of a number of *a priori* principles that concern the application of particular categories to objects of experience. In the **Axioms of Intuition** he examines the principles that govern the application of the categories of **quantity** (unity, plurality and totality) to objects of experience. In the **Anticipations of Perception** he does the same for the categories of quality (reality, negation and limitation). In the **Analogies of Experience** he does the same for the categories of relation (**substance, causation** and **community**), and in the Postulates of Empirical Thought he examines the application of the **modal** categories (**possibility, existence** and **necessity**). The most famous and influential section of the Analytic of Principles is the Second Analogy. Here Kant defends the principle that all alteration occurs in accordance with the law of the connection of cause and effect.

The second major section of the *Critique of Pure Reason* is the **Transcendental Dialectic**. Here Kant denies the possibility of rationalist special metaphysics. He argues that although we have the **ideas** of the soul, the world and of **God**, we can have no knowledge of any objects corresponding to these ideas. We cannot even know whether there are objects corresponding to these ideas. We can analyse these concepts but such conceptual analysis cannot provide us with any **synthetic** knowledge of the objects corresponding to these ideas. In the **Paralogisms of Pure Reason** he provides a critique of rational psychology. Rationalist metaphysicians had argued that we know that the soul is a simple substance that persists through time, and in this section Kant shows that these claims to knowledge are unfounded. His conclusion is that we can have no knowledge of the nature of the soul. We can have no knowledge of ourselves as we are; we can only know ourselves as we appear to ourselves. In the

Antinomy of Pure Reason Kant examines the doctrines of rational cosmology. In rational cosmology philosophers would discuss questions such as Does the world have a beginning? Are there any simple substances? Is there any real **freedom** in the world or is everything determined? Is there a **necessary** being, or is everything contingent? Kant argues that these questions cannot be answered theoretically, although he will argue in ethical writings that we have a moral reason to believe in the existence of freedom. In the Ideal of Pure Reason Kant examines the arguments of rational theology, and rejects three traditional arguments for the existence of God: the **ontological argument**, the **cosmological argument** and the **physicotheologial argument**. Although he claims that we can have no *knowledge* of the existence of God, he will argue in the *Critique of Practical Reason* that we have moral reasons to *believe* in the existence of God. In the course of his discussion of the ontological argument Kant has a very influential discussion of the concept of 'existence' arguing that 'existence' is not a real predicate.

Descartes, René (1596–1650)

Descartes is considered to be the founding father of modern philosophy. He was a mathematician as well as a philosopher, inventing the Cartesian coordinate system and analytic geometry, which allows us to understand lines and shapes in terms of equations. Descartes was a **rationalist**. He distinguishes between the imagination, our capacity to picture the world, and the intellect, our capacity to understand the world, and argues that true knowledge is purely intellectual. His discovery of analytic geometry supported this position for it suggests that shapes and figures are things that can be understood through equations and so our understanding of geometry does not require images. In his most influential work *Meditations on First Philosophy* (1641), Descartes examines our knowledge of the Soul, **God** and the **World**. Descartes equates knowledge with certainty, and believes that our knowledge of these three objects comes in a particular order. The first object of knowledge is our own soul. Thus with his famous claim, 'I think therefore I am', Descartes argues that our knowledge of the existence and nature of the soul is the foundation of all the rest of our knowledge. Now Descartes does not just argue that I immediately know *that* I am but I also know *what* I am. Thus he argues that I know that I am essentially a simple, indivisible thinking substance. He also uses this claim about the nature of the soul to defend the claims that the mind and body are distinct substances, a doctrine known as **dualism**. For, he claims, we know that mind is essentially simple and divisible, whereas we know that bodies, existing in space, are essentially extended and hence, at least in principle, divisible. Now, given the assumption that one substance cannot have two incompatible properties (being essentially indivisible and being essentially divisible), Descartes concludes that the mind and body must be distinct substances. Kant rejects Descartes' arguments for dualism, arguing in the **Paralogisms** of the *Critique of Pure Reason* that I do not know that I am a simple indivisible substance.

Having discussed the soul, Descartes turns to our knowledge of God which is next in order of certainty. In the fifth *Mediation* Descartes presents his famous version of the **ontological argument** for the existence of God, which Kant criticizes in the Ideal of Pure Reason of the *Critique of Pure Reason*. Finally Descartes explains our knowledge of the external physical universe, our knowledge of which depends upon our knowledge of ourselves and our knowledge of the existence of God. He argues that the world as it appears to us through our senses is not the way it is in itself, for the world as it is in itself is something that is to be understood through the new mathematics that he himself had developed. See: **rationalists**; **Paralogisms of Pure Reason**; **God**.

design, argument from

See: **physicotheologial argument**

desire, faculty of

Kant wrote three Critiques, each examining the *a priori* principles governing a particular faculty. The *Critique of Pure Reason* (1781/1787) examines the *a priori* principles that govern our faculty of **cognition**, the *Critique of Practical Reason* (1788), and

Kant's other major works on moral philosophy, examine the *a priori* principles that govern the faculty of desire and the ***Critique of Judgment*** (1790) examines the *a priori* principles that govern the faculty of **judgement**. Kant defines the faculty of desire as a being's capacity of becoming by means of concepts the cause of the actual existence of the objects of these concepts. What this means is that the faculty of desire is the capacity for action. In action we start with a representation, for example, of the world being in a certain way, and we attempt to bring this state of affairs into existence. The faculty of desire, then, is the capacity to act.

determining judgement

See: reflecting judgement

determinism

Causal determinism is the position that every event is necessitated by prior events together with the laws of nature. And one of the major debates in the history of philosophy has been on whether determinism and free will are compatible. Compatibilists, such as David **Hume** (1711–76), argue that free will and determinism are compatible, for all that is required for free will, and moral responsibility, is that the agent is able to do what they want or decide to do, and it does not matter if this desire or decision was itself determined by previous events external to the agent. Incompatibilists argue that free will and determinism are incompatible. Kant's position in this debate is complicated, for, on the one hand, he believes that the physical world is deterministic, and so we must regard our actions as part of this world as fully determined by past events and the laws of nature. On the other hand, he thinks that this is compatible with regarding ourselves, as we are in ourselves, as free from determination by alien causes, and he thinks that such freedom from determination by alien causes is necessary for moral freedom. Some commentators have read this position as implying a commitment to incompatibilism, whereas other commentators have argued that Kant is actually defending an unusual form of compatibilism.

dialectic

See: Transcendental Dialectic

disjunctive judgement

In the table of judgements of the *Critique of Pure Reason* (1781/1787). Kant argues that there are only three types of judgements of relation which he names categorical judgements, hypothetical judgements and disjunctive judgements. Disjunctive judgements are either-or judgements. A disjunctive judgement has the form '*x* is *a* or *x* is *b*', and Kant explains that in such a judgement the sphere of a concept is represented as a whole divided into parts (the subordinate concepts). A disjunctive judgement, then, is one in which a number of judgements somehow restrict one another and fill up a logical space. So, for example, in the disjunctive judgement 'knowledge is either *a priori* or *a posteriori*', the whole sphere is knowledge, and this sphere is divided into two exclusive parts which exhaust the possibilities. The assertion of the judgement that some piece of knowledge is *a priori* rationally excludes the assertion of the judgement that it is *a posteriori*. Kant derives the **category** of **community** (or mutual interaction) from the disjunctive form of judgement. His thought here, which becomes clearer if we bear in mind his dynamic theory of matter defended in the *Metaphysical Foundations of Natural Science* (1786), seems to be that the notion of mutual interaction involves the notion of exclusion and resistance, for one material substance fills space through its repulsive force by resisting the penetration of the force of other substances, and it is this mutual interplay of forces which lies behind the mutual interaction of physical substances. Kant then is trying to model the way in which a physical substance fills space through its repulsive force by *excluding* the penetration of other substances, on the way in which the assertion of one disjunct is logically excluded by the assertion of the other disjunct in a disjunctive judgement. It is not clear, however, whether it really makes sense to model the notion of physical exclusion on logical exclusion in this way.

dogmatism

The word 'dogmatism' comes from the Greek '*dogma*' which means belief or opinion, and in traditional Christian theology the dogmata are the articles of faith that are considered to be those beliefs that are essential to hold if one is to be a Christian. Used in this sense, the word 'dogmatic' did not originally have a negative connotation. Kant, however, uses the word 'dogmatic' in a negative sense to imply a belief that is held with insufficient justification, and he regarded rationalist metaphysics, which claimed to provide us with theoretical insight into how things are in themselves, as dogmatic in this negative sense. Kant positioned his own **critical** philosophy as occupying a middle ground between dogmatism and **skepticism**.

Dreams of a Spirit-seer elucidated by Dreams of Metaphysics (1766)

Kant's pre-critical *Dreams* is an evaluation of the eight-volume *Heavenly Secrets* (1749) written by the Swedish mystic Emanuel **Swedenborg** (1688–1772). In his work Swedenborg provides inspired biblical interpretation and recounts his mystical visions of heaven and hell. Kant in his analysis suggests that Swedenborg was probably insane, but argues that rationalist metaphysics is based on an analogous type of madness, in its belief that we can have insight into things beyond the possibility of experience. Thus, *Dreams* and Kant's engagement with Swedenborg represent a step on the path towards Kant's rejection of such metaphysics in his critical period. Although Kant rejected Swedenborg's claims to mystical knowledge, he seems to have found Swedenborg's descriptions of heaven as a community of spirits governed by moral laws, standing in non-spatial relationships to one another morally inspiring and may perhaps been one of the inspirations for his own moral ideal of a **realm of ends**. And engaging with Swedenborg probably helped Kant develop his own account of the distinction between the **phenomenal** and **intelligible** worlds. See: **Swedenborg**.

dualism

Dualism is the doctrine, defended by **Descartes** (1596–1650), that the mind and the body are distinct kinds of substance. Kant attacks Descartes arguments for dualism in the **Paralogisms of Pure Reason**. Kant argues that we have knowledge of things only as they appear and not as they are in themselves, and this applies not just to bodies, but to ourselves as well. We only know ourselves as we appear to ourselves not as we are in ourselves. As we do not know what bodies are in themselves nor what minds are in themselves, but only know these things as they appear to us, we have no way of knowing whether bodies and minds are appearances of one type of substance or not. So Kant believes that we must remain agnostic about whether or not dualism is true or not. See: **Descartes; Paralogisms**.

duty

Kant's most influential arguments about duty are to be found in the *Groundwork of the Metaphysics of Morals* where he argues that morality, at least for human beings, involves acting from duty. It is important to note the distinction between *acting in accordance with* duty and acting *from* duty. An agent might do the right thing, but if they are not doing it *because* it is the right thing to do they are not acting *from* duty. For example, Kant believes that morality requires that we do not lie to others. Now someone might tell the truth to someone in a certain circumstance, because they are afraid of the consequences of getting caught, but if they believed there was no danger of getting caught they would be quite prepared to lie. In telling the truth at this particular moment the person has *acted in accordance with* duty but they have not acted *from* duty. A moral individual does not just do the right thing, but they do the right thing because they recognize that it is the right thing to do. They tell the truth because they recognize that they have a duty to be honest. What is important here is the motive of the action. Now some moral philosophers believe that what makes a motive a good motive are the intended results. Kant, however, argues that what gives actions done out of duty their moral value is not their actual or intended results, but the **principles** on which they are based. For Kant, then, good action is *principled* action, and in the *Groundwork* he argues that the only principle that is capable of being an absolute ground of **rational** action is the **categorical imperative**.

In section two of the *Groundwork* Kant introduces four examples of specific duties, and discusses these duties for each formulations of the categorical imperative. These duties are: (1) The duty to not make a promise we have no intention of keeping; (2) The duty to not commit suicide if we have grown weary of life; (3) The duty to develop our talents; and (4) The duty to help other people (the duty of **beneficence**). Kant did not choose these four specific duties randomly, but they are examples of the four main species of duty. To understand this fourfold classification of duties, it is necessary to understand two distinctions. The first distinction is between duties towards ourselves and duties towards others. The duties to not commit suicide and to develop our talents are duties to ourselves. The duties to not make lying promises and to be benevolent are duties towards others. The second is between perfect and imperfect duties. Perfect duties specify particular actions that are to be done or are forbidden. The duties to not commit suicide and to not tell a lying promise are perfect duties as they forbid specific actions. Imperfect duties do not forbid or command specific actions, instead they demand that we promote or cultivate certain things but they do not specify how this is to be done, and so allow significant degree of freedom in deciding how to comply with the duty. The duty of beneficence and the duty to develop our talents are imperfect duties in this sense. Take, for example, Kant's understanding of the duty of beneficence. We have a duty to care about the well-being of other people, but Kant does not think that this duty specifies who or how much we should help. Unlike a **utilitarian,** he does not believe that we have a duty to maximize total happiness in society. The duty of beneficence merely tells us that it would be wrong to never help anyone, and so the duty merely doemands that we should sometimes help some people. The choice of whom and when to help is up to us. A similar story can be told about our duty to develop our own talents, for morality demands that we do not neglect developing our talents, but it does not specify which particular talents we should develop and how. Given these two distinctions we can see that duties can be classified into four classes:

	Perfect Duties	Imperfect Duties
Duties to ourselves	Not to commit suicide	To develop our talents
Duties to others	Not to make a lying promise	To be benevolent

emotions

See: **feeling**

empiricism/empiricists

The British empiricists John **Locke** (1632–1704), George **Berkeley** (1685–1753) and David **Hume** (1711–76) argued that our knowledge and ideas have their roots in experience. It is useful to distinguish between *content* empiricism and *knowledge* empiricism.

Content empiricism has got to do with the content of our thoughts and argues that all of our ideas are to be traced back to our sensible experience. In saying this, content empiricists deny the existence of innate (inborn) concepts. Hume drew very strong semantic consequences from his content empiricism as he thought that content empiricism implies that a word is only meaningful if it corresponds to some idea that has its origin in sensuous experience. And so Hume argues that if we cannot explain how a word is related to some particular experience or experiences, we should assume that the word is meaningless. This aspect of Hume's philosophy was developed by the logical positivists in the twentieth century, who used a similar doctrine to argue that the claims of metaphysicians were literally meaningless. Kant rejects an extreme form of content empiricism. Although he does not argue for the existence of innate ideas, for he believes that all our thinking has its origin with experience, he does believe that certain logical concepts, which he names the **categories**, are *a priori*, for we cannot trace their content back to experience.

Knowledge empiricism claims that our knowledge can only be justified empirically by an appeal to experience. The three classic British empiricists were only moderate knowledge empiricists, for even Hume, the most radical of the three, believed in the possibility of *a priori* knowledge. Hume, for example, thought that our mathematical knowledge had to do with the relationship between ideas and so could not, and did not, need to be justified by an appeal to experience. Later empiricists such as John Stuart Mill (1806–73) and Wilfred Van Orman Quine (1908–2000) have advocated an even more extreme form of knowledge empiricism arguing that even mathematical and logical judgements ultimately can only be justified by appeal to experience. Moderate knowledge empiricists, such as Locke, Berkeley and Hume, although they believe that mathematical and logical knowledge is *a priori*, argue that we can have no *a priori* knowledge of the world, for our judgements and beliefs about the world all need to be justified by appeal to experience. Kant rejects moderate knowledge empiricism because he believes in the possibility of **synthetic** *a priori* knowledge of the physical world.

enthusiasm (*schwärmerei*)

'Enthusiasm' was a common term of disapproval in the seventeenth and eighteenth centuries employed by defenders of **reason**, to denote the fanaticism of religious mystics, irrationalists and those who appealed to inspiration in religion. Kant was a committed opponent of religious enthusiasm. Discussions of enthusiasm were influenced by Plato's description, in his *Ion*, of the inspired poet, who has a certain type of insight but not knowledge. See: **Pietism**.

Epicureans

Epicureans are followers of Epicurus (341–270 BCE). Epicurian ethics, like that of the later **utilitarians**, identifies the good with pleasure and evil with pain, and thinks that the goal of philosophy is to help us lead a happy, pleasurable life. Unlike the utilitarians, however, Epicurus did not argue that we should aim at maximizing total pleasure in society but thought that each individual should seek their own happiness. Epicurus, then, advocated a form of rational self-interest. He thought, however, that the best way of achieving such happiness was by leading a tranquil life absent of fear and of seeking simple pleasures and friendship. And he thought that a person who sought such a life would also be virtuous as he thought that truly enlightened self-interested would naturally result in virtuous and moral behaviour towards others. Kant objects to the identification of the good with happiness, arguing that the only thing that is **unconditionally** good is a good will, and the value of happiness is conditional, for the happiness of a wicked person is not good. Kant also objected to Epicurus' claim that a happy life will also be a virtuous one, for he thinks that virtue and happiness are quite distinct things and that it is quite possible for a happy person to be wicked. Although Kant thinks that happiness and virtue are distinct, he thinks that to be virtuous is to be deserving of happiness and that what he calls the highest good, which we should all hope for, is a world in which virtue is proportional to happiness. See: **utilitarianism; happiness.**

existence

Existence is one of the 12 categories presented in the table of categories in the *Critique of Pure Reason*. Kant's most important and influential discussion of existence occurs during his discussion of the **ontological proof** for the existence of God a section of the *Critique of Pure Reason* titled the Ideal of Pure Reason. Here Kant argues that 'being is not a real predicate'. Instead he suggests that existence is what we today call a second-order predicate. A **categorical judgement** is one that has the form '*a* is *b*', and *a* is the subject term and *b* is the predicate term. When one makes a categorical judgement, one uses the subject concept to pick out an object or a set of objects and then uses the predicate concept to say something about this object or set of objects. So, for example, when one judges that 'dollars are green', one is saying that all dollars have the property of being green. On the surface it looks like something similar is going on in existential judgements. When one judges that 'dollars exist', it looks like one is pointing to dollars and claiming that dollars, in addition to having the property of being green, also have the property of existing. This is what Kant denies when he claims that 'existence' is not a real predicate. In claiming that existence is what we now call a second-order predicate, Kant is arguing that in existential judgements we are not saying something about the object the subject concept picks out but are rather saying something about the subject concept itself, namely that it is instantiated. When I claim that 'dollars exist', I am not saying anything about dollars, instead I am saying something about my concept 'dollar'; I am saying that there are things in the world corresponding to this concept. The motivation for such a position is clearer if we think about negative existential judgements, for example, the judgement that 'unicorns do not exist'. If we think that existence is a first-order predicate, like 'being green', then we would have to analyse this sentence as picking out all the unicorns and then claiming that all the unicorns have the property of not existing. So if we think of existence as a first-order concept, it looks like we are committed to the existence of non-existence objects. If we assume that existence is a second-order predicate, however, we can avoid this worry. For the judgement 'unicorns do not exist' is understood not to be making a claim about unicorns, but about the concept 'unicorn'. When one says 'unicorns do not exist', what one is saying is that the concept 'unicorn' is not instantiated, which means that there is nothing in the world corresponding to the concept 'unicorn'. Understood in these terms, the claim that unicorns do not exist is not a claim about non-existent unicorns, but a claim about the concept 'unicorn'. See: **ontological argument**.

experience

In the *Critique of Pure Reason* (1781/1787) Kant examines the necessary conditions of human experience. Kant argues that the world as we experience it is necessarily spatio-temporal, and the objects of possible experience are governed by certain **synthetic** *a priori* principles, such as the **principle** that any alteration of a substance must have a cause. Thus, Kant disagrees with **empiricists**, such as David **Hume** (1711–76), for he believes that there are certain things that we can know about objects of experience independent of any particular experience. Kant calls the world of objects of possible experience the **phenomenal** world, and he argues that although the **synthetic** *a priori* principles he proposes necessarily govern all objects of possible experience, they do not necessarily govern all objects, and so we are not justified in believing, as **rationalists** such as Gottfried Wilhelm **Leibniz** (1646–1716) believed, that they necessarily apply to things as they are in themselves. For this reason, Kant rejects a radical form of materialism which argues that if something cannot exist in space and time, then it cannot exist, for he believes that the conditions of the possibility of experience are not, necessarily, conditions for the possibility of **existence**. Although the only criterion we have for whether a kind of object can really exist is whether or not it is the sort of thing that could be experienced, there is nothing contradictory in the idea of an unexperiencable object, and so from the theoretical perspective, we have no justification for either believing in or denying the existence of such object. This leaves room for the logical **possibility** of objects that are not subject to the principles that govern phenomenal objects and Kant calls our idea of such objects intelligible. For example, Kant believes that the concept of a free or uncaused cause is not contradictory, but he thinks that no object of experience could be a free cause. This does not imply that free causes cannot exist, it just means that we have no theoretical justification for believing in the existence of such causes. See: **phenomena; Hume, empiricism.**

faculty of desire

See: **desire, faculty of**

faculty of judgement

See: *Critique of Judgment*

feeling

Kant believes that to be moral we must act *from* **duty**, and many readers assume that acting from duty is incompatible with acting on feeling. So, for example, a common but misguided criticism of Kantian ethics is that Kant believes it is immoral to act from the feeling of love. If this interpretation were correct, then if one's lover were in danger, a morally good agent would save him or her from duty not out of love. The assumption here is that acting from duty is incompatible with acting on a feeling. And there are passages that suggest that Kant is committed to such a position. Kant's attitudes towards feelings and emotions, however, are more complicated than this, and a more plausible reading is that Kant thinks that acting from duty is compatible with acting on a feeling or an emotion. Evidence for this position is suggested by the fact that in many places, for example the *Metaphysics of Morals* (1797), Kant argues that we have a duty to cultivate certain emotions or feelings, such as the feeling of sympathy. Kant's point is that feelings are not the sort of things that we can decide to have at will, and so although a good person will try and cultivate moral feelings, he or she will not necessarily succeed, and a good person will do the right thing even if he or she does not have the appropriate feelings. So, to use two of Kant's examples from the *Groundwork of the Metaphysics of Morals* (1785), Kant believes that a good person has a duty to help others and to not commit suicide. Naturally, most people have a love of life and a feeling of sympathy towards others and these feelings motivate them to care about their own preservation and to help others. In claiming that a moral person acts from duty Kant is not suggesting the person who helps others without any feeling of sympathy is a better person than one who has such a feeling. Indeed he argues in the *Metaphysics of Morals* that morality demands that we cultivate the feeling of sympathy. Instead his point is that a moral person is one who would still do the right thing, for example helping others and not committing suicide, even if they had lost these natural feelings. This suggests one possible way of understanding what is involved in acting *from* duty. To act from duty rather than merely *in accordance with* duty can be understood counterfactually. Someone who acts from duty is someone who would do the right thing even if their feelings and emotions were different. One hopes that a good friend normally enjoys helping their friends and does so with gladness and feeling. But a good friend is one who would also help their friends even if they were depressed and did not particularly feel like doing so.

In addition to believing that there are certain feelings that we have a moral duty to cultivate, Kant also argues that there are certain feelings that are a necessary condition for morality. If we lacked such feeling, we would be incapable of being moral agents. Thus, for example, in the *Critique of Practical Reason* (1788) Kant argues that morality requires the existence of a sensible impulse, which he calls the feeling of **respect** for the moral law, and he argues that this feeling must be caused by our recognition of what morality demands. Such a purported feeling is highly unusual as it has an *a priori* intelligible cause. His thought is that the existence of such a feeling is a necessary condition for the possibility of practical reason; for if reason is to be practical (i.e. if recognition of what morality requires is to result in action), then our recognition of the demands of morality must be able to motivate us, and motivation requires the existence of feeling. In the *Metaphysics of Morals* (1797) Kant argues that there are four feelings, namely (a) moral feeling (b) conscience (c) love of one's neighbour and (d) respect for oneself, that are necessary conditions for the possibility of morality. At first sight, it might look like Kant's account here is incompatible with his position in the *Critique of Practical Reason*, for there he identified a single feeling, and here he identifies four. The positions are compatible, however, if we assume that the four feelings listed here are four aspects of the feeling of respect for the moral law discussed in the earlier work. See: *Critique of Practical Reason*; *Metaphysics of Morals*; *duty*.

free will

Kant believes that practical reason and morality require a belief in freedom of the will. Practical deliberation requires choosing between alternatives and so when we engage in practical deliberation, we must regard these alternatives we are choosing between as real possibilities. So from the perspective of deliberation, we must regard ourselves as free. The fact that we must regard ourselves as free from the perspective of deliberation does not in itself imply that we actually are free. It is worth noting here that Kant is committed to the principle that ought implies can and so believes that in situations in which we recognize that we ought to do something but decide not to do it; the fact that we recognize that we had an obligation implies that we could have done it. It is this that leads him to claim in the *Critique of Practical Reason* (1788) that it is our recognition of the bindingness of the moral law which allows us to recognize our freedom.

Although practical reasoning and morality require a belief in our freedom, insofar as we regard ourselves as objects that are parts of the phenomenal world, we must regard ourselves and our actions as thoroughly determined by natural laws, for Kant is committed to the position, which he famously defends in the Second **Analogy**, that all phenomenal objects (or possible objects of experience) are subject to strict causal **determinism**. We cannot experience ourselves as objects except as thoroughly causally determined. This does not, however, imply that we are causally determined as we are in ourselves, or as **noumena**. As phenomena we are causally determined, but it is at least logically **possible** that as noumena we are free in the way that morality requires. And since morality requires a belief in such noumenal freedom, we are practically justified in believing that we possess free will. See: **freedom; determinism; autonomy.**

freedom

The idea of freedom is the cornerstone of Kant's moral philosophy, for he believes that being moral and being free mutually imply one another. This is often known by commentators as the reciprocity thesis. Kant uses a number of different conceptions of freedom.

Kant's first major discussion of freedom in his **critical** period is to be found in the Third **Antinomy** of the *Critique of Pure Reason* (1781/1787). Here what he means by freedom is the idea of being an uncaused cause; such a cause will be a first cause or a cause that is not itself an effect of some other cause. Such a free cause is essentially spontaneous and thought of as an ultimate source or origin, and such a cause is free in the sense that it is not determined by anything external to itself, and so corresponds to what Kant will later call negative freedom. Kant argues that such a spontaneous cause cannot be found in the natural phenomenal world, for, as he had famously argued in the Second **Analogy**, every event and object in time must be determined by external causes. So each cause that can possibly be an object of experience must itself be the effect of some other cause or causes and so cannot be free in Kant's sense.

A free cause, then, cannot be a possible object of experience and if the phenomenal world were all there were, a free cause would be impossible. However, although freedom is not possible in the **phenomenal** world, Kant thinks that there is no contradiction in thinking of the existence of such a cause in the **noumenal** realm, and thinking of phenomenal events as the effects of such a cause. Now, although we have no theoretical reason for believing in the existence of freedom in this sense, we do, Kant believes, have moral reasons for believing in the existence of such free noumenal causes.

In chapter three of the *Groundwork of the Metaphysics of Morals* (1785) Kant famously distinguishes between a negative and positive sense of freedom. Freedom in the negative sense involves freedom from external determination. Kant argues, however, that the idea of freedom in the negative sense implies freedom in the positive sense, where freedom in the positive sense involves determination by laws one has made oneself. Positive freedom, then, is equivalent to what Kant elsewhere calls **autonomy** and involves reason being practical. Some commentators think that in chapter three of the *Groundwork* Kant is attempting to give an argument for the existence of human freedom that does not appeal to the force of morality and so is aimed to convince the rational egoist or moral skeptic. In the *Critique of Practical Reason* (1788), however, Kant denies the possibility of such an argument (and so these commentators believe that Kant changed his mind) arguing instead that what justifies our moral belief in our freedom is our consciousness of the moral law, which Kant calls a 'fact of reason'. What he seems to mean by this is that it is the recognition of moral obligation, combined with the ought implies can principle, that allows us to recognize our own freedom. For if we recognize that we ought to do something but do not do it, we recognize that even though we did not do the right thing, we could have done so. See: **free will**; **determinism**; **autonomy**; *Groundwork of the Metaphysics of Morals*; *Critique of Practical Reason*.

genius

Kant's discussion of genius in the *Critique of Judgment* (1790) had a strong influence on later romantic philosophers and artists. Kant argues that beautiful **art** is only possible as a product of genius. To understand why Kant thinks like this, it is necessary to understand something about his theory of **beauty**. For Kant a beautiful object must appear to be both natural and artificial – it must appear to be purposive but without purpose. Thus Kant believes that nature is beautiful if it seems to be like art, that is, if they appear to be purposive, and we regard artefacts as beautiful if they seem natural. A beautiful artefact, then, must appear natural, and so Kant believes that an artist, when he or she creates a beautiful object, must produce something that appears natural. Now, the dominant artistic movement in the eighteenth century was classicism, which looked back to the artworks of the classical world as setting the standards for beauty. Neoclassical artists of the eighteenth century tried to emulate the art of the ancient Greeks and Romans and so they attempted to discover and follow the rules that governed the production of great classical art. For example, neoclassical architects and painters tried to follow classical rules of symmetry and proportion, and neoclassical poets believed in the existence of rules of correct style which they consciously tried to follow in their works. Kant's criticism of such practice is that if an artist is mechanically and consciously applying rules, the work produced will appear to be artificial, and so will not be seen as beautiful. However, in order to be an artefact, an object must be the product of some rules. Thus in order to produce a beautiful work of art, the artist must be producing the object according to some rule, but cannot be consciously doing so. In Kant's language, nature must be working through the artist to give the rule, and this is the work of genius. For, to use Kant's language, genius is the inborn predisposition of the mind through which nature gives the rule to art. And so Kant argues that beautiful art is possible only as a product of genius. An example might help here. Beautiful dancing is a rule-governed activity, it is not merely random movement, but someone who self-consciously follows the rules of a particular dance looks clumsy and self-conscious. Such a person does not dance beautifully. Dancing is beautiful when the dancer is moving in a rule-governed way but is not consciously following the rules but moving naturally. Such dancing will be the product of genius. Kant believes that the true artist cannot explain scientifically how she produces her work and does not know how the ideas for it came to her and is unable to communicate to others rules that would allow them to produce similar products. In saying this, Kant rejects a fundamental premise of neoclassical theory.

Kant's remarks on the importance of genius had a strong influence on the romantic movement, and we can see its influence in Freudian theory, which suggests that great art has its sources in the subconscious. It is important to note, however, that Kant is not advocating something like the cult of the artistic genius. Genius, for Kant, is a faculty that we all possess to a greater or lesser degree and which we manifest when we unselfconsciously, and naturally, act and produce objects in a rule-governed way. See: *Critique of Judgment*; beauty.

God

Kant discussed God in a section of the *Critique of Pure Reason* (1781/1787) called the Ideal of Pure Reason, where he examines, and rejects the traditional arguments for the **existence** of God. His discussion of the **ontological argument** is particularly influential. Kant argues that although there is no obvious contradiction in the idea of God, we have no theoretical justification in believing in the existence of God, that is, in the existence of an object corresponding to this idea. However, although Kant rejects the possibility of a theoretical proof of the existence of God, he argues in the *Critique of Practical Reason* (1788), among other places, that we have good moral reasons for believing in the existence of God. This argument, which he calls a postulate of practical reason, is based on his moral commitment to the possibility of what he calls the **highest good**. Although Kant thinks that the only thing that is unconditionally good is a good will, he argues that that the highest good involves both having a good will and being happy. Thus, Kant thinks that a commitment to morality involves the hope that ultimately happiness will be proportioned to virtue, and he thinks that this hope is only reasonable if we assume the existence of a wise, just, omniscient and omnipotent ruler of the universe, namely God. For only such a being would have the capacity to proportion happiness to virtue. Thus, for Kant, his commitment to a belief in the existence of God is based on his commitment to morality and his hope that the universe is ultimately just. See: religion; ontological argument; *Religion within the Boundaries of Mere Reason*; *Critique of Pure Reason*; *Critique of Practical Reason*; Pietism.

good will

Kant begins the *Groundwork of the Metaphysics of Morals* (1785) by claiming that the only thing that we recognize to be **unconditionally good** is a good will, and the first two chapters of the *Groundwork* should be read as offering an analysis of what it is to have a good will. Kant argues that a good will is not characterized by what it achieves but in terms of its **principle** of motivation. An agent with a good will is a being that is motivated by the moral law, and as such a good will is the idea of a being whose reason is practical.

Groundwork of the Metaphysics of Morals (1785)

Kant wrote the *Groundwork* as an entry into his ethical system, and along with Mill's *Utilitarianism* and Aristotle's *Ethics* it has been one of the most influential works in the history of ethics. Although, for a full understanding of Kant's ethical thought, one should also read the *Critique of Practical Reason* (1788) and the *Metaphysics of Morals* (1797).

It is instructive to begin by comparing Kant's conception of the function of moral philosophy with Christian **Wolff's** (1679–1754), whose philosophy was extremely influential in Germany during Kant's philosophical development. Unlike Kant, Wolff was an intellectualist who believed that there is no gap between recognizing an act as good and the act of willing it. Wolff therefore believed that immoral behaviour is always the result of mistaken beliefs about goodness. If we knew what was good for us, we would do it. As a result of this, Wolff maintains that the only way we can become better human beings is by improving our knowledge of what is truly good. Unfortunately, discovering the truth about goodness is difficult, and Wolff's response is to suggest a division of labour. It is not necessary that all people spend time putting in the work to distinguish the good from the bad; this job can be left to the philosophers. So according to Wolff, then, the function of a moral philosopher is to discover the truth about morality and to communicate this truth to people who do not have the time, inclination or capacity to think about such matters. The function of moral philosophers is, from this perspective, to communicate moral knowledge to people who are ignorant so that they can lead more virtuous lives. Kant, influenced by Jean-Jacques **Rousseau** (1712–88), has, in contrast, far more respect for the moral capacities of common men and women, and as a result of this he believes that there is no need of philosophy to know what morality requires; we all already know what morality demands; Immorality, for Kant, is not an intellectual failing; it is not the result of lack of knowledge. Instead it is a practical failure, a failure of the will, due to our propensity to listen to the call of happiness rather than the call of conscience. The task of moral philosophy, according to Kant, is not to provide us with moral knowledge; instead its primary job is to clarify and analyse what we already know, and such clarification, as we shall see, does have some practical value, for it can help us in the struggle against moral self-deception. And this is what Kant explains he is doing in the first two chapters of the *Groundwork* where he claims to be following the **analytic method**. The *Groundwork* is divided into three chapters:

In *Groundwork* I Kant promises a transition from common rational knowledge of morality to the philosophical, and so his claims in this chapter are intended to be merely a clarification of our common-sense moral commitments. He begins by claiming that the only thing that we recognize as **unconditionally good** is **good will**. There are other things that we recognize as having value, for example, **happiness**, and virtues, such as courage and intelligence. But the value of these goods is conditional on the character of the person who possesses them. Kant is not denying that happiness, wealth, health, courage and intelligence are good things; his point is that the bravery and intelligence of a serial killer or the happiness of a rapist are not good. So, Kant's claim is that having a good will is the condition of the value of all these other goods, and so a good will is the only thing we regard as unconditionally good without qualification. And the first two chapters can be understood as an analysis of what it is to have a good will. *Groundwork* I and II, then, can be understood as an analysis of what it is for a human being to have a good will.

The first important claim that Kant makes in *Groundwork* I is that having a good will has to do with one's basic motivation in acting not in the results that one achieves. A good person may be unlucky and unsuccessful in their projects, but this does not in any way detract from their moral goodness. A bad person may unintentionally cause a lot of good; a serial killer, for example, may have killed Hitler, and this would have almost certainly been a good thing, but this does not make the serial killer a good person. Having established that having a good will depends upon one's motivation, Kant continues by arguing that to have a good will, at least for beings like us, consists in acting from duty, and so he turns his attention to an analysis of duty and what duty demands. The first point he makes is that to have a good will it is not enough to act *in accordance with* duty but one must act *out of* duty. Someone who is honest because they are afraid of the consequences of being caught, being dishonest does not manifest a good will. A moral individual will be honest because they recognize that being honest is the right thing to do. But, if having a good will involves acting out of duty, we need a proper account of what duty demands. **Utilitarians** will argue that what duty demands is that we aim or intend to maximize total happiness in society. According to a **consequentialist** moral theory such as utilitarianism, the moral worth of an action has to do with the intended objective; a good action is one which aims to produce the best outcome. Kant, however, rejects such an account of duty. He argues that duty does not have to do with the intended consequences of an action but with the principle behind the action. To be moral, an action must be principled, and to act on principle is to act out of respect for law. So he argues that morality demands that I ought never to act in such a way that I could not also will that my **maxim** should become a **universal law**. A maxim is the subjective principle behind one's action, and so what Kant is saying here is that the test for whether a maxim is moral or not is whether one could or would will that everyone acted upon such a principle. To illustrate what he means by this, Kant gives the example of making a promise with no intention of keeping it. Although it is possible for an individual to make such a promise, people lie all the time, Kant argues that the maxim of making a lying promise in order to get out of difficulties is not the sort of thing that could exist as a universal law. The reason for this is that the intention in making such a promise presupposes that other people believe the promise maker. In a world in which everyone lies whenever it is convenient to do so, however, no one would trust any promises made; and so in such a world the institution of promise-making would not be possible, and the maxim of making a false promise to secure one's goals would be self-defeating. So Kant concludes that although I can will the lie, I cannot will a universal law to lie.

Kant finishes *Groundwork* I by discussing the relationship between moral philosophy and common-sense moral beliefs. He argues that his moral philosophy is not meant to be revisionary but is merely an explication of common-sense morality. Although Kant's language is philosophical, he is attempting to explain what we all already believe. His test of universalizability might be thought of as an attempt to formulate more precisely the commons-sense golden rule: do unto others as you would have them do unto you. Kant also claims that we do not need to do moral philosophy or be educated in order to know what do. The point of moral philosophy, then, cannot be to provide us with a set of rules telling us how to act morally, for we already know how to do this. So what is the point of doing moral philosophy? In *Groundwork* II Kant argues that immoral behaviour is always the result of making an exception for ourselves. We know what the right thing to do is, and we want everyone else to do it, but we decide, perhaps just this one time, to make an exception for ourselves. When we make such an exception, we normally give some excuse to ourselves for our bad behaviour and try and convince ourselves that the action was good, or at least not particularly bad. Kant believes that the value of doing moral philosophy is to help us recognize such excuses for what they are. Moral philosophy then is a tool we can use to guard against moral self-deception and the excuses we give ourselves to justify our less-than-perfect behaviour. Understood in these terms, moral philosophy does have some practical value. It does not, as Wolff thought, provide us with moral knowledge, but it can be used as a tool to help us increase our own self-knowledge and strengthen our will and resolve to do the right thing.

Although Kant is primarily concerned with giving an analysis of what it is to be moral, *Groundwork* II is best thought of as offering an analysis of practical rationality in general. For Kant, to be moral is to be practically **rational**, but practical rationality involves more than just morality, for a prudent person, who is concerned with their long-term self-interest, is also exhibiting rationally. Now, for human beings practical rationality is a matter of constraint. We are beings with needs and natural inclinations, and sometimes these needs and **inclinations** are in conflict with what we recognize to be rational. I may really want another slice of cake, but realize that eating it will probably make me sick. In such a case I recognize that although I really want another slice of cake, I *should not* eat it for prudential reasons. Similarly, although I might really want to do well in the exam and so am tempted to cheat, I know that I *should not* for moral reasons. In such cases we recognize the demands of practical rationality as commands that constrain us. Another word for a command is an **imperative**, and so Kant argues that for us practical rationality in general involves imperatives. We can conceive of a type of agent, which Kant names a **holy will**, that had no inclinations or needs that conflicted with the demands of rationality. Such a being would act rationally gladly and without constraint, and so for such a being practical rationality would not be a matter of imperatives. For human beings things are different. As beings with needs and inclinations, rationality will always involve some constraint. This is not to say, as some readers of Kant sometimes suggest, that Kant thinks that being constrained and acting against our needs and inclinations is a good thing. One might think that Kant is committed to a view that would suggest, for example, that the best, and most committed, type of partner is one who wants to cheat but through an act of will controls herself. But this is not what Kant thinks; he believes that ideally we should strive to be people who act rationally gladly, and he thinks that it is better if our inclinations and needs are in line with what rationality demands. For this reason Kant argues that we have a duty to try and cultivate our natural inclinations. His point is merely that as imperfectly rational beings, there are times when what we want and what we recognize we should do come apart, and in such cases we should subordinate our desires to the demands of rationality.

As we have seen, Kant thinks that rationality involves both the demands of prudence as well as the demands of morality, and he suggests that this distinction can be captured in terms of a distinction between two types of imperative, which he names **hypothetical imperatives** and the **categorical imperative**. A hypothetical judgement is a conditional, 'if . . . then' judgement, and so a hypothetical imperative is a conditional imperative. Such imperatives tell us, 'if you want *x*, do *y*!' Kant distinguishes between two types of hypothetical imperative, which he names imperatives of skill and imperatives of prudence. Imperatives of skill are imperatives that presuppose a contingent desire. For example, I may want to go home, and the only way to get home is to walk through the quad.

In such a case the hypothetical imperative will be: 'If you want to go home, walk thought the quad!' Now the desire to go home is a contingent desire, it is a desire that I may or may not have. Kant believes, however, that there is one desire that all human beings share, namely the desire to be happy, and imperatives of prudence have to do with this desire for happiness. They tell us, 'if you want to be happy, do x!' For example, if my conception of happiness involves having a good job, and I recognize that in order to get a good job I must work hard on my exams, I will recognize that insofar as I want to be happy I *should* work hard on my exams. Now although we all desire to be happy, we all have different conceptions of **happiness**. And so what hypothetical imperatives demand will depend upon the particular desires that one has. This is why Kant claims that hypothetical imperatives only command conditionally. I should work hard if I want a well-paying job, but if I am the sort of person whose conception of happiness does not involve having a well-paying job, prudence will not demand that I work hard, at least for this particular reason. Hypothetical imperatives, then, are contingent on the particular desires and inclinations one actually has. We may think of a rational egoist as someone who only cares about their own long-run self-interest, who is prudent but not moral. Such a person will constrain their immediate desires for the sake of their long-term self-interest, and will recognize that there are certain things that they should or should not do, but they will not recognize the demands of morality. They might behave honestly if they believe that honesty is the best policy in the long run, but they will not behave honestly if they believe lying will benefit them in the long run. Morality, then, involves recognizing some other 'should' than the 'should' of prudence and Kant calls this 'should' the **categorical imperative**.

Kant argues that unlike hypothetical imperatives which are always conditional on the existence of particular contingent desires, the categorical imperative, the demand of morality, commands unconditionally and absolutely. This, Kant believes, captures our everyday moral intuitions. The demands of morality do not depend upon the existence of particular desires and inclinations; there are particular types of action that we recognize that are just wrong, regardless of how we feel or what we happen to want. Now Kant thinks that just by thinking about the notion of an unconditional command we can recognize what such an imperative must demand.

In this respect, the idea of the categorical imperative is very different from the idea of a hypothetical imperative. Understanding what a hypothetical imperative is, does not give me any insight into what I should do. With a conditional command to know what the command commands, I must know the condition; in other words, to know what a hypothetical imperative tells me to do, I must already know what I want. Things are different with an unconditional command. Kant assumes that a command has to be law-like, and in the case of the categorical imperative there can be no condition limiting the law. So the only think that the categorical imperative can command is that our maxims be law-like. At this point in the argument a political analogy may be helpful. Let us define a decree as an order backed by threats made by someone who has power, and let us assume that those in power give orders in order to satisfy their desires. Understanding this definition of a decree will not tell us what decrees will be issued, for this will depend upon the actual contingent desires of those in power. Things are different, however, with the idea of a constitution. For merely by understanding what a constitution is we know something about what it demands. Any constitution demands that decrees be law-like. So, understanding what the idea of a constitution is tells us something about what a constitution demands, and a similar story can be told about our idea of a categorical imperative. We can think of an individual with a good will as one who is ruled by something like a constitution, whose maxims are law-like, rather than arbitrary. And Kant thinks that thinking about what is involved in the notion of law can tell us a lot about what morality demands, for one aspect of law is that law must be universal and this leads Kant to the first of his three formulations of the categorical imperative.

The first formulation of the categorical imperative is the **formula of universalizability**. Kant states this formula as follows: 'Act only on that maxim by which you can at the same time will that it become a universal law.' The basic idea here is that all the categorical imperative demands is that our actions be law-like, and law is something that must be universal. To illustrate the force of this maxim he discusses four examples of particular **duties**: (1) the duty against suicide if one is weary of life, (2) the duty to not make a lying promise, (3) the duty to develop one's talents and (4) the duty to help others in need. Kant returns to these four examples for each formulation of the categorical imperative. Kant argues with regard to the first two examples, that we cannot even *conceive* of a world in which the maxim to commit suicide if one is sick of life were a universal law, or a world in which everyone made lying promises whenever it was to their benefit. In the case of the second two duties Kant argues that although we can conceive a world in which everyone adopted the maxim never to develop their talents or adopted the maxim never to help others in need, we cannot will the existence of such a world.

The second formulation of the categorical imperative is the **formula of humanity**. Kant states this formula as follows: 'Act in such a way that you treat humanity, whether in your own person or in any other person, always at the same time as an end never merely as a means.' By 'human' here Kant does not mean the member of a particular species, but means a rational agent. So this formulation demands that we respect our own rational nature and other rational beings. The relationship between this formula and the previous one is the subject of much debate. It is not clear what respecting humanity has to do with law. Kant himself suggests that the existence of some being whose existence has absolute worth, something, as he puts it, that is an end in itself, is necessary if there are to be any definite laws. Perhaps Kant's thought here is that the notion of law, and with it the notion of universalizability, presupposes the existence of some beings that are ends in themselves. Universality presupposes the existence of a universe or plurality of beings over which to universalize, and if these beings are to be potential lawgivers, then they must have the authority to make law, and only beings who are ends in themselves and whose existence has unconditional value could possibly have such authority. If this interpretation is correct, then it suggests what it is to be human in the morally relevant sense is to have the capacity to give law. And so what the formula of humanity demands is that we should respect the **autonomy** of ourselves and others. Other interpreters, however, argue that Kant means something weaker by the notion of humanity. According to this notion, what it is to be human in the morally relevant sense is merely to have the capacity to set ends.

The final formulation is the **formulation of the realm of ends** (or, in some translations, the *kingdom* of ends). According to this formula, morality demands that we always regard ourselves as law-giving in a realm of ends. Kant suggests that this final formulation in some ways combines the first and second formulations. Once again it is not exactly clear what Kant means by a realm of ends. But one suggestion is that this notion is modelled on **Rousseau's** (1712–78) political ideal of a republic, as developed in his *On the Social Contract* (1762). Rousseau argues that in an ideal society, which he calls a republic, each member will be a citizen, and to be a citizen involves being both sovereign and subject. In a republic, then, each citizen will be both the source of the law and subject to the law, and so in such a political system each individual will only be subject to laws they have made themselves. This interpretation helps to explain the relationship between the idea of a realm of ends and the idea of **autonomy**. For Kant argues that another way of stating the basic principle of his ethics is to call it the principle of **autonomy**, and he contrasts this with the notion of heteronomy. To be autonomous (*auto* = self, *nomos* = law) is to be subject to a law one has made oneself, and this is exactly how Rousseau characterizes the situation of a citizen living in an ideal republic.

Groundwork III is probably the most difficult section of the *Groundwork*. In *Groundwork* I and II Kant claims to have been following what he calls the **analytic method**, and merely providing an analysis and clarification of our common-sense moral commitments, and in so doing he was not attempting to provide a justification of these moral commitments that might persuade a moral skeptic. In Groundwork III, however, he claims to be adopting the **synthetic method** and in so doing he is attempting to prove some sort of justification of our common-sense moral beliefs. Kant begins *Groundwork* III by distinguishing between **freedom** in the negative sense and freedom in the positive sense, and he argues that the positive conception of freedom somehow flows from the negative conception. The negative conception of freedom is the idea of a type of causality that can be effective independent of alien causes determining it. A free cause, in the negative sense, is one that is not determined by external objects or laws. The positive conception of freedom is the idea of an autonomous cause, which has the property of being a law to itself. And Kant seems to think that the only way we can make sense of a free cause in the negative sense is if we think of it as free in the positive sense, or as autonomous; so only beings that are free in the positive sense can be free in the positive sense. His argument is that a cause must be law-governed, but if the law is external to the cause, then the cause will be determined by an alien cause and so will not even be free in the negative sense. So the only way we can think of a cause that is free in the negative sense is if we think of it as governed by a law that it has given itself, that is if we think of it as autonomous.

There is much disagreement, however, about what exactly Kant is trying to prove in *Groundwork* III and how his argument is supposed to work. One suggestion is that Kant is attempting to provide an argument against the rational egoist. The rational egoist is a particular type of moral skeptic who in their action only cares about their long-term self-interest. As such, the rational egoist is committed to the principle of prudence and so recognizes the binding force of hypothetical imperatives and is rational in the sense that she is willing to sacrifice some pleasure in the short run for the sake of greater, long-term gratification of her desires. The rational egoist, then, is capable of taking the practical perspective and deliberating about which of their inclinations to act on. In so doing the rational egoist cannot but help acting under the idea of freedom, for insofar as she is engaged in deliberation as to which of her inclinations to act on, she has to assume that she is free in the negative sense and that she has a real choice about whether or not to satisfy a particular inclination. Now, if being free in the negative sense implies being free in the positive sense, then this argument would show that even the rational egoist is implicitly committed to a belief in freedom in the positive sense and suggests that the egoist is being inconsistent in recognizing the binding force of hypothetical imperatives while denying the binding force of the categorical imperative.

The argument just presented does not assume that we know that we are free, it just claims that insofar as we engage in practical deliberation we must implicitly assume that we are free in the negative sense. The argument does, however, give an argument for the bindingness of the moral law that takes as its starting point some sort of consciousness of freedom. Because of this some commentators think that the argument that Kant makes here in the *Groundwork* (1785) is inconsistent with the position he defends in the **Critique of Practical Reason** (1788) and that Kant must have radically changed his position between writing these two works. For in the *Critique of Practical Reason* Kant explicitly rejects any argument that begins with consciousness of our freedom and from this draws a conclusion about the force of morality. Instead he argues that the consciousness of the moral law is what he calls a fact of reason and that it is only the consciousness of this fact, and the recognition of the demands that morality places on us that provides the source, and practical justification, of our belief in our own freedom. One implication of Kant's later position would seem to be that it is impossible to give an argument to a moral skeptic to convince them of the binding force of morality that takes as a starting point the consciousness of freedom, because we are only justified in believing in our own freedom if we already recognize and accept the binding force of the moral law. So if Kant was attempting to offer such an argument in *Groundwork* III, it is an argument that he would have rejected 3 years later when he wrote the Second *Critique*. See: **Critique of Practical Reason**; **freedom; categorical imperative; hypothetical imperative; maxim; duty; obligation; universalizability, formula of; humanity, formula of; realm of ends, formula of; autonomy**; *Metaphysics of Morals*; **law; reason; unconditional value; perfectionism.**

happiness

The role of happiness in Kant's moral philosophy is complicated. Kant does not think as many philosophers had thought that the function of practical reason is to direct us to our own happiness. The purpose of reason cannot be to obtain happiness, for reason is so bad at this task and often interferes with our achievement of happiness. Instinct is a far better means to happiness than reason. In addition, in contrast to the utilitarians, Kant does not think that happiness is unconditionally good, for the only thing that is **unconditionally good** is a **good will.** This is not to say that Kant thinks that happiness is not intrinsically good and desirable for its own sake, but that the value of happiness is conditioned by the possession or lack of a good will. What Kant means by this is that the moral state of one's character is what makes one deserving or worthy of happiness and so he thinks that the happiness of a vicious person is a bad thing for such a person does not deserve to be happy. As evidence for this he appeals to the fact that an impartial spectator would not approve of the happiness of an individual who is vicious. The happiness of a good person, however, is an intrinsically good thing, and the unhappiness of someone with a good will a bad thing. Thus, although the only thing that is unconditionally good is a good will, insofar as we are virtuous we deserve to be happy; and the happiness of someone with a good will is itself something that is intrinsically good and the value of happiness is quite a distinct thing from the value that is involved in having a good will. Morality and happiness are quite distinct things, both of which are intrinsically valuable – although the value of happiness is conditioned by having a good will, so although happiness is intrinsically valuable, it is not unconditionally valuable. Having a good will is the only thing that is **unconditionally good**. However, someone who has a good will and is not happy is lacking something valuable, namely happiness. It is better to be a good person and happy rather than being a good person and unhappy! Thus, what Kant calls the **highest good** involves the combination of a good will (the condition) with happiness (the conditioned).

In terms of his account of what happiness is, Kant offers two seemingly incompatible accounts. On the one hand, he sometimes suggests that happiness consists in well-being and the enjoyment of life, which suggests that happiness essentially involves pleasure, and so the happy life is the pleasurable life. On the other hand, he more often suggests that happiness involves desire satisfaction, with the ideal of happiness being the ideal of the complete satisfaction of the sum total of all one's desires. And this second account of the nature of happiness seems to be his official position. The idea of happiness, in this sense is the ideal of getting everything one wants, of satisfying *all* of one's desires. Now Kant argues that happiness, understood in these terms, is what he calls an ideal of the imagination, and is indeterminate because our desires are contingent and the satisfaction of one nearly always leads to a new one coming into being and so the notion of the sum of *all* one's desire is indeterminate. The two accounts of happiness are in tension because, for Kant, the notions of pleasure and desire satisfaction are quite distinct, and involve quite different faculties. Pleasure is a feeling, and for Kant the faculty of **desire** and the faculty of **feeling** are distinct faculties. Pleasure does not always involve the satisfaction of a desire, as Kant makes clear in his account of the disinterested feeling of pleasure we have in the experience of **beauty**. And the satisfaction of a desire does not always lead to pleasure. For example, a parent may desire that their children get good jobs and this desire may be satisfied only after their death in which case it would not lead to pleasure.

In terms of our duties regarding happiness, Kant believes we have a **duty** to promote the happiness of other, which he calls the duty of **beneficence**, but he thinks that we do not have a direct **duty** to promote our own happiness as this is something that we naturally seek anyway. Kant's point here may be understood in the following terms. If one has a desire then one is naturally inclined to satisfy it, as this is just what it is to have a desire. So when it comes to ourselves what is important is having the right desires and motivation and only acting on those desires that are permissible. When it comes to others, however, we cannot force them to have or choose to satisfy the right desires, but we can help them satisfy their desires, and insofar as their desires are permissible, we should take account of the desires of others in our decision-making procedures and make the satisfaction of the desires of others one of our goals or ends. This is not to say that we have a duty to maximize the total happiness in the world. Our duty to make the happiness of others one of our ends is a wide or imperfect duty. It tells us that we should aim to promote the happiness of others, but it does not tell us how we should do this, and so this duty leaves a lot of latitude for free choice. Kant does not think that it would be morally wrong to focus on promoting the happiness of those closest to us or to choose to promote the happiness of a few rather than the many. Finally, it is important to note that Kant distinguishes between the duty of **beneficence**, which concerns how we should act, and the feeling of **benevolence**, which is the feeling of being satisfied or pleased by the happiness of others. Although we have a duty to cultivate our feeling of benevolence insofar as this is possible, we do not have a duty to be benevolent, for Kant believes that ought implies can, and we cannot have feelings on demand.

highest good (*summum bonum*)

Kant's discussion of what he calls the highest good has to do with the relationship between morality and happiness. Unlike the Stoics who thought that virtue was its own reward, and so who thought that the virtuous man would be happy even if he were being tortured, and unlike the **Epicureans** who thought that the person who sought their true long-run happiness in an enlightened manner would naturally behave virtuously, Kant thought that being moral and being happy are quite different things. It is possible to be good and unhappy, for example the person of principle may end up being imprisoned and tortured, and it is possible to be bad and happy, as the examples of many tyrants throughout history suggest. Now, although there is no natural link between being moral and being happy Kant thinks that the two concepts are related because he thinks that morality is the condition of the value of happiness, for he thinks that to be moral is to be worthy or deserving of happiness. And he also thinks that the happiness of a bad person is actually a bad thing, as is indicated by the fact that we do not approve of the happiness of the wicked. Now although Kant thinks that having a good will is the only *unconditioned* good, he does not think it is the *highest* good, for a person who has a good will but is not happy lacks something of value. Thus Kant argues that in an ideal world, or what Kant calls a moral world, the happiness of individuals would be proportional to their virtue, and this proportionality between virtue and happiness is what Kant calls the highest good. In a just world people would get what they deserved.

Kant's two most substantial discussions of the highest good are found in the Doctrine of Method of the *Critique of Pure Reason* (1781/1787), and the Dialectic of the *Critique of Practical Reason* (1788). In these passages Kant argues that morality demands that we assume that the highest good is possible, for the virtuous person should at the very least be able to reasonably hope for their own happiness. He argues, however, that such hope is only reasonable if we believe in the existence of God, for Kant thinks that the idea of a just world is one in which there is a necessary relationship between one's moral character and the happiness one obtains, and he thinks that naturally there is not such a relationship between these two quite distinct things, and so the necessity of the relationship must be established by something external, and the only type of being that could establish such a necessary relationship between morality and happiness, and guarantee justice, would be a wise, omnipotent, omniscient and good ruler of the universe – in other words, God. So, insofar as our belief in the possibility of justice in the world is reasonable we must believe in the existence of God as the ruler of the universe. In the *Critique of Practical Reason* he calls these two beliefs postulates of practical reason.

history

Although Kant did not write a major book on the philosophy of history, many of his works deal with questions having to do with history, and he wrote a number of shorter works dealing with history, especially in the 1780s and 1790s, such as *Idea for a Universal History with a Cosmopolitan Aim* (1784) and *Conjectural Beginning of Human History* (1786) and *Perpetual Peace* (1795). Kant's philosophy of history is best understood as attempting to offer an account how the realms of freedom and nature are related to one another, as he sees the natural progress of human history as the gradual progress of man from a purely natural being to a state of freedom and morality. The progress Kant sees in human history is not to be understood in terms of the gradual increase in human happiness and well-being, but in terms of the gradual establishment of a condition of right and justice, and of the emergence of states ruled by law, with the hope for goal of such history being a world of free republics living in perpetual peace with one another. In human history the intelligible slowly becomes visible. This sounds paradoxical given Kant's strict division between the **intelligible** and **phenomenal**, but it is important to remember that Kant regards **law** and right as themselves intelligible. A truly just society would be one in which each and every human individual in the world was autonomous and sovereign in the sense of fully endorsing, indeed willing, the legal order that governed them. This ideal of a just world order is an intelligible ideal and as such is unachievable at any moment in time, for our human laws at any moment in time are only provisionally just and they are so only insofar as they can be regarded as steps on the road to this ideal. So, in a sense, positive laws at any particular moment are not fully laws, as they do not come from all and apply to all, but even though at no moment in time can we ever achieve complete legitimacy of the laws, we can reasonably hope that over time, in history, we can and will gradually approach and approximate this ideal.

Kant's goal in writing on history is primarily to justify the reasonableness of the hope that human history is progressive in this sense. His account is not meant to suggest that he regards such progress as inevitable. He merely wants to show that the hope that such progress is possible is not unreasonable. His main motivation here is that he believes that we have a moral duty to enter and develop what he calls the civil condition – a condition in which human relations are governed by law rather than by force or the threat of force. He is also, however, committed to the principle that ought implies can. As a result of this he thinks that for this duty to enter into the civil condition to be real, it must be possible, at least in principle, for us to bring such a condition into being, and so at the very least it must not be unreasonable for us to hope that such a condition can gradually be brought into existence. And in order to justify the reasonableness of this hope he argues that there are elements in human nature, understood in descriptive naturalistic terms, that suggest that such progress is not impossible. Indeed he tries to show, using arguments similar to Hobbes, that the selfish elements in human nature themselves tend to promote the development of what he calls the civil condition. In particular he argues that what he names our **unsocial sociability** is a natural driving force in the natural progress of human civilization, which suggests that progress is something that can occur naturally. See: *Idea for a Universal History with a Cosmopolitan Aim*; *Conjectural Beginning of Human History*; *Perpetual Peace*.

holy will

The idea of a holy will is the idea of a perfectly good will that obeys the moral law spontaneously and without inner conflict. For such an agent morality would not be a matter of imperatives or obligations, but such an agent would always gladly do what morality demands. Human beings cannot have such a will, for as beings with needs and contingent inclinations, there is always the possibility of conflict between our desires and what morality demands of us. And so, although we must assume that it is possible for us to resolve to always obey the **moral law**, it is not possible for us to always do the right things gladly. This is why for beings like us morality is a matter of **obligation** and why the moral law presents itself to us in the form of an **imperative**. Although it is not possible for human beings to have holy wills, Kant thinks that the idea of such a will is an ideal that we can strive towards and although it is impossible for a human being to have a holy will at any particular moment in time, it is an ideal we can gradually approach. Such striving involves cultivating our character so that we are more likely to be able to satisfy the demands of morality, and this cultivation will involve both attempting to strengthen our positive emotions, such as the feeling of benevolence, and working to weaken our negative feelings, such as anger and envy. See: *Groundwork of the Metaphysics of Morals* (1785).

humanity, formula of

The formula of humanity is the second of Kant's three formulations of the **Categorical Imperative** found in the *Groundwork of the Metaphysics of Morals* (1785). According to this formulation the practical imperative is: 'So act that you use humanity, whether in your own person or in the person of any other, always at the same time as an end, never merely as a means.' There are a number of important questions about this formulation. First, it is not clear how this formulation relates to the other two formulations. In particular, it is not at all clear how it is supposed to be related to the formula of **universalizability**. Secondly, it is not clear what Kant means by 'humanity'. It is clear that humanity in this moral sense should not be identified with being the member of a particular natural biological species. Kant is open, for example, to the possibility that there might be non-biologically human rational beings on other planets, and although such beings would not be biologically human it seems clear that Kant would think that if we encountered such beings they would be deserving of respect, and so they should be thought of as human in the morally relevant sense. It seems clear that Kant identifies the notion of humanity in the morally relevant sense with that of being a rational agent, but this notion is also quite vague and there have been a number of different interpretations of what Kant means by this. There have been weaker and stronger interpretations of what is necessary to be a rational being in the morally relevant sense. And there are at least three quite distinct accounts of what Kant means by humanity in the context of this formulation of the categorical imperative:

(1) Some commentators have argued for a weak interpretation of what it is to be human in the morally relevant sense arguing that

all this requires is a capacity to set ends or a capacity to engage in practical reasoning, which might be limited to the capacity to recognize hypothetical imperatives. Such a reading would suggest that psychopaths, who for this purpose can be defined as individuals who are capable of prudential reasoning but not moral reasoning, should be regarded with some (minimal) moral respect. Some Kantians, however, who defend a weak interpretation of what is deserving of respect, argue that any individual who is capable of prudential reasoning must be capable of moral reasoning, and so deny the real possibility of psychopaths as so defined. (2) A stronger interpretation of what Kant means by humanity in this context is that he identifies it with the capacity to engage in moral reasoning. According to this interpretation, any being capable of recognizing the force of moral demands should be regarded as an end in itself and treated with respect. Let us define a true psychopath as an individual who is capable of setting ends but unable to recognize the demands of morality. Now some Kant scholars believe that Kant thought that such a being is impossible for they think that Kant is committed to the view that any being capable of setting their own ends is able to recognize the force of moral demands. However, if such a being was possible, according to this interpretation it should not be regarded as an end in itself and we are not required to treat such a being with respect. We are on this interpretation, however, required to regard a vicious person who recognizes the demands of morality but chooses to act immorally as an end in themselves and deserving of some sort of respect. It is important to note here that respect here does not mean to esteem. We can regard someone as despicable, but as worthy of respect, in the sense that we believe that they should, for example be treated fairly and honestly. (3) An even stronger interpretation identifies 'humanity' with having a good will. According to this interpretation, we should only regard beings with good wills as ends in themselves and deserving of respect.

These different interpretations suggest different ways of interpreting the formulation. If, for example, one thinks that the capacity to set ends is what is demanding of respect this might suggest an understanding of Kant's ethics that suggests that we should respect the choices of others even if they are bad, whereas if one identifies humanity with actually having a good will, one might think that we do not need to respect the bad choices of others.

Finally, once we have an adequate interpretation of what Kant means by 'humanity', we need a more detailed account of what it means to treat someone as an end never merely as a means. For example, if I employ someone to work for me, is the fact that we have a contractual relationship, and that our relationship is consensual, enough to satisfy this requirement? The formula of humanity, with its requirement that we treat others as ends and not merely as means involves that idea that we should not treat other people merely as objects, has had an influence on recent feminist critiques of objectification. See: **categorical imperative**; *Groundwork of the Metaphysics of Morals*; duty.

Hume, David (1711–76)

David Hume was a philosopher of the Scottish enlightenment. He was committed to a radical form of **empiricism** and defended a form of **skepticism**. His two most important works are *A Treatise of Human Nature* (1739–40) and *An Enquiry Concerning Human Understanding* (1748).

Hume was an **empiricist** in at least two senses: he was a *content empiricist*, believing that the contents of all of our thoughts must be derived from sensible experience, and he was a *knowledge empiricist*, denying the possibility of *a priori* knowledge of the world and arguing instead that all of knowledge of the world was *a posteriori*. Hume's *content empiricism* involved two radical claims, one about the content of our thought and another about the meaning of words. Hume argued that all of our ideas were ultimately derived from sensation and so that the content of our thought has to be explained entirely in terms of sensation. But he also assumes that words get their meaning from the ideas they are associated with, and argues that if we cannot explain the meaning of a word in terms of the sensations that produced an idea we should assume that the word is meaningless. Much of his theoretical philosophy involved explaining the meaning of some central philosophical concepts, such as the notion of causation, in such empiricist terms. Kant rejects such content empiricism, arguing that there are certain *a priori* logical concepts which he names **categories**. Hume was also a *knowledge empiricist* for he thought that all of our knowledge of the world is empirical and, in Kant's terms, *a posteriori*. Kant rejects knowledge empiricism for he believes in the possibility of **synthetic *a priori*** knowledge.

In addition to being a radical empiricist, Hume also defended a form of skepticism. Hume argued that many of our most fundamental beliefs about the world are not justified but are produced merely as a result of habit. One such belief is our confidence in induction. Inductive arguments draw conclusions about what has not been observed from what has been observed. Many of our beliefs about the world are based upon inductive arguments. For example, our beliefs about the future are based upon our prior experience. When one lets go of a heavy object, say a cup, one expects it to fall to the ground, and the reason we expect the object to fall is that this is what has always happened in the past. But is this expectation justified? Hume argues that it is not, for the belief that the cup will fall will only be justified if it we have good reason to believe that the future will resemble the past. But what reason do we have to believe that the future will resemble the past? One might try and argue that in the past it was always the case that the future resembled the past, but this will only count as good evidence for believing that the future will resemble the past if we already have good reasons for believing that the future will resemble the past. So, our belief that the future will resemble the past does not seem to be the sort of belief that can be justified by appeal to past or present experience, but past and present experience is the only experience we have, so if we think that the only way a belief about the world can be justified is by appeal to our experience, we have to conclude, with Hume, that our practice of inductive reasoning is unjustified.

Kant was very stimulated by Hume's **skepticism** and claimed that Hume woke him from his '**dogmatic** slumbers', and many commentators in the English-speaking world have read Kant's **critical** project as primarily intended to provide an answer to Hume. Although Hume had an important influence on the development of Kant's thoughts, however, it is important to remember that Kant was educated in the German philosophical tradition, and was perhaps more strongly influenced by **rationalist** thinkers from this tradition such as Gottfried Wilhelm **Leibniz** (1646–1716), Christian **Wolff** (1679–1754) and Alexander Gottlieb **Baumgarten** (1714–62).

hypothetical imperative

In the *Groundwork of the Metaphysics of Morals* (1785) Kant famously distinguishes between hypothetical imperatives and what he calls the **categorical imperative**. An imperative is a command, and a **hypothetical judgement** is a conditional, 'if . . . then', judgement, and so a hypothetical imperative is a conditional command. Such imperatives tell us, if you want *x*, do *y*! Kant distinguished between two types of hypothetical imperative, which he names imperatives of skill and imperatives of prudence. Imperatives of skill are imperatives that presuppose a contingent desire. For example, I may want to go home and the only way to get home is to walk through the quad. In such a case the hypothetical imperative will be: 'If you want to go home, walk thought the quad!' Now the desire to go home is a contingent desire, it is a desire that I may or may not have. Kant believes however, that there is one desire that all human beings share, namely the desire to be happy. So an imperative of prudence will tell us that 'if you want to be happy, do *x*!'. Kant believes that the **principle** behind hypothetical imperatives is **analytic**, for hypothetical imperatives tell us that if we will an end we should also will the necessary means to the end, and if we do not will the necessary means to an end we have not really willed the end. See: **categorical imperative**; *Groundwork of the Metaphysics of Morals*.

hypothetical judgement

The hypothetical form of judgement is the second of the three judgements of relation enumerated in the table of **judgements** in the *Critique of Pure Reason* (1781–87). A hypothetical judgement is an 'if . . . then' judgement that relates two judgements. For example, 'if Istanbul is in Turkey, then Taksim is in Turkey' is a hypothetical judgement. The first clause here is the ground, the second is the consequence. Kant derives the **category** of **causation**, the second of the categories of relation in the table of categories, from the hypothetical form of judgement. It is important to note that Kant does not identify the cause-effect relation with the ground-consequence relation, for the former is a real relation whereas the latter is a merely logical relation. Kant explains this distinction between the logical notion of a ground and the notion of a real cause in the Schematism of the Pure Concepts of the Understanding. Kant also claims that the hypothetical form of judgement is the principle of the **series**, and this claim is important for his discussion of number and **causation**. See: **Causation; Analogies of Experience; judgements, table of.**

idea

Whereas the **understanding** is the faculty of **concepts, reason** is the faculty of principles and ideas, and Kant identifies three ideas of pure reason corresponding to the three **categories** of relation (the concepts of **substance, causation** and **community**). Our idea of the *soul*, or an absolute substance, is derived from the category of substance; our idea of the *world* as a whole and the idea of freedom are derived from the category of causation; and our idea of *God* is derived from the category of community. The way in which both the idea of the world as a whole and the idea of freedom are derived from the category of causation will be explained below. Kant argues that the three ideas of reason are what he calls problematic concepts. That is, they are concepts that are not logically inconsistent, and so they are thinkable, but we have now way of knowing whether or not there really is any object corresponding to these ideas. Kant argues in the Dialectic of the *Critique of Pure Reason* that rationalist metaphysicians mistake the fact that we possess these three concepts for knowledge of the putative objects of these concepts.

In explaining the relationship between the three categories and the ideas, Kant claims that an idea is the concept of the totality of conditions of a given conditioned. This sounds quite complicated, but Kant's thought is quite simple. The three categories of relation all involve the relationship between something that is conditioned and its condition. The category of causation, for example, involves the relation of cause and effect, and in this case the effect is the conditioned and the cause the condition. If we take a particular effect, say the state of the world at the present moment of time, as the conditioned, then the concept of the totality of the series of causes that produced this effect is the concept of the totality of conditions. This idea of the totality of conditions, or the complete series of events that proceeded and produced the present state of the world, is an idea of reason. But this idea is, Kant thinks, an empty concept, for there is no object in experience corresponding to it, for, Kant thinks, that every event in time must have a cause and so the series of causes that produced any particular effect is infinite, and like nearly all early modern philosophers he believes that an infinite totality is impossible. For to say that something is infinite just is to say that however many things you have enumerated there will always be more, and so the idea of the whole series of past events is incoherent. There is, however, nothing contradictory in the idea of an uncaused cause, although an uncaused cause is not something that can exist in space and time, for every event in space and time must be the effect of some prior cause. And if we think of an event or series of events as the effect of an uncaused cause then we are thinking of the totality of the conditions (the cause) of the conditioned (the event). Now the idea of an uncaused cause is the idea of freedom, for the idea of such a cause is the idea of something that is not determined by any thing external to itself. And Kant argues that although nothing that can exist in space and time can be free in this sense, morality demands that we think of ourselves in such a way and there is no contradiction in doing this if we regard ourselves, as free, as not existing in the spatio-temporal phenomenal world but in the intelligible realm.

Kant's account of the relationship between the **category** of **community** and the idea of **God** is more complicated. The category of community is derived from the **disjunctive** form of judgement and it is easiest to understand Kant's account of the origin of the idea of God in terms of how it is derived from the disjunctive form of judgement. Disjunctive judgements are exclusive either-or judgements which divide a given concept into two spheres, and it is through disjunctive judgements that we divide a genus into species. For example, we may have the concept 'object' and in making the judgement 'all objects are either living or non-living beings' we divide the concept of object into two species of object, living and non-living object. We may then divide the concept of living objects in a similar way into animals and plants, and animals into rational animals and non-rational animals. The conditioned here is the concept of the highest genus and all the species that fall under this genus are the conditions. So our idea of reason here is the idea of a completely systematic and exhaustive conceptual scheme. In such a scheme there will be lowest species, that is, species that cannot themselves be subdivided onto further species. These lowest species will not be general concepts but will be the complete concepts of individuals being determinate with regard to every possible concept. And Kant thought that the idea of a completely determined lowest concept is impossible for whenever we have a particular concept it is always possible to divide it into species. Now although this idea of a completely specified conceptual scheme is empty as it is not the sort of thing that could ever be given in experience or even in thought, it can and does function as a **regulative idea** or what Kant calls a *focus imaginarius*, and it is this idea of complete **systematicity**, which involves the unobtainable goal of complete specification of all our concepts, that is the object of reason's desire. Now, Kant thinks that this regulative idea of complete systematicity is the origin of our theoretical idea of God. For the idea of complete systematicity requires a set of principles from which all of our conceptual distinctions can be derived, and Kant thinks that we are led by what he calls transcendental illusion, to mistake this idea of reason for the representation of an object – God. For our idea of complete conceptual specification and systematicity involves the idea of a set of principles from which all of our conceptual distinctions can be derived, and this ideal set of principles for which reason searches, would, if found, be the source for the whole structure of our thinking and of all of our conceptual distinctions. As such they would be the source of all of our concepts. The transcendental illusion is to take this idea of a set of principles from which all conceptual distinctions could be derived, that is, a set of principles that would be the source of all of our concepts, as the cognition of a being that is the source of all beings. See: **reason; categories, table of; God.**

Idea for a Universal History with a Cosmopolitan Aim (1784)

In this short essay Kant provides his most detailed account of his views on **history**. He offers a teleological account of the progress in human history, the goal of which is to show that it is not unreasonable to hope that the goal reason has of producing a world in which relations between human beings is governed by **law** rather than force or threats of force is also the goal of nature.

His account of this goal is cosmopolitan because he thinks that the goal of reason is for the relation between all human beings to be governed by law, and so this does not just require the existence of individual states governed by law, but also a law-like and peaceful relationship between states – a theme which will be developed in his influential later essay *Perpetual Peace* (1795). In order to show that this goal of reason can also be a goal of nature, he argues for a natural mechanism that explains why human history can naturally be thought of as developing towards such a condition. He suggests that this mechanism is the **unsocial sociability** of human nature, and paradoxically he suggests it is the natural antagonism that exists between human beings living together in society that is the driving force behind history and which pushes the development of human culture, technology and the building of political institutions that will hopefully make peaceful coexistence based upon a respect for law possible. His thought seems to be that it is the existence of such antagonism and conflict that propels us to build political institutions and institute laws. In offering a teleological and progressive account of human history, Kant does not want to defend a form of historical determinism, or to suggest that progress is in any sense inevitable. Instead, his aim is far more modest. The fact that morality has a certain goal implies that we must hope that progress towards this goal is achievable, and his teleological account of history is meant to explain the reasonableness of this hope. Given what we know of human nature and human history, it is quite possible to despair about the possibility of human progress and the creating of a more just world. Kant's point is that even given what we know of human nature such hope in progress is not unreasonable, and indeed it is precisely those forces that are the most destructive and negative in human nature that are likely in the long run to lead to progress. Kant's goal then is to show that it is not unreasonable to hope and hence to believe that nature and morality have the same goal. See: *Perpetual Peace*; **history**.

ideal

Kant rejects the Platonic theory of ideas. According to Plato's theory, the world as we experience it is a pale copy or shadow of a world of ideal forms, which serve as archetypes of the material objects that we experience, and the goal of philosophy is to acquire knowledge of these ideal forms. According to this Platonic theory the material world is dependent for its existence on this world of ideals. However, although Kant rejects this theoretical role of ideals, rejecting their theoretical power, he does think that they have practical power, serving as **regulative** principles which can ground the possibility of the perfection of both knowledge and action. Thus, the ideal of **systematicity** plays an important role in Kant's account of the development of our knowledge and the formation of empirical concepts. And ideals play an extremely important role in his ethics. There are good reasons to think that what Kant calls a **good will** in the *Groundwork of the Metaphysics of Morals* (1785) is at least partially to be thought of as a practical ideal. In the section called the Ideal of Pure Reason of the *Critique of Pure Reason* (1781/1787) Kant explains the distinction between an **idea** of pure reason and an ideal, explaining that with an ideal we understand an idea not merely concretely but as an individual thing that is determined through the idea alone. And he suggests that whereas we can think of ideas as providing rules for our thinking we can think of an ideal as serving as something like an original picture which we can use to judge how accurate a copy is. As such, Kant suggests, although ideals can never be realized as objects of experience, they can play an indispensable role as standards of reason and of judgement. See: **beauty, ideal of; Ideal of Pure Reason.**

idealism

See: **Refutation of Idealism; Transcendental Idealism; realism**

idealism, formal

Although Kant generally calls his position **transcendental idealism** he sometimes, especially in the *Prolegomena to Any Future Metaphysics* (1783), calls his own position 'formal idealism'. The main reason for using this expression in the *Prolegomena* is to make clear the difference between his own species of idealism and the subjective idealism of **George Berkeley** (1685–1753). Berkeley had denied the real existence of material objects arguing that all that really exist are ideas and minds. Kant, however, makes distinction between the form and matter of the objects of intuition, and argues that although the matter of the objects of intuition is real, the spatio-temporal form of the objects is ideal and subjective. Thus, in claiming to be a formal idealist Kant is suggesting that, unlike Berkeley, he is not denying the real existence of material objects, for it is only the form of material objects that is ideal. See: **Berkeley.**

identity of indiscernibles, principle of the

According to this principle, which is sometimes called Leibniz's law because it was advocated by Gottfried Wilhelm **Leibniz** (1646–1716) and his followers, if two substances have all the same properties then they are the same substance. Kant rejects the principle of the identity of indiscernibles, arguing that Leibniz mistakes a logical principle for a real principle. Thus, in the **Amphiboly of the Concepts of Reflection,** Kant argues that Leibniz is mistaken to take this logical principle, which can legitimately be applied to concepts, and assume that it also applies to objects. It is true, Kant agrees, that if two concepts contain all the same predicates then they are the same concept. But our criterion for the identity of objects is different from our criterion for the identity of concepts. In the case of physical objects our criteria of identity involves the spatio-temporal position of objects. But this, Kant argues, provides a counterexample to the principle of the identity of indiscernible because two object, say two points in space, can be exactly the same in all of their properties but be in different places, and so although they cannot be distinguished conceptually they are distinct objects because they are in different places. See: **Leibniz.**

imagination, productive

In the **Transcendental Deduction** of the *Critique of Pure Reason* (1781/1787), Kant explains that the imagination is the faculty for representing an object even without its presence in intuition and he argues that what he calls the **productive imagination** is necessarily involved in all experience. There is much disagreement about how to read the *Deduction*. One explanation is that the productive imagination is necessarily involved in all spatio-temporal experience because such experience involves the capacity to represent that which is not spatially or temporally present. For Kant argues that we can only experience objects as given in space and time and as such all objects of experience are necessarily experienced as conditioned. The experience of the 'presence' of objects is a fundamental feature of temporal experience. To experience something in time, then, is to experience it as present, as existing now, in the present time. But a condition of experiencing something as present is the implicit awareness that there is a past. In other words, the experience that something *is present* involves an awareness (or what Kant calls a 'representation') that there *was* something prior to what is now being experienced. Thus, everything experienced in time is experienced as conditioned, for it implies or points to something that existed in some prior time that is not-present, and not presently experienced, something in the past. A similar argument can be made with regard to our experience of space. When we experience something as occupying a particular space we experience the space as bounded, for we are always implicitly aware that what is given in any particular space of which we are immediately aware is necessarily only a part of what there is. This is the sense in which the experience of an object as occupying a particular space is conditioned by the thought of the 'larger space' to which the particular space belongs. This 'larger space' is not immediately experienced but the thought of some 'larger space' is a necessary condition for the experience of any particular space, and hence is a necessary condition for the experience of any object in space. Another way of putting this is that no space or time can be thought without at the same time thinking of a much larger space or time and so every space and every time we experience is experienced as bounded. But, we can only experience a space or a time as bounded, however, if we are somehow implicitly aware of a space or time beyond the boundary. Thus every object of experience, being experienced as in space and/ or time, 'points to' something beyond itself that is not experienced.

The 'productive imagination', then, is just Kant's name for the capacity we have to implicitly represent the past and spaces beyond our visual field while we are experiencing something as here and now. And Kant argues that this capacity is judgemental. What he means by this is that the productive imagination has a conceptual structure, governed by the categories. Our implicit awareness of, say, the past while we are experiencing something as present is somehow dependent upon the categories, and in particular the categories of relation. In the **Analogies of Experience** Kant explains why the categories of relation are necessarily involved in our experience of objects in space and time. And one should note that Kant chose the title of this section carefully. Analogies are a way of representing that which is not present and thus the capacity to make analogies is to be understood as a particular instance of the faculty of productive imagination. Experiencing the phenomenally given as conditioned involves the categories of relation, because to experience something as conditioned is to experience it as having a relation to something else. The **Transcendental Deduction** provides a general account of the role of the productive imagination in experience whereas the **Analogies of Experience** examine in more detail the conceptual structure of the productive imagination showing how the concepts of relation play a role in representing that which is not immediately present. See: **Transcendental Deduction; Analogies of Experience.**

imperatives

See: **categorical imperative; hypothetical imperative,** *Groundwork of the Metaphysics of Morals*

inclinations

The notion of inclination plays an important role in Kant's ethics and in his theory of action. An inclination is a species of impulse or movement towards action and Kant often refers to inclinations as 'sensible impulses'. In particular, inclinations are impulses which are combined with an expectation or representation of pleasure at the actualization of the impulse. Although Kant does value pleasure, and believes that ideally a virtuous individual should act morally gladly and with pleasure, he thinks that immorality is the result of choosing to do something because we have an inclination to do it rather than because it is the right thing to do. See: **feelings; duty; categorical imperative;** *Groundwork of the Metaphysics of Morals.*

incorporation thesis

The incorporation thesis is a name given by some commentators to Kant's claim that an incentive can determine the will to an action only in so far as the individual has incorporated it into a **maxim.** The main idea behind this claim is that action is always for some reason and it is only insofar as we take an incentive, such as the feeling of hunger, as a sufficient reason for action that we actually act on the incentive. A commitment to the incorporation thesis involves a rejection of a balance of forces account of the relationship between desire and action. According to such a balance of forces account, desires are thought of as pushing and pulling us in various directions, with the strongest desire ultimately causing action.

inner sense

Kant distinguishes between two forms of experience which he names inner sense and **outer sense.** Through inner sense we are aware of ourselves. Inner sense consists of a temporal stream of felt experiences and the science of the objects of inner sense is psychology. Although inner sense provides us with a type of self-knowledge, in the **Paralogisms of Pure Reason** Kant rejects the possibility of Rational Psychology, the discipline that claims to provide us with *a priori* knowledge of the nature of the soul, and argues that through inner sense we are not aware of ourselves as we really are but only as we appear to ourselves. Through outer sense we are aware of physical objects existing in space, and the science of the objects of outer sense is physics. In the **Refutation of Idealism,** a section that Kant added to the second edition of the *Critique of Pure Reason* (1787), Kant argues that immediate experience of physical objects through outer sense is a necessary condition for the possibility of inner sense, for he argues that the only way we are able to experience our inner experiences as having a determinate temporal order is through the immediate experience of objective change and persistence. For example, we are able to date our subjective experiences by appeal to the motion of the sun or the movements of the hands of a clock. In claiming that outer sense is a necessary condition for the possibility of inner sense, Kant is rejecting the way of ideas, the doctrine that what we are immediately aware of are our subjective ideas or sense data and that we construct physical objects from this essentially subjective experience. Instead Kant defends what he calls empirical realism, or what we would today call direct realism, the doctrine that we are immediately aware of physical objects in space.

intelligible

The distinction between the intelligible and the phenomenal is one of the most important distinctions in Kant's philosophy, playing a central role in both his theoretical and practical philosophy. Something is intelligible if it can be thought but not experienced. The phenomenal is that which is a possible object of experience. Now, because Kant thinks that **space** and time are our forms of **intuition**, he thinks that only objects that can exist in space and time are possible objects of experience. Therefore anything that we can think but which cannot be experienced in space and time is intelligible. The intelligible can be thought, but we do not know if there is, or even could be, an object corresponding to the thought. So if Kant calls something 'intelligible' this means that we possess an idea that purports to refer to something, but that we have no knowledge of the purported referent of the idea. So, for example, Kant thinks that the idea of God is not obviously contradictory, and so the idea of God is thinkable. However, Kant thinks that God is not a possible object of experience and so God is *not knowable*. In Kant's terminology, the idea of God is intelligible.

Kant often contrasts the phenomenal world with the intelligible world. The intelligible world is the idea of a community of individuals that are not in space and time and there is no contradiction involved in this idea, so it is thinkable, but no object corresponding to this idea can be intuited. From the theoretical perspective it is the idea of a world of objects that are not in space and time. Although Kant thinks that we have no theoretical justification for believing in the existence of such objects, from the practical, moral perspective we are committed to the existence of such objects. For insofar as we believe in the possibility of morality, we have to regard ourselves and others as free, and Kant thinks that anything that can exist in space and time must be determined and so cannot be free. And so the idea of a community of free individuals, or what Kant calls in his moral writings a realm of ends, is an intelligible idea, the idea of the intelligible world. Even though such a world cannot be a possible object of **cognition**, morality demands that we strive to be a member of such an intelligible world. See: **phenomena**; **Transcendental Idealism**; *Critique of Pure Reason*; **character**.

intrinsic value

Something has intrinsic value if it is valued for its own sake. The value is extrinsic if it is valued for the sake of something else. Money, for example, has merely extrinsic value for most people because we value money because of what we can do with it. It is important to distinguish between the notions of intrinsic value and **unconditional** value, for some things can have intrinsic but conditional value. Kant thinks that a **good will** has both intrinsic and unconditional value. Pleasure and **happiness**, however, have intrinsic but conditioned value. They are desirable for their own sake, but are only good if the individual who attains them also has a good will, for Kant thinks that the pleasure and happiness of a vicious person is not a good thing, so having a good will is the condition for the value of happiness. See: **unconditional value**.

intuition

Kant believes that experience involves two distinct faculties which he names **understanding** and intuition. The understanding is the faculty of concepts. Intuition is the faculty through which objects are immediately present to the mind. And Kant argues that our intuition has a certain form, for the only objects that we can immediately be aware of are spatio-temporal objects, so he claims that space and time are our forms of intuition. In claiming that experience necessarily involves both understanding and intuition, Kant means that in experience there must be both an immediate awareness of an object and that the object must be conceptualized. In the **Transcendental Aesthetic** of the *Critique of Pure Reason* (1781–87) Kant argues that human intuition is limited in two distinct ways. First, our intuition is necessarily sensible, for the only way we can intuit an object is through sensation, and for us the activity of intuiting does not create the object intuited. What he means by this is that the only way we can intuit objects is if we are affected by them and that our relationship to objects in intuition is in part passive. We can, however, conceive of a being very unlike ourselves whose intuition is active and creative and Kant names such a being an 'intuitive intellect' and this is how many theologians think of God. The idea of God is the idea of a being that is not passively affected by objects, but that actively creates them. In claiming that human intuition is necessarily sensible Kant is claiming that our experience is not God-like. Some rationalist and mystical philosophers sometimes seem to disagree with Kant and suggest that human beings are sometimes capable of non-sensible intuition. Secondly, Kant argues that our form of intuition is necessarily spatio-temporal. What he means by this is that we can only experience objects that exist in space and time. We can have the idea of things that do not exist in space and time, for example, God, but such beings are not the sort of things that can be experienced by us and so we have no way of knowing whether such beings really exist or not; we do not even know if such a being is really possible. See: **Transcendental Aesthetic; space; time.**

Jacobi, Friedrich Heinrich (1743–1819)

Jacobi was an important early critic of German rationalist and enlightenment philosophy. He thought that philosophy, insofar as it is based on the principle of **sufficient reason**, inevitably leads to atheism and fatalism and the denial of human free will and individuality. As a result of this, Jacobi thought that one had to choose between faith and reason and advocated a leap of faith – a view that was influential on Soren Kierkegaard (1813–55). Jacobi's critics accused him of **enthusiasm** and of advocating irrationalism. His correspondence with Moses **Mendelssohn** (1729–86), published in 1785, concerning the alleged Spinozisim of their mutual friend Gotthold Ephraim Lessing (1729–81), who had been one of the great figures of the German enlightenment, sparked the **pantheism controversy**, one of the major intellectual events of late-eighteenth-century Germany, and led to a renewed interest in the works of Baruch **Spinoza** (1632–77) among subsequent German philosophers. See: **Spinoza; Mendelssohn; pantheism controversy.**

judgements, table of

The table of judgements presented in the *Critique of Pure Reason* (1781/1787) and the **table of categories** derived from it play a central role in Kant's thought, and the structure of many of his works are based upon the structure of these two tables. Kant argues that all judgements have four aspects as they have a **quantity**, a **quality**, a certain **relation** and a certain **modality**. In terms of their quantity, judgements can either be universal, particular or singular. **Universal judgements** are of the form 'all *a*s are *b*s', **particular judgements** are of the form 'some *a*s are *b*s' and singular judgements are of the form 'this (or the) *a* is *b*'. Kant argues that the categories of unity, plurality and totality are derived from these three forms of judgement. In terms of their quality, judgements can either be affirmative, negative or infinite. An affirmative judgement is of the form '*a* is *b*', a negative judgement of the form 'it is not the case that *a* is *b*' and infinite judgements have the form '*a* is non-*b*'. The categories of reality, negation and limitation are derived from these three forms of judgement. In terms of relation, judgements can either be categorical, hypothetical or disjunctive. **Categorical judgements** are subject-predicate judgements and they are the basic building blocks of the other two judgemental relations. The judgement 'the cat is white' is a categorical judgement. In this judgement 'the cat' is the subject concept, whereas 'white' is the predicate concept. **Hypothetical judgements** are 'if . . . then' judgements, and what are related in such judgements are themselves judgements. For example, 'if the cat is white, then the cat is beautiful' is a hypothetical judgement. **Disjunctive judgements** are 'either . . . or' judgements, and once again these judgements relate judgements. For example, 'either the cat is white or the cat is not white' is a disjunctive judgement. The categories of **substance, causation,** and **community** are derived from these three forms of judgement. In terms of their **modality,** judgements can either be problematic, assertoric or apodictic.

Kant thinks that the modality of a judgement does not contribute to the content of the judgement but has got to do with its status with regard to its truth. In a problematic judgement, the truth of the judgement is merely regarded as **possible**; in a disjunctive judgement neither of the disjuncts is actually asserted, but is held problematically. So for example if one asserts the judgement 'either the dog is on the mat or the dog is not on the mat' one asserts neither 'the dog is on the mat' nor 'the dog is not on the mat' but each of these two constituent judgements has merely problematic status within the whole disjunctive judgement; all the disjunctive judgement commits me to is that it is *possible* that 'the dog is on the mat' is true. In an assertoric judgement, one claims that the content of a judgement is actual or **true**. In an apodictic judgement one claims that the content is **necessarily** true. See: **categories.**

justice

See: **right; law**

kingdom of ends

'kingdom of ends' is one translation of the German '*Reich der Zwecke*'. Most recent translations, however, prefer to translate this expression as 'realm of ends' as Kant thought that in an ideal community the citizens would be sovereign, not a king. The German word '*Reich*' literally means 'empire' and when Kant was writing, this word did not have the negative connotations that it has today. In using this word, Kant probably had in mind the Holy Roman Empire which was abolished after Kant's death in 1806. Legally, although not in practice, this empire was a confederation of free sovereign princes, and so it was legally a community of sovereign individuals. See: **realm of ends.**

knowledge

See: **cognition**

law

For Kant there are two distinct types of law. On the one hand there are laws of nature, which govern the natural world. On the other hand there is the moral law, which governs the wills of free beings (if any such beings exist). These two laws have something in common as both involve necessity. Laws of nature do not tell us what does happen but what has to happen. Moral laws do not tell us what we will do, but what we should or must do. Since such laws involve the idea of necessity, they must be based on *a priori* **principles**, for Kant believes that necessity is one of the two marks of *a priority*. In his theoretical philosophy Kant attempts to account for such *a priori* principles in nature. Thus, in the *Critique of Pure Reason* (1781/1787) and the *Metaphysical Foundations of Natural Science* (1785) one of Kant's major goals is to explain the possibility of laws of nature. As these laws involve necessity, and hence have an *a priori* element, but also govern objects in the natural world, Kant thinks that the principles behind such laws must be **synthetic** *a priori*, and so his goal in the *Critique of Pure Reason* is to discover and justify the synthetic *a priori* principles that govern the natural world and hence explain the possibility of the necessity involved in laws of nature.

In his ethics writings, and particularly in the *Groundwork of the Metaphysics of Morals* (1785) and the *Critique of Practical Reason* (1788), Kant wants to explain the possibility and content of the **moral law**, or what he calls the laws of freedom, and he explains that the moral law presents itself to us in the form of a **categorical imperative**. The moral law determines what a free will, insofar as it is free, must or should do. In terms of the relationship between the laws of nature and the moral law, Kant argues that laws of nature and laws of freedom can only co-exist if they govern two distinct realms. The laws of nature govern the natural, phenomenal world, and so the moral law, if it is to be really **possible**, must govern individuals that occupy some other realm, which Kant calls the **intelligible** world. Although we have no theoretical justification for believing in the **existence** of non-phenomenal intelligible individuals, insofar as we recognize the demands of morality and the force of the moral law, we must regard ourselves as free and as members of such an intelligent world, governed not by the laws of nature but by moral law. See: *Metaphysical Foundations of Natural Science*; *Groundwork of the Metaphysics of Morals*; **categorical imperative**; **causation**.

Leibniz, Gottfried Wilhelm (1646–1716)

Along with René **Descartes** (1596–1650) and Baruch **Spinoza** (1632–77), Leibniz was one of the most important **rationalist** philosophers, and had a strong influence on German philosophy in the eighteenth century due to the popularization and systematization of his ideas by Christian **Wolff** (1679–1754). He was, along with Isaac **Newton** (1643–1727), one of the discoverers of calculus. In his *Monadology* (1714) Leibniz argues that the world consists of indefinitely many individual substances, which he names monads. A monad is essentially active and its activity is that of having representations, so a monad can be thought of as a unified series or stream of representations that flow out of the nature of the individual. As all representations must have their source in the individual, Leibniz argues that this implies that there can be no real interaction between individual substances, but only what he calls a pre-established harmony. When I raise my arm and you see me doing this it looks as if my activity is really causing a change in your consciousness. Leibniz argues, however, that this is an illusion, for although God has set up the universe in such a way that a change in one individual corresponds to a change in another, there is, strictly speaking, no real influence of one individual on another. Kant was very influenced by the philosophy of Leibniz, but disagreed with him about the impossibility of interaction and many of his **pre-critical** writings involved an attempt to explain the possibility of real interaction between substances from within a fundamentally Leibnizian framework. In his ethics Leibniz, unlike Kant, was an intellectualist who believed that immorality is a result of ignorance of what is truly good. See: **rationalists; Wolff.**

Locke, John (1632–1704)

John Locke was a British **empiricist** who believed that all knowledge and all our ideas have their origins in experience. In his *Essay Concerning Human Understanding* (1690) Locke attacked the doctrine of innate ideas, arguing that before experience the mind is a blank sheet (or what others have called a *tabla rasa*, although Locke does not actually use these famous words, which are often attributed to him, in the *Essay*). He also denies the existence of innate principles and innate knowledge. Locke was also an important political theorist. His *Two Treatises on Government* (1689) is one of the most important works in the liberal tradition. In this work he argues that men are naturally free and equal and that a legitimate state is one that respects this freedom and equality and this requires the rule of law. His account of the relationship between **freedom** and **law** is an important stage in the development of the idea of **autonomy**. Thomas Hobbes (1588–1679) had argued in his *Leviathan* (1651) that the opposite of freedom is to be subject to constraint, and he also argued that law is a type of constraint on our actions. Hobbes concluded that the more law there is the less freedom there will be; but he thought that because the state of nature (that is a state of society without any government) was a state of war, it is rational for us to relinquish much of our freedom in exchange for peace and security. Hobbes thought, then, that without law and a strong government there would be chaos and that it was in everyone's long-run self-interest to live in a society governed by law, and this meant giving up some of our freedom in return for peace. Locke strongly disagreed with this Hobbesian definition of freedom arguing that freedom, properly understood, does not mean being able to do whatever we want but instead means being ruled by law. For, he argued, the opposite of being free is being a slave, and to be a slave is to be subject to the arbitrary will of another. Now, the opposite of being subject to the arbitrary will of another is to be subject to law, and so Locke concluded that to be free was to be subject to law. Jean-Jacques **Rousseau** (1712–88) develops this idea in his *On the Social Contract* (1762) but argues that real freedom requires not just that we are subject to law, but that we are subject to a law that we have *made ourselves*. Rousseau, then, identifies freedom with **autonomy**. See: **empiricists; Rousseau; autonomy; law; freedom.**

logic, general

In the *Critique of Pure Reason* (1781/1787) Kant distinguishes between what he calls general logic and **transcendental logic**. General logic is the most abstract and formal conception of logic and has to do purely with the form of thinking, in abstraction from any relationship to objects, and so is best understood as providing us with a criterion of thinkability. General logic, then, studies the form of thought as such and abstracts from all content of cognition, that is, from all reference of cognition to objects. Thus, general logic is concerned with the relations concepts have to one another and as such only examines laws of thought and not laws of **truth**. In claiming that general logic does not provide laws of truth, Kant is denying the possibility of rationalist metaphysics and is disagreeing with Christian **Wolff** (1679–1754) and his followers who thought that we could discover truths about being, the soul, the **world** and God merely by analysing our concepts.

The principle that governs general logic is the principle of **non-contradiction**, and Kant believes that this principle can only supply us with a negative criterion of truth, for the fact that a claim or concept does not contradict itself merely means that it is thinkable and not that it is true, for strictly speaking truth involves the relationship between thought and an object. Kant argues that rationalist metaphysicians make the mistake of taking general logic, which merely provides us with a criterion of thinkability and nothing more, as providing us with knowledge of objects. Taking general logic as providing us with objective knowledge leads to what Kant calls dialectic, and in the **Transcendental Dialectic** of the *Critique of Pure Reason*, Kant examines the negative consequences of mistaking general logic, which he argues can serve merely as a **canon** for judging, for an **organon** for the production of objective assertions about things-in-themselves. General logic and the principle of non-contradiction, then, merely provide us with a criterion of thinkability and can provide us with no knowledge of objects. See: **logic, transcendental; possibility, real versus logical; non-contradiction, principle of; rationalists.**

logic, transcendental

In the *Critique of Pure Reason* (1781–87) Kant distinguishes between general and transcendental logic. Whereas **general logic** is purely formal, and deals merely with the form of thought, transcendental logic is concerned not only with the form of thought but with *a priori* objects of thought and Kant argues that the only *a priori* object of human thought is spatio-temporality, or what Kant calls our form of **intuition**. Transcendental logic, then, examines the relationship between the concepts of the understanding and spatio-temporality. General logic has no object at all but merely examines the form of thought, whereas transcendental logic has an object even if only a very general one. As a consequence of this, Kant believes that general logic can only provide us with a negative criterion for truth, for truth does not have to do with the purely logical relationship between concepts, but has to do with the relationship between concepts and objects. The principle of general logic is the principle of non-contradiction, and Kant believes that although a cognition may be in complete accord with logical form, that is, not contradict itself, yet it can still always contradict the object. What Kant means by this is that general logic can only tell us whether a concept (or proposition) is self-contradictory or not. Whether or not a concept is self-contradictory, however, is not an adequate criterion of truth, for it may be the case that although proposition does not contain a contradiction, the proposition is not true because there cannot (in fact) be an object corresponding to the subject concept. For example, there is no logical contradiction in the thought of an object that is totally red and totally green, but in reality these two properties oppose each other. In other words, although general logic can determine whether a concept is thinkable, which is to determine whether or not it contains a contradiction, it cannot tell us whether a thinkable concept has what Kant calls **objective validity** or reality, for inspecting a concept cannot tell us whether or not there could actually be an object corresponding to the concept. Transcendental logic, in contrast, can be a logic of truth, for it has to do with the *a priori* relationship between **concepts** and objects in general. There can be a logic of truth because the faculty through which objects are given to us (the faculty of **intuition**) has a certain form that we are aware of *a priori*. Thus, the positive part of transcendental logic examines *a priori* the relationship between the faculty of concepts (the understanding) and the faculty through which objects are given (the faculty of intuition). Such a logic can provide us with a positive touchstone for truth because there are certain things we know *a priori* about what type of objects can be given in intuition, for we know *a priori* that space and time are our forms of intuition.

As a result of this, we can know *a priori* that an object can exist corresponding to certain concepts if the object is the sort of thing that can be given in space/time. See: **logic, general;** *Critique of Pure Reason.*

love

In the *Groundwork of the Metaphysics of Morals* (1785) Kant distinguishes between practical and **pathological** love, and argues that we can only have a duty of practical love towards others. The word 'pathological' is derived from the Greek *pathos* which means a feeling or affection that the mind suffers, and so when Kant talks about pathological love he is talking about a type of love which involves a particular type of feeling towards others. It is important to note that Kant does not use the word 'pathological' in the most common contemporary sense to mean diseased or mentally disordered. By practical love Kant means a desire to benefit others out of the motive of duty. Kant argues that we cannot have a duty of pathological love towards others and one reason he believes this is because he is committed to the principle that ought implies can, and believes that we are not able to have feelings at will. Thus Kant thinks that we have a **duty** of practical love towards others which Kant names **beneficence.** That is we have a duty to care about the welfare of other people. Some readers of Kant have taken the fact that he believes that we do not have a duty of pathological love love towards others to imply that Kantian thinks that practical love is the only type of love that is relevant to ethics and that he does not give enough emphasis to the role of feelings in morality. Kant's attitude towards **feelings**, however, is more complicated than this. In the *Metaphysics of Morals* (1797) Kant argues that there are four feelings, including the feeling of love of one's neighbour, that we cannot have a duty to have because they are necessary conditions for the possibility of morality; without these feelings we would not be capable of morality. He also thinks that although we cannot have a duty to have particular feelings we do have, insofar as it is possible, a duty to cultivate our feelings. So, for example, he argues that we have a duty to cultivate our feeling of sympathy towards others, a feeling which is closely related to pathological love. See: **feeling; beneficence; duty; virtue, duties of.**

mathematics

When talking of mathematics Kant is primarily thinking of arithmetic and geometry and he famously argues that mathematical judgements are **synthetic** *a priori*. This claim has been interpreted in many different ways, and has also been the subject of much criticism. The claim that mathematical truths are known *a priori* means that mathematical judgements are not justified by appeal to experience. The claim that mathematical truths are *a priori* has been subject to less criticism than the claim that they are **synthetic**. Some philosophers, such as John Stuart Mill (1806–73) and Willard van Orman Quine (1908–2000) have argued that mathematical judgements are not *a priori*. Quine, for example, argues that although mathematical and logical beliefs occupy a central place in what he calls our web of beliefs, and so are far more stable than others, this whole web stands or falls as a whole and in principle all beliefs, even mathematical and logical beliefs, are revisable. The claims that mathematical judgements are **synthetic** means that mathematical judgements do not merely have to do with the logical relation between concepts, and this claim has been the subject of far more criticism, especially with the development of modern logic. There have been at least three strategies used by contemporary philosophers to defend the claim that mathematical judgements are synthetic, all based on slightly different account of what it is for a judgement to be synthetic.

The first strategy is to argue that although mathematical theorems can be derived from a set of definitions and axioms by using the laws of logic, this does not imply that mathematical judgements are analytic, as the axioms and definitions themselves can only be justified by appeal to intuition, and it is the synthetic nature of the axioms and definitions of mathematics that makes the theorems logically derived from them synthetic. The second strategy, is to argue that it is the nature of mathematical reasoning and inferences that makes mathematical judgements synthetic, for mathematical proofs require the construction of objects, such as **numbers** and shapes, and such objects can only be constructed in intuition. Thus, for example, Kant argues that in order to prove that the angles of a triangle must add up to 180 degrees we cannot just examine our concept of a triangle but must begin by constructing a triangle. Although contemporary mathematicians do not think that geometrical proofs require the construction of triangles in space, there are some philosophers of mathematics, influenced by the work of the Dutch mathematician, Luitzen Egbertus Jan Brouwer (1881–1966), who defend a form of intuitionism in mathematics. According to this view mathematical proofs require the mental construct of mathematical objects and so are not analytic. A third strategy is to argue that the reason mathematical judgements are synthetic is not because an appeal to intuition is needed to provide justification for mathematical judgements, but such an appeal is needed to explain the objectivity of such judgements, and in so doing to explain how mathematical concepts and judgements are contentful. For Kant mathematics involves more than the manipulation of a set of symbols, for mathematical judgements are the sort of things that can be true or false and Kant thinks that **truth**, strictly speaking, always involves the relationship between concepts and objects, and so an account of how mathematical judgements can be objective and have content is also an account of how it is that mathematical judgements can be true. Thus, Kant thinks that mathematical judgements involve certain existential commitments, and to give content to these commitments requires an appeal to intuition. Thus, for example, arithmetic presupposes commitment to the principle that any two numbers can be added together. This is why Kant claims that when we make the judgement $7 + 5 = 12$, the representation '12' is not contained in the representation '7 + 5', for $7 + 5$ is something like a command and for us to understand that this command is meaningful we must presuppose that we can add 5 can be added to 7, and that ultimately the practice of arithmetic presupposes the *a priori* principle that any two numbers can be added together to produce a new number. Now, Kant does not in any way doubt this principle, but he is interested in explaining what justification we have for accepting it. His answer is that the grasp of this principle is based on the fact that our capacity to understand numbers requires the representation of a line. Numbers, for Kant, are constructed by adding units together and the so the existential presupposition behind the principle that any two numbers can be added together is that however many units you have there will always be more. And he thinks that our representation of a line provides us with a representation of arbitrarily many units, for we immediately recognize when we intuit a line that we can introduce as may divisions, or points, as we want. By appealing to the intuition of a line Kant is not trying to provide an anti-skeptical argument for the principle that any two numbers can be added together, but is instead giving an account of how we know *a priori* that the principle is true and how it can be grasped by the human mind. See: *a priori*; analytic/synthetic; synthetic *a priori*; series.

maxim

A maxim is a subjective **principle** of action. A principle is a **universal** rule, and so a maxim is something like the rule that a particular action expresses. There is some disagreement as to what Kant thinks is included in the maxim of an action, but maxims might be expressed linguistically as having something like the following form: 'in situations *a*, do *b*, in order to achieve *c*, unless *d*'. So, for example, if I decide to wear a suit to an interview for a job that I want, the maxim behind my action might be something like: 'at interviews for jobs that one wants to get, wear a suit, in order to produce a good impression, unless there is good evidence that the interviewers are very informal'.

Maxims, then, are the rules we implicitly follow when we act and Kant thinks that the morality of an action is determined by the permissibility of the maxims that lie behind our actions. Now, many readers and commentators of Kant assume that what he is primarily concerned with in his ethics are individual actions. But what he is most concerned with is the gradual improvement of our character and motivational set over time. Most of the time, action does not consist in explicitly formulating rules and consciously acting upon them, and even at times when we convince ourselves that this is what we are doing, the rule we explicitly and consciously formulate may not be the true motive for our action. And so most of the time we are not conscious of the maxims behind our actions. In acting we are not transparent to ourselves, and when behaving immorally it is easy for us to convince ourselves that we are in fact acting on a permissible maxim. So morality requires that in order to weed out impermissible maxims we need to strive to understand our true motivation in acting. Thus, in the *Metaphysics of Morals* (1797), Kant argues that the first command of all duties to oneself is 'know yourself!' and he claims that only the descent into the hell of self-knowledge can pave the way to godliness. What Kant is particularly concerned with here is that the possibility of moral improvement involves working out what the real maxims behind our actions are. And it is only through gradually obtaining insight into what our maxims are that we are able to weed out those that are impermissible. For example a member of an interview panel may believe themselves to be non-sexist and have convinced themselves that the maxim behind their action in choosing whom to hire at the interview is something like 'in an interview, in order to pick the best candidate for the job, only pay attention to the candidates qualifications and capacity to perform the job', but, because he feels uncomfortable about working with women, the true maxim behind his action might actually be more like 'in an interview, in order to pick the best candidate for the job, only pay attention to the candidates qualifications and capacity to perform the job, unless she is a woman', a maxim that if he were conscious of it he would reject as impermissible. As human beings, subject to what Kant calls **radical evil**, we are all morally corrupt and suffer from what could be thought of as a type of motivational sickness, for the structure of our motivations is not one we can ultimately endorse rationally. Working out what the true maxims of our actions are is extremely hard, but recognizing the ways in which we are sick is the first step in finding a cure. See: **categorical imperative**; *Groundwork of the Metaphysics of Morals*.

Mendelssohn, Moses (1729–81)

Moses Mendelssohn, the grandfather of the composer Felix Mendelssohn (1809–47), was one of the leaders of the Berlin enlightenment. His book *Phädon, or On the Immortality of Souls* (1767) was one of Kant's targets in the **Paralogisms** in the second edition of the *Critique of Pure Reason* (1787). Mendelssohn was a practicing Jew and although he admired Jesus for his moral character he refused to abandon his religion despite some unpleasant attacks upon him by evangelical Christians who demanded that he convert to Christianity. His book *Jerusalem* (1783), which was greatly admired by Kant, was an influential plea for religious freedom of conscience. His correspondence with Friedrich Heinrich **Jacobi** (1743–1819) concerning the alleged Spinozism, which at this time was considered to be synonymous with atheism, of their mutual friend Gotthold Ephraim Lessing (1729–81) was published in 1785. The publication of this correspondence sparked the **pantheism controversy** and inadvertently led to a revival of interest in the philosophy of **Baruch Spinoza** (1632–77) among the younger generation of German philosophers, and explains the greater number of references to Spinoza in the second edition of the *Critique of Pure Reason* (1787). See: **Jacobi; pantheism controversy.**

Metaphysical Foundations of Natural Science (1786)

In this work, Kant attempts to provide a bridge between the *a priori* principles introduced in the *Critique of Pure Reason* and natural science, particularly Newtonian physics. The most significant chapter is the third one on Mechanics in which Kant attempts to provide an *a priori* justification of what he calls the three 'laws of mechanics', which are closely related to **Isaac Newton**'s (1643–1727) three laws of motion. The three **laws** that Kant identifies are: (1) the law of the conservation of the total quantity of matter in the world, (2) a version of the law of inertia, namely that every change of matter must have an external cause and (3) the law of the equality of action and reaction. These laws are specifications of the three *a priori* principles introduced in the **Analogies of Experience.** In the first Analogy Kant defended the principle that in all change of appearances **substance** persists, and its quantum is neither increased nor diminished in nature, and the first law of mechanics is a more specific version of this principle, specifying that what must remain constant is the total quantity of matter in the world. In the Second Analogy Kant defended the principle that all alterations occur in accordance with the law of the connection of cause and effect. In making this claim he is particularly concerned with the causal relation between states of an individual substance. In the second law of mechanics Kant makes this principle more specific, claiming that the law that governs the relationship between states of an object at different times is one of inertia. In the third Analogy, Kant defended the principle that all phenomenal substances are in thoroughgoing interaction, and the third law of mechanics is a more specific version of this principle. Although it is clear that there is some sort of relationship between the principles of the analogies and the laws of Mechanics Kant's justification of these laws is not particularly clear.

Another interesting aspect of this works is Kant's defence of a dynamic theory of matter according to which the basic properties of material substances, such as impenetrability, solidity, hardness and density, are constituted by the interplay of the forces of attraction and repulsion. The **pre-critical** Kant had defended a similar theory of material substance in his *Physical Monadology* (1756). There he had defended the **Leibnizian** position according to which material substances are monads: simple, unextended and indivisible, point-like substances. A theory like this has a problem explaining how such substances can fill or occupy space, as they are dimensionless. Kant solved this problem in the *Physical Monadology* by suggesting that such monads should be thought of as point-like centres of attractive and repulsive forces. Such point-like substances can be thought of as the centres of spheres of activity and the solidity or impenetrability can be explained in terms of repulsive force. This explains how unextended points can, in a sense, fill and occupy space. The **critical** Kant accepts a similar account of matter in the *Metaphysical Foundations of Natural Science*, but by this period he has come to reject the view that matter is composed of point-like monads. Instead the critical Kant argues that all the parts of a material substance occupy space and are extended and potentially divisible, and so there are no smallest parts of matter. Matter is indefinitely divisible although not infinitely divided. So he rejects his pre-critical commitment the existence of material monads. Kant's arguments for this claim can be found in the second **Antinomy** in the *Critique of Pure Reason*. See: *Critique of Pure Reason*; experience; causation; laws; *Physical Monadology*.

metaphysics

In the eighteenth century, German metaphysics was strongly influenced by the **rationalists** Gottfried Wilhelm **Leibniz** (1646–1716) and Christian **Wolff** (1679–1754). The rationalists believed that metaphysics could provide us with knowledge of things beyond our experience. Eighteenth-century rationalist metaphysics textbooks, including the text by Alexander Gottlieb **Baumgarten** (1714–62) that Kant used as the textbook for his metaphysics lectures for over 20 years, divided metaphysics into general metaphysics (ontology) and special metaphysics. Ontology (general metaphysics) was understood to be the study of being as being in general and examined the categories and principles that had to be applied to objects in general, irrespective of the type of object involved. The most important principle of rationalist ontology was the principle of **sufficient reason**: the principle that absolutely everything must have a cause or explanation. Special metaphysics was concerned with our *a priori* knowledge of particular objects or types of object and was divided into three special sciences corresponding to the three objects of rational cognition: the soul, the world and God. Rational psychology was concerned with *a priori* knowledge of the *soul*; rational cosmology dealt with *a priori* knowledge of the *world*; and rational theology dealt with *a priori* knowledge of *God*.

Although Kant rejected the possibility of rational cognition of **transcendent** objects, the structure of the *Critique of Pure Reason* (1781/1787) follows this traditional plan. Although Kant rejects the possibility of ontology in the traditional sense, the **Transcendental Aesthetic** and Transcendental Analytic of the *Critique of Pure Reason* can be understood as corresponding to the traditional role of general metaphysics, although ontology, in the strict sense of the science of being has been replaced by an examination of our cognitive faculties. The goal of such a project was to examine the principles that govern these faculties, and their limits. Kant rejects the possibility of traditional ontology because he thinks that we can have no knowledge of **things as they are in themselves**; an examination of the **categories** does not, as Aristotle thought, provide us with an understanding of the way in which things-in-themselves must be, but only an understanding of the way in which we must think of the world, and the fact that we must experience the world in a certain way does not mean that the world as it is in itself must actually be this way. So instead of providing us with an account of the nature of things-in-themselves, Kant is content to provide us with an account of the way in which the world must appear to us.

In the **Transcendental Dialectic** Kant examines the doctrines of traditional special metaphysics. In the **Paralogisms of Pure Reason** he examines the doctrines of rational psychology, in the **Antinomies of Pure Reason** he examines the doctrines of rational cosmology and in the Ideal of Pure Reason he examines rational theology. His conclusion is that rational psychology, cosmology and theology are impossible as sciences, for although we do have the ideas of the soul, the world as a whole and of God, no objects corresponding to these three ideas can ever be objects of experience, and so we do not even know if such objects are really possible. See: *Critique of Pure Reason*; **rationalists**.

Metaphysics of Morals (1787)

Having given a clarification and justification of the supreme principle of morality, the **categorical imperative**, in his earlier *Groundwork of the Metaphysics of Morals* (1785) and the *Critique of Practical Reason* (1788), in the *Metaphysics of Morals* Kant applies this principle to provide a systematic account of the whole system of human duties.

The *Metaphysics of Morals* is divided into a Doctrine of Right and a Doctrine of Virtue. By drawing this distinction Kant wants to draw a line between the political sphere and the ethical sphere. The German word *recht*, is much broader than the English word 'right' and can also be translated as '**law**' or '**justice**'. The Doctrine of **Right** is concerned with outer freedom and deals with laws that can govern external behaviour of individuals and can be coercively enforced by state power. Such laws can demand or prohibit the external actions of individuals, and exclude considerations of an agent's motive in acting. From the perspective of right, it does not matter if a shopkeeper is honest out of duty or merely from prudence. What is important is her behaviour. The doctrine of **virtue** is concerned with inner freedom and deals with duties of virtue which have to do with an agent's moral disposition and which cannot be coercively enforced.

Kant's main concern in the Doctrine of Right is to examine and justify the coercive power of the state. Kant argues that the universal law of right is that one should act externally so that the free use of one's choice can coexist with the freedom of everyone else in accordance with universal law. What this means is that we should regulate our behaviour in such a way as to allow others to act in an unconstrained way, so that compelling others to act in a particular way through force, threats or deception is wrong. Coercive power is legitimate if (and only if) it is used to check such wrong. So, coercive state laws limiting the external freedom of citizens are justified insofar as they allow the freedom of one citizen to coexist with the freedom of others. And the main way the state does this is through the creation and enforcement of laws concerning property rights.

The Doctrine of Right is itself divided into sections on Private Right and Public Right. Private right is concerned with the relationship between citizens, whereas public right concerns the relationship between citizens and the state. The main topic in the section on Private Right is Kant's account of the metaphysics of property and the nature juridical laws. Because we own things it seems natural to assume that ownership should be understood as a relationship between an individual and an object. For Kant, however, this is a fundamentally mistaken way of conceiving of property, for to *own* something is to have a (legitimate) right to it, and to have a legitimate right to something is not to be understood in terms of the relationship between an individual and a thing owned, but instead in terms of the owner's relation to other agents regarding objects. To claim a right is to claim that others should recognize your possession and not interfere with your use of the object. It is to claim that others should not *resist* your use of an object, and Kant believes that such a claim can only be made against others who have commonly willed the same set of juridical laws. To have a property right ultimately involves an **intelligible** relationship and such intelligible rights are only possible in the civil condition. Such a condition, which for Kant is an **ideal** which can never be realized but only approached asymptotically, is only possible if the juridical laws are willed by all members of the community. In an ideal juridical community each member of the community consents to the laws of the community and it is the existence of these laws that makes us all members of the same community and it is only the existence of such commonly willed laws that makes (fully legitimate) property rights possible. The existence of juridical rights, then, presupposes the existence of juridical laws and it is the existence of such laws that allows us to act upon one another in an intelligible juridical way.

Public Right, in contrast to Private Right, has to do with the relationship between citizens and the state. For in order to create and enforce property laws we require a state and so Kant's discussion of Public Right has to do with those laws that are necessary for bringing about a condition of Private Right, or what Kant sometimes calls 'the rightful condition', and Kant argues, as what he calls a postulate of public right, that we have an obligation to enter civil society. Public right has to do with those laws that have to do with the organization and well-functioning of the state, and the relationship between a state and citizens. So for example, Kant believes that in order to function properly the state requires certain resources, and so can pass laws that, for example, require citizens to pay taxes or to perform military service. For human beings the existence of state institution, and hence of public right, is a necessary condition for the possibility of private right, for without a state such laws cannot be created and enforced.

Whereas the Doctrine of Right has to do with the regulation of external action and involves laws that can be coercively enforced, the Doctrine of Virtue has to do with inner freedom and with the moral disposition of particular agents, and virtue is not something that can be enforced coercively by the state, although, as Kant argues in **Religion within the Boundaries of Mere Reason** (1793), it is something that can be encouraged through the existence of an ethical community which is a non-coercive community which has the purpose of helping and encouraging its members to develop their moral dispositions.

Kant defines virtue in general as 'moral strength of will' and although there is disagreement in exactly how to interpret this notion, it is clear that one thing this definition implies is that the possession of virtue is not an either-or thing, but is a matter of degree. Virtue is, then, what Kant elsewhere calls an **intensive magnitude**. As such we can think of the degree of virtue of a particular individual as being somewhere on a scale between 0 and 1, with 1 denoting perfect virtue. Kant believes, however, that given human nature perfect virtue is unobtainable by human beings. However, although Kant thinks that human beings can never at any particular moment of time achieve such perfect virtue, the idea of perfect virtue, which Kant sometimes calls the idea of a **holy will**, can and must serve as our ethical ideal, for morality demands that we strive for such perfection. And although it can never be achieved we can hope over time to gradually improve morally and to approximate and approach this ideal. When it comes to particular **duties of virtue**, Kant argues that they can be divided into two classes: duties to ourselves and duties to others. Our principle duty towards ourselves is to develop our talents and to strive for self-perfection. Our principle duty towards others is to promote their **happiness,** and Kant calls this the duty of **beneficence.** See: *Groundwork of the Metaphysics of Morals; Critique of Practical Reason*; duty; categorical imperative; law; virtue; feelings; right.

modality

In his table of **judgements** in the *Critique of Pure Reason* (1781/1787) Kant lists the three different modalities that a judgement can have. Judgements can either be **problematic,** assertoric or **apodictic.** Problematic judgements are judgements that are represented as **possibly** truel; assertoric judgements are judgements that are presented as actually true; and apodictic judgements are judgements that are represented as necessarily true. The three categories corresponding to these three forms of judgement are the categories of **possibility, existence** and **necessity.** See: **judgements, table of; categories, table of; possibility; existence.**

moral law

Kant distinguishes between the **laws** of nature, which govern the **phenomenal world,** and the moral law, or laws of freedom, which govern the wills of free agents, if any such beings exist. Both kinds of law, as laws, involve necessity and hence are based upon *a priori* principles. Laws of nature determine what has to happen. The moral law determines what a free will, insofar as it is free, must or should do, and for beings like us the moral law presents itself to us in the form of a **categorical imperative.** See: **law; categorical imperative;** *Groundwork of the Metaphysics of Morals.*

necessity

Necessity, along with **existence** and **possibility,** is one of the three **categories** of modality. The opposite of necessity is contingency. The notion of necessity plays a central role in Kant's philosophy. In the *Critique of Pure Reason*, Kant argues that the two marks or criteria of *a priori* knowledge are universality and necessity. The notion of necessity also plays a central role in Kant's ethical thought as he thinks that morality has to do with **obligation**, and obligation is a type of necessitation. See also: *a priori*: **obligation**.

Newton, Isaac (1643–1727)

Newton was a British natural philosopher and mathematician, who, simultaneously with Gottfried Wilhelm **Leibniz** (1646–1716), discovered calculus and developed what is now known as classical mechanics. His major work the *Mathematical Principles of Natural Philosophy* (1687), which is usually just called the one of the most important scientific works ever published. In this work Newton formulated the law of universal gravitation, according to which the attractive force between two objects is proportional to their mass and inversely proportional to the square of the distance between them. He also formulated the three laws of motion, which form the basis of classical mechanics. These three laws are: (1) Every object persists in its state of rest or uniform motion in a straight line unless it is compelled to change that state by forces impressed on it – often called the law of inertia. (2) For a constant mass, force equals mass times acceleration. (3) For every action, there is an equal and opposite reaction. Newton also defended an absolute theory of **space**, according to which space and time exists independently of the objects that exist in them. This theory was opposed by **Leibniz** and his followers who defended a relative theory of space according to which space is constituted by the relations between objects which are in themselves extensionless. Newton engaged in a major and acrimonious dispute with Leibniz about who discovered calculus, with Newton accusing Leibniz of plagiarism. Modern historians now generally agree that Newton and Leibniz discovered calculus almost simultaneously and independently. Evidence of this is provided by the fact that Leibniz' notation, which is closer to the notation we use today, was very different from Newton's. This personal dispute however led to a sometimes strained relationship between followers of Newton and followers of Leibniz.

Kant was a great admirer of Newton and one of the major aims in his theoretical philosophy is to provide a philosophical foundation, and justification, for Newtonian physics. This is one of the major aims behind the *Critique of Pure Reason* (1781/1787), but is most explicit in the *Metaphysical Foundations of Natural Science* (1786) where Kant attempts to offer a justification of three laws of mechanics which are close to Newton's. Kant argues that his three laws of mechanics are specifications of the three principles defended in the **Analogies of Experience**, with Kant's principle of **causation** defended in the Second Analogy being the ground of Newton's principle of inertia. Although Kant agreed with much of Newton's work, he rejected the Newtonian theory of space, arguing in the **Transcendental Aesthetic** that space is not a mind-independent entity in which objects exist, but is instead what he calls our form of **intuition**. See: *Metaphysical Foundations of Natural Science*; *Critique of Pure Reason*; Transcendental Aesthetic; Analogies of Experience; law.

non-contradiction, principle of

The principle of non-contradiction is the logical principle that states that contradictory statements cannot both be true. Kant argues that this principle is the principle that governs what he calls **general logic**, and he insists that it does not provide us with a positive criterion of truth and cannot be the basis for any real knowledge of the world. The German **rationalist** Christian **Wolff** (1679–1754), in contrast, had tried to derive the metaphysical principle of **sufficient reason,** the principle that everything must have a ground, cause or explanation, from the logical principle of non-contradiction. As such Wolff believed that the logical principle of non-contradiction could provide us with real knowledge of the world. Kant rejects this rationalist point of view and argues that the principle of non-contradiction is merely a criterion of thinkability and provides us with a merely negative criterion of **truth.** Truth, however, has to do with the relationship between our thoughts and objects, and the mere fact that a concept is thinkable does not imply that there is, or even could be, an object corresponding to the thought. As a result of this Kant concludes that general logic, governed by the principle of non-contradiction, cannot provide any knowledge of the world and he dismisses the attempts of rationalist metaphysicians to provide such knowledge as **dogmatic** and dialectical. See: **logic, general; Leibniz; Wolff; sufficient reason, principle of.**

noumenal

See: **world, noumenal; intelligible**

objective validity/objective reality

To claim that a **concept** has objective validity or objective reality is to say that there are some objects that it applies or refers to. In the **Transcendental Deduction** of the *Critique of Pure Reason* (1781/1787) Kant attempts to prove the objective validity of the **categories**. What this means is that he wants to prove that these *a priori* concepts can, and must, be applied to objects of experience. The problem is that the categories are logical concepts that structure our thought, and it is not immediately obvious that such concepts can be applied to objects, for why should we assume that the structure of reality mirrors the structure of thought? Kant's answer to this question is that because the mind is active in cognition, the application of the categories is a necessary condition for the possibility of experience, and so the structure of reality, at least insofar as it is experiencable must in some sense mirror the structure of our thinking. Although some scholars think that Kant uses the expressions objective validity and objective reality interchangeably, others think that that to claim that a concept has objective *reality* means that it has *some* instances in experience, whereas to claim that a concept has objective *validity* is to say that it must necessarily apply to *all* possible objects of experience, which is a much stronger claim. See: **Transcendental Deduction; logic, transcendental; concept; understanding; categories, table of.**

obligation

For human beings morality is always a matter of obligation, as for us, as finite beings with needs, there is always the possibility of a conflict between what morality demands and our needs and inclinations. For us, then, morality always involves a willingness to sacrifice the satisfaction of our needs and desires for the sake of the **moral law,** and in cases where we actually make such a sacrifice we cannot obey the moral law gladly. This is the reason why morality for human beings is always a matter of **imperatives.** We can have the idea of a type of agent for whom morality would not be a matter of obligation or constraint, and Kant calls the idea of such an agent the idea of a **holy will.** Such an individual would be perfectly rational and there would be no conflict between its needs and inclinations and the demands of practical reason. Such an agent would always do what morality demands and would do so gladly. Kant argues that the idea of such a holy will is the ideal that we should strive to approach. Thus, although Kant thinks that, for us, morality is a matter of obligation and as such always involves the possibility of inner conflict, he does not think that such conflict is a good thing that should be encouraged. He does not think that someone who does the right thing, such as being willing to help a friend in need, with a heavy heart and against their inclinations and feelings is necessarily morally better than someone who does the same thing gladly. A virtuous person is someone who, when there is a conflict between the demands of morality and their natural desires, subordinates satisfying their inclinations and needs to what morality demands. But a virtuous person will also strive, insofar as it is possible, to cultivate their feelings and inclinations in such a way so that they can do what duty demands gladly. So, for example, Kant thinks that we have a duty to cultivate our capacity to feel benevolence, which is the feeling of enjoying helping others, and doing this will make it more likely that we will be able to do the right thing gladly. See: **categorical imperative; duty; feeling;** *Groundwork of the Metaphysics of Morals*; *Critique of Practical Reason*; *Metaphysics of Morals*.

ontological argument

The ontological argument for the existence of **God** was originally made by St Anselm of Canterbury (1033–1109) but the best-known version of this argument is the one found in **Descartes'** (1596–1650) fifth *Meditation*. The argument attempts to show that we can prove that God exists merely by analysing the concept of God. The basic idea is that our concept of God is the concept of a perfect being. Now, Descartes argues, existence is a perfection and so our idea of a perfect being must be of a being that exists. Merely by thinking about then concept of God, then, we realize that God must exist. **Leibniz** (1646–1716), objected to this argument by claiming that it was missing a premise, namely that God is possible. So the most that Descartes is entitled to claim is 'if God is possible then God exists'. Leibniz, however, had an argument designed to show that God is possible. For our idea of God is the idea of a most perfect or real being and Leibniz believed that realities could not oppose one another and so there would be no contradiction in the concept of a most perfect being. Kant has two interrelated objections to the ontological proof. First, Kant makes an important distinction between what he calls logical and real **possibility** and he argues that just because something is thinkable, which means that the concept is non-contradictory and so logically possible, this does not necessarily imply that an object corresponding to the concept is really possible, for just because we are able to combine two concepts in thought does not imply that the properties these concept refer to can be combined in reality. Thus, Kant rejects Leibniz' assumption that realities cannot oppose one another. For example, if we think of the concepts of red and green we can see no reason why a single thing cannot be totally red and totally green, but we know that in reality being red all over precludes something from being green all over. Kant's conclusion from this was that we have no reason to accept Leibniz' assumption that realities cannot oppose one another. Secondly, as Kant argues in a section of the *Critique of Pure Reason* called the Ideal of Pure Reason, the ontological argument assumes that existence is a first-order predicate. Kant argues, however, that 'existence' is not a first-order predicate but a second-order predicate. 'Existence' is not a property that God may or may not have, it is not the sort of thing that could be contained in the concept 'God'. When I claim that God exists I am not making a claim about God, or a claim about what is contained in my concept 'God', instead all I am claiming that there is an object corresponding to the concept 'God'. If Kant is right here, then existence is not the sort of thing that could be a perfection. See: **Descartes; God; existence; possibility, real and logical.**

organon

See: **canon**

outer sense

In the *Critique of Pure Reason* (1781/1787) Kant distinguishes between **inner sense** and outer sense. Outer sense is our capacity to experience external objects, and Kant argues that objects of outer sense are necessarily experienced as in space. Inner sense, in contrast, is our capacity to experience our own states, and Kant argues that inner sense is necessarily temporal for we experience our own subjective states as flowing. See: **inner sense**.

pantheism controversy

This controversy was one of the major intellectual events in late-eighteenth-century Germany. It started in 1785 with the publication of the correspondence between Moses **Mendelssohn** (1729–86) and Friedrich Heinrich **Jacobi** (1743–1819) concerning the religious beliefs of their mutual friend the recently deceased poet, playwright and philosopher Gotthold Ephraim Lessing (1729–81), who had been one of the great figures of the German enlightenment. The correspondence started when Jacobi wrote to Mendelssohn, who he had learnt was planning to write a biography of his friend Lessing, claiming that Lessing had confided in him that he was a follower of Baruch **Spinoza** (1632–77). Mendelssohn was shocked by this claim as Spinozism was at that time generally regarded as synonymous with atheism and he felt a need to defend his friend against this charge. Jacobi's most influential argument in this correspondence was that reason, which he identified with the principle of **sufficient reason**, necessarily leads to atheism and fatalism for the principle of sufficient reason leaves no room for either the existence of God or free will. Jacobi thought that the consequence of this was that individuals had to choose between faith and reason, and Jacobi himself defended a form of fideism, arguing that we should reject the claims of reason and make a leap of faith. The publication of this correspondence led to a renewed interest in the philosophy of Spinoza among younger German philosophers, and explains the greater number of references to Spinoza in Kant's works after this date, including in the second edition of the *Critique of Pure Reason* (1787). Ironically, perhaps Jacobi's most influential legacy was to popularize Spinoza, and in the nineteenth century many philosophers came to agree with Jacobi that reason leads to atheism and a denial of free will, but instead of taking this as a reason to reject reason, took this to be a reason to deny the existence of God and free will. See: Jacobi; Spinoza; Mendelssohn; sufficient reason, principle of.

Paralogisms of Pure Reason

In this section of the *Critique of Pure Reason* (1781/1787) Kant Presents his critique of rationalist psychology. **Rationalists** such as René **Descartes** (1596–1650), Christian **Wolff** (1679–1754) and Alexander Gottlieb **Baumgarten** (1714–62) had argued that we know that the soul or mind is a simple **substance** that persists through time. Kant argues that we only have knowledge of how we appear to ourselves and not as we are in ourselves, and so the rationalist conclusions about the nature of the soul are unjustified, and he provides an analysis of what he takes to be the fallacies in the rationalist arguments for such self-knowledge.

A 'paralogism' is, literally, an illogical or fallacious argument, but Kant seems to use the word in a more specific sense to refer to a **syllogism** in which there is equivocation, with the middle term being taken in two senses. For example, consider the following fallacious argument:

Premise 1:   All rivers have *banks* next to them
Premise 2:   All *banks* have money in them
Conclusion: One can always find money next to a river.

In this argument there is equivocation on the middle term 'banks', for it is used in one sense in the first premise but in a totally different sense in the second premise. Kant argues that rationalist arguments for the claim that the soul is a simple substance involve a similar type of equivocation.

In the *first* Paralogism he discusses the claim that the soul is a substance and argues that the rationalists equivocate between thinking of the I as the logical subject of thought and as the real subject of inherence, or as a substance. Kant had argued in the **Transcendental Deduction** for the necessity of what he calls the transcendental unity of **apperception**. What he means by this is that the representation 'I think' is necessary to supply unity to our thought. Our representation of 'I' however, is purely formal and empty. An example may help to illustrate Kant's idea here. Think about the difference between thinking 'the cat sat on the mat' and three individuals one of whom thinks 'the cat', one of whom thinks 'sat' and the third of whom thinks 'on the mat'. Only in the first case do we have a complete unified thought, so Kant argues that the existence of a single logical subject is a necessary condition for the existence of a unified thought. But, Kant asks: what do we know of the nature of this logical subject? And his answer is: nothing apart from the fact that it has the role or function of unifying thought. We know that there is something that plays the role of unifying our thought and we represent the thing that plays this role with the expression 'I', but apart from the fact that 'I' plays this role we know nothing about 'I'. We know the function of the representation 'I', for its role is to unify thought, but we do not know what, if anything, this representation refers to. And Kant argues that the rationalists confuse the representation of a logical subject with the representation of a substance; they confuse the knowledge that something plays a certain role with knowledge of what it is that plays this role. An analogy might be made here to the game of chess. To understand what it is to be a chess king is to understand the moves a king can make and its role in the game of chess. To be a chess king is not to be a certain type of physical object (or substance). We can use anything we want to play this role, and good chess players do not even need to use physical objects to play chess as they can play it in their head. The fact that one owns a wooden chess set does not mean that a chess king is a particular type of wooden object. A child may think that a chess king is a particular type of wooden object, but they are confusing the role a chess king plays in a game of chess with a particular object we use to represent this functional role. And Kant thinks that rationalist psychologists are confused in a similar way, mistaking our knowledge of a particular functional role with knowledge of a particular type of substance. In the *second* Paralogism, Kant attacks the rationalist arguments for the claims that the 'I' is something simple, that is, without parts. The claim that the I is simple and without parts plays a central role in **Descartes'** argument for **dualism** – the position that the mind and body are different substances and distinct types of substance. Descartes argues that we know that the mind is simple and without parts whereas bodies exist in space and are necessarily extended and so have parts, and as one thing cannot be essentially both divisible and indivisible, we must conclude that the mind and body are two distinct substances. Kant argues that the rationalist confuse the simplicity of the representation 'I' with the representation of something simple. We represent the logical subject as something simple because we just represent it as fulfilling a certain role in thought; however, just because we represent the I as something simple this gives us no good reason for assuming that the thing represented is simple. I may represent Istanbul on a map by a small red dot, but this does not mean Istanbul itself is small and red. Kant believes that the rationalist makes a similar kind of mistake in their argument for the claim that the mind is essentially simple and without parts, for they mistake the simplicity of the representation for the simplicity of the thing being represented. Kant makes a similar type of criticism in the *third* Paralogism of the rationalist argument for the position that we know that the soul is a substance that persists through time.

In the *fourth* and final Paralogism Kant discussed **dualism**, the doctrine defended by Descartes that the mind and body are distinct substances. Kant argues that we do not know what minds are in themselves and we do not know what bodies are in themselves, so we have no way of knowing if that which appears to us through **inner sense** as our mind is the same thing as that which appears to us through our **outer sense** as our body. As we have no knowledge of what our mind is in itself and no way of knowing what our body is in itself we have no way of knowing whether they are the same or distinct things. We just have no theoretical criteria for individuating and distinguishing things-in-themselves. So although Kant rejects Descartes' arguments for dualism he is ultimately agnostic as to the truth of the doctrine. See: **dualism; Descartes; Transcendental Deduction.**

particular judgement

In the table of judgements of the *Critique of Pure Reason* (1781/1787) Kant claims that, when it comes to their **quantity**, all judgements are either **universal**, particular or **singular**. Particular judgements are of the form 'some As are Bs' and Kant derives the

category of plurality from this form of judgement. Kant's idea here is that when we make a particular judgement we think of a domain as necessarily comprised of a plurality of members. For example, if I judge that 'some swans are white' this implies that some swans are not white, so for a judgement like this to be true there must be at least two objects falling under the subject concept; in the case of this judgement, the truth of the judgement presupposes there are at least two, and hence a plurality of, swans. See: **judgements, table of.**

pathological

The word 'pathological' is derived from the Greek *pathos* which means an experience or a feeling that the mind suffers. The word 'passion' has a similar etymology and can either mean feeling or suffering. In Kant's work the word 'pathological' implies a relation to the feelings or emotions. For example, in both the *Groundwork of the Metaphysics of Morals* (1785) and the *Metaphysics of Morals* (1797) Kant distinguishes between practical and pathological **love.** All he means by pathological love in this context is a love that is based on feeling or emotion. It is important to bear in mind that Kant does not use the word 'pathological' in the most common contemporary sense to mean diseased or mentally disordered. See: **feelings; love; beneficence.**

perfectionism

Eighteenth-century perfectionists such as Christian **Wolff** (1679–1754) and his follower Alexander Gottlieb **Baumgarten** (1714–62) believed that the principle of morality is to seek perfection. Wolff argues that perfection involves unity in manifoldness, and he believes that this implies that perfection is relative to kind, for he believes that unity is provided by a thing's function or goal. What it is to be a perfect watch is different from what it is to be a perfect flower or trampoline. A perfect watch is one that tells the time perfectly. In such a watch we find unity in manifoldness. The components from which a perfect watch are made are put together in such a way that they all work towards the same function, telling the time well.

Human perfection can be explained in similar terms. Humans have many drives and desires, and do many particular things. A perfect human is one who unifies this manifold of actions and desires, and this can be achieved if they are all directed to one end. Kant does not deny that morality demands that we seek perfection. He believes, however, that the principle 'seek perfection' lacks content, and the principle of perfection is merely a negative criterion of morality in the same way that the principle of non-contradiction is merely a negative criterion of truth. Kant's objection is that for Wolff it does not seem to matter what goal we set ourselves as long as we follow it rigorously. If, for example, one succeeded in subordinating all of one's inclinations to the goal of being a serial killer one would, presumably, be perfect in Wolff's sense – a perfect serial killer; but being a perfect serial killer is clearly not morally good. So Kant concluded that having **a good will** involves more than perfection. See: **Wolff; categorical imperative; universalizability, formula of.**

Perpetual Peace (1795)

For Kant the idea of world at peace is both a moral ideal and a realistic political goal. Kant argues that in order to promote world peace we must (a) encourage the rule of law and a respect for human rights, (b) maintain international law and promote the development of international institutions and (c) promote international economic development. And it is no coincidence that these are the three goals that are stressed in the preamble to the charter of the United Nations, which was founded in 1945, exactly 150 years after the publication of *Perpetual Peace* and which had its inspiration in Kantian ideas.

For Kant and, seventeenth- and eighteenth-century liberals in general, peace is *the* political ideal for to really live in peace with others involves more than not being engaged in open conflict for it requires that one's relations with others is based upon law and right, rather than on force or the threat of force. In this point all the major classical liberals, including Kant, were in agreement. Peace and law go hand in hand. Although Kant is clearly not a liberal imperialist, he is a strong universalist, believing that the ultimate moral community includes the whole of humanity. Thus, his ideal is that the relations between *all* human beings should be governed by law and not by force, for ultimately the human race constitutes a single society and hence the ideal legal order would be one that encompasses all human beings. Now one way that such an ideal could be achieved would be through the creation of a single world state, of which every human being was a citizen. Such an ideal was advocated by a number of eighteenth-century liberals, most famously by the Abbe Saint Pierre (1658–1743), who believed that for the whole human race to be ruled by law, there would have to be a single universal law and hence a world state. Kant, however, rejects this ideal and instead argues that the universal rule of law can be achieved through the establishment a league of nations, or a world federation of independent sovereign states living at peace with one another. So Kant's moral **ideal** is of a world of free and independent sovereign republics living at peace with one another. But he also argues that it is a realistic goal that we can hope to achieve. World peace is *both* a moral goal that any moral statesman should work towards *and* a state of affairs that could even by realized by a world of devils dominated purely by self-interest.

Kant hopes to show us that many of the aspects of human nature that tend to lead to war and conflict are precisely those elements that also ground the possibility of peaceful co-existence. In this aspect of his project Kant is clearly walking in the footsteps of that arch realist Thomas Hobbes (1588–1679). Hobbes had argued in his *Leviathan* (1651) that the primary cause of conflict and war between individuals is self-interest. Each individual desires to satisfy not only their present desires but also to secure the means to satisfy their desires in the future. And in a world of limited resources this can only lead to conflict. Thus, as Hobbes famously argues, the state of nature, and by this Hobbes means the way things would be in the absence of a political state, is a state of war, and in such a state the life of man would be 'solitary, poore, nasty, brutish and short'. Hobbes believes, however, that the same natural facts about humans that lead us to conflict are also those elements of human nature that promote peace, for we can all recognize that the best way of achieving our long-run interests is to live at peace with our neighbours if possible, and that the only way we can do this is to compromise. To the degree that we are motivated by enlightened long-run rational self-interest we are willing to submit to a law that forces us to renounce some of our desires on the understanding that our neighbours will do the same. Now some of us might do this out of a respect for morality, but if this does not do the job cold-hearted selfish rational calculation will. Kant takes this analysis and applies it to the sphere of international relations between states rather than the relations between human individuals and Kant agrees with the Hobbsian realist that the natural relation between states is one of war.

Kant, then, agrees with Hobbes that peaceful relations and law are not natural but need to be created or established. Now, Hobbes believed that the only way that the state of peace can be formally instituted is through the introduction of an absolute sovereign. Kant, however, argues that perpetual peace can be *guaranteed* by nature. By 'guaranteed' here Kant does not mean 'made inevitable'. Instead what he means by this is that we do not need a world sovereign to guarantee world peace, for given certain conditions, namely the spread of republican constitutional regimes, the creation of international institutions and the globalization of trade relations, peaceful relations would naturally follow, and he also argues that these conditions could arise naturally, even given what we know of human nature. It is important to recognize that in examining the conditions that would naturally guarantee peace, Kant is not suggesting that he believes that the institution of perpetual peace is *inevitable*, all he wants to show is that even given what we know of human nature perpetual peace is really possible, and hence a realistic ideal. Thus, at the heart of his essay Kant introduces what he calls three 'definitive articles' for the establishment of perpetual peace. These are the conditions that Kant believes, if realized, will make peaceful relations between states possible.

The *first* article is that 'The Civil constitution of Every State shall be Republican'. Kant's conception of a republic is modelled on **Jean-Jacques Rousseau**'s (1712–78) *On the Social Contract* (1762). A republic is a political regime in which each member is a free and equal citizen, being both sovereign and subject to the laws. Kant has a number of arguments for suggesting that republics are likely to establish lasting peaceful relations. First he believes that most wars are started by leaders for their own benefit and that wars (especially between republics) are not to the benefit of citizens, and so they will be hesitant in engaging in wars. He also suggests that in republics, at least over time, there will emerge a public culture of respect for law and that this will spread to relations with other states, or at least to other republics. Kant's *second* article is that 'The Right of Nations shall be based on a Federation of Free States.' For he argues that lasting peace cannot be inaugurated nor secured without a general agreement between nations, and this require the creation of particular kind of league, which he calls a *pacific federation*. Such a federation is necessary for the establishment of any sort of international law, the purpose of which is not to regulate the relations between human individuals but between states. International law does not require a world state, but it does require international institutions and agreements. Finally, Kant argues that economic growth and international trade are also natural factors that make lasting peace between nations possible. His thought is that globalization, in enmeshing nations in a web of mutually beneficial trading relations will also encourage lasting peace, for in such an economically globalized world, war will become increasingly damaging to the economies of the countries involved.

Kant is not arguing that there is a law of **history** that requires the emergence of such a state of affairs. He is not arguing that democratization and the growth of international institutions and trade are inevitable. Rather he is arguing that given what we know of human nature it is not unreasonable for us to hope that the world could develop in such a way, and that a world of free republics that subjected themselves to international law, something that is only possible if they were members of an international federation, and which engaged in mutual trade relations would be a peaceful world and that such a world, is not a utopian ideal but something that could emerge naturally and that we should and can work to bring such a condition into being. See: **history**; *Idea for a Cosmopolitan History*.

phenomenal

See: world, phenomenal

Physical Monadology (1756)

In this **pre-critical** work Kant defends a fundamentally Leibnizian metaphysical position and develops an interesting, and influential, dynamical conception of matter. In his *Monadology* (1714) Gottfried Wilhelm **Leibniz** (1646–1716) had argued that all composite substances must ultimately be composed of individual substances, which he named monads (from the Greek '*monas*' which means 'one'). These monads must be simple, unextended and indivisible, point-like individuals that are essentially active. A theory like this has a problem explaining how such substances can fill or occupy space, as they are dimensionless. And it seems to suggest that interaction between monads is impossible, for if monads are essentially active it is difficult to explain how they can be acted upon, which seems to require that they be passive. In his *Physical Monadology* Kant tries to explain how point-like monads can fill and occupy space by suggesting that such monads should be thought of as point-like centres of attractive and repulsive forces. Such point-like substances can be thought of as the centres of spheres of activity and the solidity or impenetrability of matter can be explained in terms of the limits of the sphere of activity of such an individual. This explains how unextended points can, in a sense, fill and occupy space. Physical monads, then, do not literally fill the space they occupy by existing in all parts of it, but by excluding other monads from occupying the space through repulsive force. According to such a theory the properties of solidity and impenetrability are not basic properties of matter but are constituted by the relations, explained in terms of attractive and repulsive force, between monads.

The **critical** Kant rejected his pre-critical position and in the Second **Antinomy** of the *Critique of Pure Reason* (1781/1787) rejects the position that material substance must be composed of simple, indivisible substances. Instead he argues that every part of matter is potentially divisible and so there can be no smallest part of matter. Although the critical Kant rejects the possibility of physical monads, he does still advocate a dynamical conception of matter according to which material properties such as impenetrability, hardness and density are constituted by the interplay between attractive and repulsive forces. His most detailed defence of this position in his critical period is found in his *Metaphysical Foundations of Natural Science* (1786). See: **Leibniz**; **metaphysics**; *Metaphysical Foundations of Natural Science*.

Physico-theologial argument

The physico-theological argument for the existence of God is Kant's name for the traditional argument from design. Unlike the **cosmological argument**, which takes as its starting point the mere fact of the existence of the world, this argument takes as its starting point some determinate features of the universe, in particular its beauty, order and purposiveness. From these facts it argues to the necessary existence of an intelligent cause. Kant discusses and rejects this argument in the Ideal of Pure Reason of the *Critique of Pure Reason* (1781/1787). However although he thinks that the argument from design is not valid, he does argue in the Critique of Teleological Judgment in the *Critique of Judgment* (1790) that when we try to think about the nature of living beings, we are naturally led to believe that the existence of such beings implies the existence of a wise designer. And he suggests that the natural attractiveness of this argument shows our desire to find order and purposiveness in the universe, a theme that will feature prominently in the *Critique of Judgment*. He also points out that at the very most such an argument could, if successful, merely provide an argument for the existence of an architect of the universe not of an all-powerful creator. See: design, argument from; God; *Critique of Judgment*.

Pietism

Pietism was a protestant religious movement that was founded in the seventeenth century by Phillip Jakob Spener (1635–1705). It had a strong influence on the development of modern Christianity. For example, John Wesley (1703–91), the founder of Methodism was strong influenced by it, and much contemporary born-again Christianity has its roots in Pietism. Pietism stressed the importance of one's individual emotional relationship to God and thought that this could only be achieved by a radical **conversion** experience, which they thought of as a change of heart or rebirth. Kant himself was brought up as a Pietist, receiving a Pietist education at the *Collegium Fridericianum*. Kant's attitude towards Pietism is complicated. By the time of his education, Pietism had been institutionalized in Prussia and was, in effect, the state religion, and Kant did not enjoy his early education and was strongly opposed to state-sponsored Pietism. To get ahead in the Prussian state bureaucracy and educational institutions it helped if you professed the faith, which involved being able to appeal to some personal moment of conversion or breakthrough. This, of course, resulted in much hypocrisy among students, and those seeking state office, and it is clear that Kant was disgusted by this hypocrisy. What had stated as a religious movement that had stressed inwardness had gradually been institutionalized into a practice that stressed the external proclamation of one's inner emotional experience. He also disliked their stress on **feelings** and emotions over **reason** and the tendency of Pietists to irrationalism and **enthusiasm**. On the other hand, however, he was sympathetic to their individualism and stress on inwardness with the idea that what is important is the state of one's heart, or inner disposition, rather than one's external behaviour. Despite his reservations about Pietist practice which made the outward public proclamation of one's piety and conversion experience central, it is clear that the Pietist idea of a moral rebirth or breakthrough plays an important role in his ethics, for he argues for the importance of a moral conversion, modelled in many ways on the Pietist idea of a change of heart, most notably in *Religion within the Boundaries of Mere Reason* (1793) and *Anthropology from a Pragmatic Point of View* (1798). See: **conversion; religion;** *Religion within the Boundaries of Mere Reason.*

possibility, real versus logical

Central to Kant's **critical** turn and his rejection of rationalist metaphysics is his distinction between logical and real possibility. Logical possibility has to do with the relationship between concepts and is our criterion for thinkability. If two concepts can be combined in thought without contradiction then the new concept is logically possible and hence thinkable. However, Kant thinks that just because a concept is thinkable this does not imply that an object corresponding to this concept is really possible. For just because there is no contradiction is combining two concepts in thought this does not necessarily imply that the properties corresponding to these concepts can coexist in a single object in reality. For example, the concepts of red and green can be combined to produce the concept of something that is totally red and totally green, and so, Kant thinks the concept of a totally green and totally green object is logically possible, but the fact that redness and greenness can be so combined in thought does not imply that that they can really be combined in an object, and we know that a material object that is totally red and totally green is not really possible.

Kant thinks that the only criterion we have for whether something is really possible is whether or not an object corresponding to the concept can be intuited. And because our form of **intuition** is spatio-temporal, which means that we can only intuit things in space and time, the only objects that we can know are really possible are objects than can exist in space and time. The fact that the only objects that we can know are really possible are objects that can exist in space and time does not, however, imply that objects that cannot exist in space and time are really impossible, it just means that we have no way of knowing whether or not such objects are really possible or not. So, for example, our ideas of the soul, the intelligible world and of **God** are thinkable without contradiction so these three things are logically possible. However, objects corresponding to these three ideas are not the sort of things that could ever be experienced in space and time, and so we have no way of knowing whether or not such objects are really possible. This fact provides one reason for Kant's rejection of René **Descartes'** (1596–1650) **ontological argument** for the existence of God, for in this argument Descartes makes the assumption that God is really possible, and Kant thinks that this claim cannot be justified. Kant's distinction between logical and real possibility and his claim that the only criterion we can have for real possibility is whether or not something could be experienced in space and time, lies behind Kant's claim that we can have no knowledge of **things as they are in themselves**. The reason for this is that we have no reasonable theoretical criteria for judging that putative objects that that transcend the limits of human cognition are really possible. But we also have no criteria for judging that such objects are impossible. See: **logic, general**; **ontological argument**; *Critique of Pure Reason*.

pre-critical

Kant radically changed many of his philosophical positions by the time he wrote the *Critique of Pure Reason* (1781). In particular he radically changed his attitude towards the possibility of **metaphysics**. When he was younger he believed that metaphysics could provide us with real knowledge of the nature of things as they are in themselves. By the time of the first *Critique* he reached the conclusion that such knowledge is impossible, and all *a priori* knowledge of the world is restricted to things as they appear to us, not as they are in themselves. When commentators talk of the pre-critical Kant they are referring to his ideas before he worked out the ideas he presented in the *Critique of Pure Reason*. See: **metaphysics**; *Physical Monadology*; *Dreams of a Spirit-Seer*.

principle of non-contradiction

See: non-contradiction, principle of

principle of sufficient reason

See: sufficient reason, principle of

principle

Kant distinguishes between the **understanding**, which he calls the faculty of **rules**, and **reason**, which he calls the faculty of principles. From the theoretical perspective a principle is a universal rule that can function as a major premise in a **syllogism**. From the practical perspective principles are practical **laws** that have the function of governing our rational choice of maxims. Both the **categorical imperative** and **hypothetical imperatives** are principles in this sense. See: **law**; *Critique of Pure Reason*; categorical imperative; *Groundwork of the Metaphysics of Morals*.

private use of reason

In *What is Enlightenment?* (1784) Kant distinguishes between what he calls the private and **public use of one's reason**, and argues that although enlightenment requires the freedom in public use of reason, the state may legitimately regulate and control the private use of reason. One uses one's reason privately when one speaks as an officeholder or representative of a particular organization. Kant was particularly interested in state officeholders because in his day pastors were state officeholders. When speaking as an officeholder, that is when engaged in the private use of reason, one has an obligation to not contradict the doctrines of the organization. Thus the state can legitimately regulate the speech of state officeholders insofar as they are speaking as officeholders. Such officeholders, however, can also speak as members of the public, for example when they write a scholarly article for the scholarly public, and the state has no legitimate right to regulate or control the speech of individuals, even if they are officeholders, when they engage in such speech. See: *What is Enlightenment?*; **public use of reason.**

problematic

Kant talks of both problematic judgements and problematic concepts. Problematic **judgements** are the first of the three judgements of **modality** presented in the **table of judgements.** In a problematic judgement, the content of the judgement is not asserted to be true but is merely presented as possibly true. This is why Kant derives the category of possibility from this form of judgement. When a disjunctive judgement is asserted, for example, neither of the two disjuncts is asserted, but within the disjunctive judgement they are held problematically, the judgement 'either the cat is on the mat or the cat is not on the mat' contains the judgements 'the cat is on the mat' and 'the cat is not on the mat', but neither of these judgements is actually asserted but merely hold problematically, both of them are presented within the whole disjunctive judgement as possibly true. A problematic **concept** is one that contains no contradiction but the objective reality of which can in no way be cognized. Such concepts can be thought, but we have no way of knowing whether an object corresponding to the concept actually exists or even if such an object is really possible. The concepts of **God** and **freedom,** for example, are such concepts. They are not contradictory, but we have no way of knowing theoretically whether God or freedom exist or not. See: **logic, general; possibility, logical versus real.**

Prolegomena to Any Future Metaphysics (1783)

A 'prolegomena' is an introduction to or preparatory remarks on a particular subject. The *Prolegomena* was published 2 years after the publication of the first edition of the *Critique of Pure Reason* (1781) and was intended to popularize this work and to respond to criticisms and what Kant took to be misreadings. He was particularly concerned to respond to accusations that he was advocating a form of subjective idealism akin to George **Berkeley**'s (1685–1753). He distinguishes what he calls his own **transcendental idealism**, which in the *Prolegomena* he prefers to calls formal idealism, from the dogmatic idealism of Berkeley, who denied the existence of mind-independent physical objects, and the skeptical idealism of René **Descartes** (1596–1650), who was unable to provide a satisfactory justification for our belief in the existence of mind-independent material objects. Kant argues that his idealism is merely formal for it does not claim that the matter of experience is mind dependent but merely its form.

The *Prolegomena* covers much of the same ground as the ***Critique of Pure Reason*** (1781/1787), except that whereas in the *Critique* Kant pursued what he called a synthetic method, in the *Prolegomena* he pursues the **analytic method**. The analytic or regressive method starts with the conditioned (or the whole, or the consequence) and provides an analysis of the condition (or the part, or the ground). The synthetic method proceeds from the condition (or the part, or ground) and proceeds to the conditioned (or the whole, or the consequence). In the *Critique of Pure Reason*, Kant pursues the synthetic method because he attempts to justify the claim that we can and do have **synthetic *a priori*** knowledge. He starts by examining the elements of human cognition, including the **categories,** (the conditions) and attempts to show that there must be synthetic *a priori* principles that govern the application of these categories to objects of experience (the conditioned). In the *Prolegomena*, in contrast, Kant begins with the assumption that we have synthetic *a priori* knowledge and he does not attempt to provide a justification of this assumption, but is content merely to give an account of what must be the case for such knowledge to be possible.

In the Preface to the *Prolegomena* Kant presents his philosophy as providing a response to David **Hume**'s (1711–76) **skepticism** about **causation**, and makes his famous remark that it was Hume who woke him from his 'dogmatic slumbers'. Hume's skepticism about causation raised the problem of the possibility of **synthetic *a priori*** knowledge and Kant's answer to Hume is to show how synthetic *a priori* knowledge is possible. The *Prolegomena* is divided into three main sections in each of which Kant examines the possibility of a particular type of synthetic *a priori* knowledge. In the first two sections, which cover material that Kant examined in the **Transcendental Aesthetic** and Transcendental Analytic, Kant discusses the possibility of **mathematical** knowledge and the possibility of pure natural science. In the second of these sections he is particularly interested in explaining our knowledge of causation. In the third section, which covers some of the material covered in the **Transcendental Dialectic** of the *Critique of Pure Reason*, Kant examines the possibility of **metaphysics** as a science, and rejects the key claims of traditional rational psychology, rational cosmology and rational theology, arguing that we can have no *a priori* knowledge of the soul, the world as it is in itself or of **God**.

An important distinction that Kant makes in the *Prolegomena*, but not in the *Critique of Pure Reason*, is that between what he calls 'judgements of experience' and 'judgements of perception'. Judgements of experience are objectively valid and necessarily involve the categories whereas judgements of perception are merely subjectively valid judgements and do not necessarily involve the categories. For example, Kant claims that when the sun shines on a stone and it becomes warm, this is a judgement of perception for it involves no necessity. However, if I judge that the sun *warms* the stone, this is a judgement of experience because it necessarily connects the concept of sunshine with that of heat by using a causal concept. Judgements of experience, then, have a synthetic *a priori* element because they involve the recognition of some necessity in the world, such as causal relationships. In the *Prolegomena*, however, Kant seems to suggest that human cognition begins with judgements of perception and the question is how such judgements can be transformed into judgements of experience. Unfortunately, it is difficult to explain how this position is compatible with Kant position in the *Critique of Pure Reason*, especially with the position defended in the **Refutation of Idealism**. For here Kant seems to argue for a form of direct realism and claims that it is our objective experience of material objects through **outer sense** which makes **inner sense** possible. This would suggest that it is our capacity to immediately make judgements of experience that makes it possible to make judgements of perception. In the Refutation of Idealism, then, Kant seems to suggest that judgements of experience are somehow prior to judgements of perception, and make such judgements possible. See: *Critique of Pure Reason*; synthetic *a priori*; analytic method; Refutation of Idealism; Berkeley; formal idealism.

public use of reason

In *What is Enlightenment?* (1784) Kant distinguishes between the public and **private use of reason**, and argues that enlightenment requires freedom in the public use of reason. That is, Kant believes that the state should not interfere or regulate public discussion of ideas. One uses one's reason publically when one speaks as a member of the public to other members of the public, as, for example, when one writes as a scholar for other scholars. Such speech should not, Kant argues, be subject to state regulation or control. One can also, however, speak as an officeholder or representative of an organization, and in such cases one is using one's reason privately, and such speech can be subject to state regulation and control, for insofar as one is speaking as the holder of a particular office or as a representative of an organization one has an obligation to not contradict the positions or teachings of the organization. One can, of course, always resign one's office if one is unable to defend the doctrines of the organization, and even an officeholder should, Kant argues, be allowed to criticize the doctrines of the organization when speaking not as an officeholder but as a member of the public, as for example when a member of an organization criticizes the policies of an organization in a scholarly article. See: *What is Enlightenment?*; private use of reason.

quality

Kant argues that all judgements have a **quantity**, a quality, a **relation** and a **modality**, and in the table of **judgements** of the *Critique of Pure Reason* (1781/1787) he enumerates the three different qualities a judgement may have. Thus he argues that all judgements are either affirmative, negative or infinite. An affirmative judgement has the form '*a* is *b*', a negative judgement has the form 'it is not the case that *a* is *b*' and an infinite judgement has the form '*a* is non-*b*'. Kant argues that the categories of reality, negation and limitation are derived from these three forms of judgement, respectively. In the **Anticipations of Perception** Kant argues that the categories of quality form the basis for our grasp of **intensive magnitudes** or degrees of reality. See: **judgements, table of**; **Anticipations of Perception**.

quantity

Kant argues that all judgements have a quantity, a **quality**, a **relation** and a **modality**, and in the **table of judgements** of the *Critique of Pure Reason* (1781/1787) he lists the three possible quantities a judgement may have. In terms of its quantity a judgement can either be **universal** ('all *a*s are *b*s'), **particular** ('some *a*s are *b*s') or **singular** ('this or the *a* is *b*'). Kant derives the categories of unity, plurality and totality from these three forms of judgement, and argues in the **Axioms of Intuition** that our capacity to recognize **extensive magnitudes** involves these three categories. He also argues that that our concepts of **number** involve all the categories of quantity, for a number is a totality constructed from a plurality of units. The number 2, for example, is the concept of a unity consisting of a two units. See: **judgements, table of; Axioms of Intuition.**

race

Although Kant believes that all human beings belong to the same natural species, defending the principle that all animals which can produce fertile young with one another belong to the same species, he thinks that the human species is divided into different races, which are distinguished by the possession of distinct sets of inherited characteristics. He also believes that all members of the human species originally belonged to one race and that racial differences **emerged** with the spread of human populations into different environments with differing climatic conditions. For Kant, the primary distinguishing characteristic between races is skin colour, and he argues that there are four principal races: the 'white race' (Europeans), the 'yellow race' (Asians), the 'black race' (Africans) and the 'red race' (native Americans). Although Kant's account of racial difference starts as an attempt to offer a descriptive account of natural human differences, like most Europeans of his time, he unfortunately also believes that these cosmetic natural differences also correspond to different practical capacities, believing that members of some races are incapable of culture and lack a sufficient drive to activity. Although Kant clearly expresses unacceptable racist views, such views were characteristic of his times, and unlike many Europeans of his time, his racist beliefs did not lead him to conclude that racial differences justify the unjust treatment of members of other races. He was a sharp critic of what he took to be unjust European colonial practices, criticizing, for example, what he took to be the unjust treatment of native Americans by European colonists, and thought that all human beings, regardless of their race, were deserving of respect. He was particularly critical of Europeans appropriating the land of other peoples in the name of spreading civilization, and this criticism was based on his belief that it is contradictory for an individual to will the perfection of another individual, or another group of individuals, as their end. Other individuals, and Kant thought other societies, have a duty to perfect themselves, and this perfection also involves the development of what Kant calls the civil condition; Kant is insistent, however, that such perfection cannot be imposed from outside. Thus, although we can, and should, condemn Kant for his racist beliefs, we should recognize that he was ahead of his time in criticizing unjust European practices and actions, which were often perpetrated under the banner of 'spreading civilization'.

radical evil

Radical evil is Kant's reinterpretation of what in traditional Christian theology was called original sin. For Kant, radical evil is not a form of guilt for the actions of our most distant ancestors, but is the result of the corruption of our character and our predisposition to (often) put the demands of self-interest before the demands of morality. It is important to note that Kant does not think radical evil involves doing evil for evil's sake. Such motivation would be diabolic, and is not the cause of human evil which, Kant thinks, is always motivated by self-interest and a desire for happiness. Paradoxically, Kant thinks that radical evil is a freely chosen form of corruption; it is a freely chosen predisposition to not do what we recognize to be the reasonable thing to do.

One way of understanding why Kant thinks that our radical evil is freely chosen is in terms of our development. Before we reach adulthood and the capacity to obey reason, we have already to a large degree developed our characters and formed a set of **maxims**.

The set of maxims we find ourselves possessing by the time we have reached adulthood has been formed unsystematically and many of our maxims are immoral. The formation of our motivational set, however, was the result of the free, perhaps arbitrary, choices we made in childhood and young adulthood. In childhood, we often have contradictory impulses which pull us in opposite directions. In such cases we are forced to make arbitrary choices, and these choices are not governed by any maxims. Through experience and repetition, we slowly and unconsciously develop a set of maxims that govern our choice between impulses. As we become older, our unconscious maxims become more complex, and when we are faced with new and unusual circumstances our maxims sometimes provide contradictory guidance. However, over time we develop the capacity to represent our maxims and to choose between them and order them in a hierarchical structure. When we first acquire the capacity to do this, we are guided by the principle of self-love, for it is only later in our development that we are able to formulate the principle of **universalizability**. By the time we reach maturity, then, we have developed the capacity to represent maxims and reason about which maxims to adopt, we have acquired a set of dispositions to have certain impulses in given situations, and through our arbitrary choices we have developed a large, incoherent and inconsistent set of maxims for choosing in particular situations which impulses to actualize. These maxims are not only inconsistent, but have been formed largely on the basis of the principle of self-love. And it is the moral task of adulthood to sort out the mess. See: *Religion within the Boundaries of Mere Reason*; *Conjectural Beginning of Human History*.

rationalists

Histories of the early modern period tend to divide philosophers into **empiricists**, who stress the importance of experience in human knowledge, and rationalists, who stress the role of **reason**. Kant often presents himself as presenting a middle ground between rationalism and empiricism. The most important rationalist philosophers with whom Kant engages are René **Descartes**, (1596–1650), Baruch **Spinoza** (1632–77), Gottfried Wilhelm **Leibniz** (1646–1716), Christian **Wolff** (1679–1754) and Alexander Gottlieb **Baumgarten**

(1714–62). See: **Leibniz**; **Wolff**; **Baumgarten**; **Spinoza**; sufficient reason, principle of; metaphysics; empiricists.

Rawls, John (1921–2002)

John Rawls, who taught for most of his career at Harvard University, is perhaps the most important American political philosopher of the twentieth century, and also had a strong influence on recent Kantian ethics. His most important works are a *Theory of Justice* (1971) and *Political Liberalism* (1996). His work is strongly influenced by Kant and his ideas have strongly influenced recent Kantian ethics. In particular, he has advocated what he calls a **constructivist** reading of Kant's ethics, according to which the concept of the right is prior to the good. See: **constructivism**; *Groundwork of the Metaphysics of Morals*; *Critique of Practical Reason*; universalizability, formula of.

realist

See: **empirical realist**; transcendental realism

realm of ends, formula of

The formula of the realm of ends (in some translations 'kingdom of ends') is the third formulation of the **categorical imperative** presented in the *Groundwork of the Metaphysics of Morals* (1785). According to this formulation all **maxims** as proceeding from our own lawmaking ought to harmonize with a possible realm of ends as a realm of nature. What Kant means by this is that when we formulate and revise our maxims of action we must think of ourselves, and all other human beings, as constituting a single community potentially governed by laws that all could will, and we should ask when formulating our maxims whether they could serve as laws for such a community. Kant identifies the idea of being a member of a realm of ends with the idea of **autonomy**, for to be autonomous is to be the law giver for such a community.

See: *Groundwork of the Metaphysics of Morals*; categorical imperative; universalizability, formula of; humanity, formula of; kingdom of ends.

reason

Kant explains that whereas the function of the **understanding** is to bring unity to **appearances** by making judgements applying **concepts** to objects given in **intuition**, the function of reason, which is the faculty of making syllogistic inferences, is to provide unity to the concepts, or rules, of the understanding by bringing them under **principles**. And, in its inferences, reason attempts to create **systematicity** in our conceptual scheme by bringing the great manifold of our set of concepts under the smallest number of principles possible, and in so doing it attempts to bring unity to our cognitive faculty. In this characterization of reason Kant rejects both the **rationalist** and the **empiricist** conception of reason. Rationalists, such as René **Descartes** (1596–1650), who often speaks of the 'light of reason', conceive of reason as a quasi-perceptual faculty that is the source of immediate knowledge of God, the world and the nature of the soul. Empiricists such as David **Hume** (1711–76), however, had thought of reason as completely passive and lacking in any sort of desire or motive force. Thus Hume could famously proclaim that reason is and can only be a slave to the passions. Kant rejects the rationalist account of reason as a capacity for intellectual intuition, but he also rejects the empiricist conception of reason as totally inert, arguing that reason does have some motive force for it is or involves a particular desire, a desire to bring unity or systematicity to our conceptual scheme.

For a fuller understanding of Kant's conception of reason, it is necessary to understand Kant's account of its relationship to the other cognitive faculties. Both rationalists and empiricists, for very different reasons, had assumed that the mind has only one cognitive faculty which is the source of our knowledge of the world. The rationalists explain cognition purely in terms of the operation of the intellect, whereas the empiricists explain it purely in terms of the operation of sensibility. Kant, in contrast to both, argues that human cognition requires the cooperation of two faculties: sensibility, which he names the lower faculty of cognition, and the intellect, which he names the higher faculty. In the *Critique of Judgment* (1790) Kant divides this higher faculty into three distinct faculties: the faculty of **understanding**, the faculty of **judgement** (which Kant seems to understand as being the faculty for what he calls **reflecting judgement**) and the faculty of **reason**, and he suggests that the faculty of judgement somehow mediates between reason and the understanding. In the *Critique of Pure Reason* (1781/1787), however, Kant focuses on the distinction between the understanding and reason, and there is disagreement among scholars as to whether it is appropriate to interpret the first *Critique* in terms of the tripartite division of the higher faculty of the later third *Critique*.

Kant explains the difference between the understanding and reason in at least four distinct, but interconnected, ways. First, the understanding is the faculty of **concepts**, whereas reason is the faculty of **ideas**. Second, the understanding is the faculty of **judgements** whereas reason is the faculty of **syllogisms**. (The German word for 'syllogism' is '*vernunftschluss*', which literally means 'inference of reason'.) Third, the understanding is the faculty of **rules**, whereas reason is the faculty of **principles**. Finally, Kant explains that reason is a faculty that seeks or demands the unconditioned.

In claiming that reason seeks the unconditioned Kant means that reason seeks complete explanation or justification. Reason is the faculty of syllogistic inferences, and a syllogism is an inference with two premises and a conclusion. The premises are the conditions and the conclusion is the conditioned in the sense that in a valid inference the truth of the preemies are the conditions of the truth of the conclusion. Reason, however, does not merely demand that the conclusion follows from the premises but also that the premises themselves are justified, and as such the premises must be regarded as the conclusions of yet further syllogisms, and as such they themselves must be regarded as conditioned. In claiming that reason seeks the unconditioned, then, Kant means that reason demands and seeks complete justification. It demands a foundation for our thinking. However, just because reason demands such a foundation this does not mean that such a foundation is possible. The demand for such a foundation is a subjective demand of reason; we, however, mistake this demand of reason for something that actually does or could exist, and this is the source of what Kant calls **transcendental illusion**, the mistaking of a subjective principle for an objective fact.

Because we seek the unconditioned we naturally assume that there must be some object to be found corresponding to the idea of the unconditioned, and this is the source of the illusion. Now the fact that reason naturally seeks the unconditioned does not imply that it can be found, and what Kant calls the **dialectic** of reason is the result of confusing this subjective desire of reason with an objective fact about the way the world is. See: *Critique of Pure Reason*; **understanding**.

reflecting judgement

In the *Critique of Judgment* (1790) Kant distinguished between two forms of judgement: reflecting judgement and determining judgement. In the determining use of judgement we start with a given universal (which could be a concept, a principle or a law) and the task is to find a particular that falls under the universal. So, for example, one may already possess the concept 'cat' and when one sees a particular cat one may judge: 'this is a cat'. This would be an example of the determining use of judgement. The reflecting use of judgement begins with the awareness of a particular object or objects and the task is to find or create a concept under which to subsume the particular object or objects. Kant suggests that there are three main types of reflecting judgement which he names the logical, the aesthetic and the teleological. The logical use of reflecting judgement is involved in the discovery of new empirical concepts and laws. Although Kant believes that our most general concepts of nature, such as the concept of **substance**, are *a priori*, in order to apply these concept we need to make them more specific, for example we need to classify the world into particular types of substance. And Kant argues that there are *a priori* principles that govern this activity of specification, for we should aim at making our conceptual scheme systematic, and so he argues that **systematicity** is a **regulative idea** for theoretical reason and that in our reasoning about the world we must presuppose that nature is such that it allows for this systematization. The **aesthetic** use of reflecting judgement is involved in our experience of **beauty** and the **sublime**. The teleological use of reflecting judgement is involved in our experience of living organisms, for when we experience such organisms we have to think of them as having an internal structure that is teleologically organized. This form of reflecting judgement is involved in our judgement of the **purposiveness** of nature as a whole. See: *Critique of Judgment.*

Refutation of Idealism

In this short, but influential, section added to the second edition of the *Critique of Pure Reason* (1787) Kant argues that **outer sense** is a necessary condition for the possibility of **inner sense**. What he means by this is that our capacity to immediately experience physical objects in space is a necessary condition for us to be able to experience the flow of our subjective felt experiences as a flow. His argument for this is that it is only through the experience of both changing and persisting physical objects in space, such as the hands of a watch or the movement of the sun, that allows us to determinately order our inner experiences in time. In making such a claim Kant is defending a form of direct realism, the position that the immediate objects of experience are physical objects and not our subjective states or ideas. See: *Critique of Pure Reason*; realism; inner sense; outer sense.

regulative principles

See: constitutive principles

religion

Although Kant was hostile to many traditional religious beliefs and practices, Kant was not in principle hostile to religion, although he believed that religion must ultimately be in the service of morality and believed that true service to God consisted in morally good conduct and having a morally good disposition.

Kant was brought up as a Pietist. **Pietism** was a protestant revival movement that stressed the individual's emotional relationship to God and the **conversion** or rebirth experience, and was opposed to rationalist interpretations of Christianity which were regarded as overly intellectual. Contemporary born-again Christianity is at least partially a descendent of eighteenth-century German Pietism. Kant's attitudes towards Pietism are complicated. On the one hand, he was opposed to their attacks on reason in religious matters, frequently criticizing irrationalism in religion, which he dismissed as 'enthusiasm' (*Schwärmerei*), and he thought that Pietism as an institutionalized movement encouraged hypocrisy. Perhaps the most popular genre of eighteenth-century Pietist literature were conversion narratives. In them, Pietists told the stories of their own rebirths. Such narratives were extremely popular and were presented as models to be followed, and professing to have had such a conversion experience was important if one wanted to be promoted in the Prussian bureaucracy. What had started as a religious movement that stressed the individual's inner relationship towards God had become a movement that demanded external profession of such an emotional relationship, and this naturally led to hypocrisy with unscrupulous individuals being the loudest in their professions of faith and inner devotion in order to get ahead in the world. In addition Kant was opposed to the idea of taking the conversion experience of another human being, rather than the pure moral **ideal** known through reason, as our ideal to imitate. On the other hand, although Kant was opposed to enthusiasm in religion he himself wished to limit the role of theoretical reason in religious matters attacking the traditional rationalist arguments for the **existence** of God and arguing that we can have no knowledge of God, for we can only have knowledge of objects of possible experience and there can be no object given in our experience corresponding to our idea of God. Although he denies the possibility of any knowledge of God, he does not want to undermine belief in God, thus in the Preface to the second edition of the *Critique of Pure Reason* (1787) he explains that he has denied knowledge to make room for faith or belief. And in the Postulates of Practical Reason of the *Critique of Practical Reason* (1788) he argues that although we can have no theoretical proof of the existence of God, we have good, practical reasons for believing in the existence of God, for morality requires that it is reasonable for us to hope that the virtuous will ultimately be happy, and this hope is, Kant argues, only reasonable if we believe in the existence of an omnipotent, omniscient and just ruler of the universe who has the capacity and will to proportion happiness to virtue, being the ground of what Kant calls the **highest good**. Thus, Kant argues, morality demands that we believe in the existence of God because the existence of a moral God is what he calls a postulate of practical reasoning. Like the Pietists Kant puts an emphasis on inwardness in practical matters believing that what is central in practical matters is the state of one's intelligible **character** or disposition. However, unlike the Pietists who focused on our emotional felt relationship to God, for Kant what is essential is that one's disposition is ruled by reason and although feelings play an important role in his account of morality, he does not make feelings central in the way the Pietists did.

In terms of organized religion Kant was opposed to religious communities or churches that were governed by religious laws that demanded particular external behaviour from their members. But he did think that the existence of a 'moral community' or 'church' was necessary for human beings to fulfil their moral vocation. Such a church, Kant argues in his *Religion within the Boundaries of Mere Reason* (1793), would be a voluntary community of free and equal individuals who were united by their inward disposition rather than external coercive laws, and its goal would be to strengthen the moral disposition and **virtue** of its member and to combat what Kant called the **radical evil** in human nature. See: *Religion within the Boundaries of Mere Reason*; conversion; Pietism; feeling.

Religion within the Boundaries of Mere Reason (1793)

Although Kant denies the possibility of a theoretical proof of the existence of God, he also denies the possibility of a such a proof of the non-existence of God. However, although Kant is, from the theoretical perspective, agnostic about the existence of God, he argues famously in the *Critique of Pure Reason* (1781/1787) that he had denied knowledge to make room for faith. Such faith is, Kant argues, rational but has its source in practical rather than theoretical reason, for he believes that morality requires a belief in the existence of God and striving to have a good will is the only thing we can do to be well pleasing to God and as such constitutes worship or true service to God.

Religion within the Boundaries of Mere Reason (henceforth, *Religion*) is an account of the type of religion that morality requires. Although Kant is critical of much of traditional Christianity, he tries to interpret much of traditional Christian doctrine in terms of his rational morality. One of the main themes of *Religion* is the notion of original sin and what Kant calls the **radical evil** in human nature. Kant argues that radical evil does not have to do, as many Christians believe, with a primordial guilt at the sins of our earliest ancestors, but with a freely chosen perversion within human motivation. For Kant morality is absolute, and his **ideal** of a **good will** involves having a perfect moral disposition and strictly obeying the **moral law**. What morality demands is that we have a holy will, but we are human, and human beings, however, have a natural, but, Kant argues, freely chosen, propensity to make exceptions for themselves and subordinate the demands of morality to self-interest. And it is this propensity that he calls radical evil. One problem with this account is that it is difficult to understand how this propensity can be both natural and freely chosen. Kant himself argues that the only way we can understand the nature of such a free choice is to understand it as **intelligible** and outside time, and many commentators have raised objections to this notion. It is also important to note that Kant does not identify radical evil with doing evil for evil's sake. This would be to have a diabolic will and Kant thinks that it is impossible for human beings to have such a will. Human evil has to do with placing the demands of self-interest above the demands of morality.

Given the fact of radical evil, Kant is worried about how human beings can ever be justified in their own eyes and in the face of God. For morality demands perfection but we are always morally imperfect. And, given this fact, Kant needs to explain how we can ever come to have a good will and be pleasing to ourselves and to God who knows the secrets of our hearts, for at any moment in time, it is impossible for us to have such a will. Kant's solution to this problem is to appeal to a dynamic rather than static notion of moral character. What is important morally is not what we are now and what we have done, but where we are going. Although we cannot be perfect at any particular moment in time, we can strive for a gradual and continuous improvement of our moral character over time, and we can reasonably hope that given enough time we can gradually approach the moral perfection that morality requires. And it is this gradual but constant progress that our inner judge, and we hope God, can find morally pleasing. Although Kant's primary account of moral development is gradualist, involving the idea of gradual but constant moral improvement, he also finds room for the **Pietist** idea of a radical change of heart or **conversion**. For he thinks that starting on the road to constant and gradual improvement requires a radical change of heart, and a turning towards the good.

Another major topic in the *Religion* is the moral status of organized religion. Although Kant is a critic of much traditional organized religion, especially what he took to be its coercive aspect, he argues that a church, understood as an ethical community, plays an essential role in moral life, with the moral function of such a community being the help and encourage its members in their striving for moral perfection and to allow them to help one another to cultivate and develop their moral **virtue**. As such, the church and state have distinct moral purposes. The role of the state is to make and enforce laws of justice or **right**. As such the state is necessarily coercive, regulating the external behaviour of its citizens with the threat of sanctions. The role of the church is to encourage the virtue of its members and so must be a purely voluntary organization as it has to do with the internal motivation of its members and this motivation cannot be coerced by external threats, for the laws of virtue are not the sort of laws than can be enforced by coercive human institutions, as they have to do with an agent's character rather than with external actions. See: **religion; Pietism;** *Metaphysics of Morals*; **history.**

respect, feeling of

David **Hume** (1711–76) had famously argued that **reason** is incapable of producing motivation and is and can only be the slave of the passions. Kant, of course, denies this. Sometimes Kant suggests that Hume was wrong to think that only passions can motivate and seems to propose that reason can motivate us directly. In other places, however, Kant seems to accept Hume's claim that reason cannot be a motive for actions directly, but suggests that reason is capable of motivating us by causing a certain passion or feeling within us. Thus, in the *Critique of Practical Reason* (1788) Kant argues that consciousness of the moral law produces a certain feeling within us which he calls the feeling of respect for the **moral law**. This feeling is unlike all other feelings, for it has an **intelligible** *a priori* origin and the existence of such a feeling is a necessary condition for the possibility of morality. Without such a feeling it would be impossible to be moral. With his account of the feeling of respect, Kant is suggesting that practical reason can be the cause of its own motive.

Critics of Kant often accuse him of motivational rigorism. According to this criticism, Kant believes that actions are only morally good if they are motivated by this feeling of respect for the moral law, and this would seem to imply that being motivated by other feelings, such as love for your partner or friends, is immoral. If this interpretation of Kant were correct, then this would make his moral theory very unattractive, and there are such passages that suggest such a reading. There are, however, more charitable and plausible ways to interpret Kant. For example, in the *Metaphysics of Morals* (1797), instead of claiming that morality requires the existence of a single feeling of respect for the moral law, he argues that there are four feelings that lie at the basis of morality, which he calls (a) *moral feeling*, (b) *conscience*, (c) *love of one's neighbour* and (d) *respect* for oneself. There are good reasons to think that the four feelings listed here are four aspects of the single feeling of respect for the moral law identified in the *Critique of Practical Reason*. This gives us a way of understanding the way in which being motivated by love of one's partner or friends is compatible by being motivated by respect for the moral law. For, the feeling of love of others is part of the feeling of respect for the moral law, and as long as our love for others is a moral love, then there is no incompatibility between being motivated by love and being motivated by respect for the moral law. See: **feelings; love;** *Critique of Practical Reason.*

right (*recht*)

The German word *recht* can be translated either as right, law or justice, and so the notion of 'right' in Kant is broader than the word as it is normally used in English. Kant's most detailed discussion of right is to be found in the Doctrine of Right of the *Metaphysics of Morals* (1797). The Doctrine of Right is divided into sections on Private Right and Public Right. The main topic in the Private Right is Kant's account of the metaphysics of property and the nature juridical laws. Public Right, however, has to do with those laws that are necessary for bringing about a condition of Private Right, or what Kant sometimes calls 'the rightful condition'. So public right has to do with those laws that have to do with the organization of the state. See: **law**; *Metaphysics of Morals*; **duty**.

Rousseau, Jean-Jacques (1712–78)

Rousseau was an important Swiss-born French philosopher, whose thought played an important role in the French revolution (1789). His thought had a major impact on Kant's ethical thinking and apparently a portrait of Rousseau was the only picture Kant kept on display in his house. In his *Discourse on the Origin of Inequality* (1754) Rousseau argues, rejecting the traditional Christian doctrine of original sin, that man is born good with a natural feeling of sympathy to the suffering of other human beings, but is corrupted by society and culture that creates unnatural vices such as competitiveness. In his most influential work, the *On the Social Contract* (1762), Rousseau describes what he takes to be the only truly legitimate form of political society, which he names a republic, and Kant's idea of a **realm of ends** is modelled on Rousseau's account of a republic. In a republic each member of the society will be a citizen, and a citizen will be both the sovereign and subject to the laws of the society. For a law to be legitimate it must be truly general, which for Rousseau meant that it must come from all and apply to all and he thought that this was only possible if the society as a whole and each individual member had what he called a general will, the existence of which requires some sort of unanimous agreement between citizens. The problem here, however, is to explain how each individual member of a society, each of whom has their own particular will (which is the result of their particular contingent desires) could possibly reach any sort of unanimous agreement and hence acquire a general will. Rousseau's solution is to suggest that although individuals within a society cannot be expected to come to a unanimous agreement about particular decisions the society is to make, they may be able to come to such agreement as to the basic constitutional and institutional structure of the society. His solution can be illustrated by an example. Suppose a group of tourists are having a holiday together but only have a single means of transportation. Some of them would like to go and visit the ancient ruins at Ephesus, while others want to go to the beach. Now although this group may not be able to reach a unanimous decision about what to do, they might be able to reach unanimous agreement about how to decide what to do. For example, they might all be able to agree that the best way to make the decision is to toss a coin, or to have a vote. If, for example, everyone agrees to vote on it, then no one can complain if the decision goes against their own particular preference, for in a sense the decision was their decision even though the decision is not the decision they wanted; such a decision can be regarded as an expression of the group's general will, and if the decision procedure was really fair and all had really accepted it, then even if some individuals may not be happy with the decision, they have all in a sense willed it, and so the decision can be thought of as the expression not just of *all* of them but of *each* individual. Those individuals who agreed to the procedure but did not vote for the policy decided upon have in a sense two wills. They have both willed the decision, by agreeing to abide by the result of the procedure, but do not want to do what was decided upon. Their general will has endorsed the decision, even though what Rousseau calls their particular will is opposed to the decision. In such a case the moral thing to do is to submit one's particular will to one's general will. Similarly, in a society, individuals might not be able to agree unanimously on particular policies, but they might, in principle, be able to agree unanimously on the constitutional and institutional set up of the society, which is not about any particular decisions but determines, in a general way, the way in which particular decisions are made. And Rousseau argues that in becoming a member of a republic we give up our natural freedom to do whatever we want, but gain something much more valuable, which he calls 'moral freedom', and he defines moral freedom as being subject to laws one has made oneself. Rousseau's notion of 'moral freedom' had a strong influence on Kant's development of the idea of **autonomy**. See: **realm of ends**; *Conjectural Beginnings of Human History*; **autonomy**; **freedom**; **history**.

rules

Kant claims that whereas **reason** is the faculty of **principles**, the **understanding** is the faculty of rules. What Kant means by this is that **concepts** function as rules for classifying objects. They do this by serving as rules to potentially divide any set of objects into two classes: those that fall under the concept and those that do not. See: concepts; principles.

sensibility

Kant believes that human **cognition** involves the cooperation of three distinct faculties, which he calls sensibility, **understanding** and **reason**. Sensibility is the faculty to which objects are given to us through **intuition**. Kant argues that space and time are our forms of intuition so that we are only capable of intuiting objects that can exist in space and/or time, and so our sensibility is necessarily spatio-temporal. It is also partially passive, for in order to sense an object an object has to be given to us. Now, Kant argues the intuition of an object through sensibility is necessary for **cognition** for without sensibility no object would be given to us and our thoughts would be empty and lack significance. Thus, disagreeing with the **rationalists**, Kant argues that understanding and reason divorced from sensibility can provide us with no real knowledge. In claiming that sensibility and understanding are two distinct faculties, Kant is disagreeing with Leibniz who had argued that sensibility is merely a confused conceptual grasp of the world. Kant thought that Leibniz failed to sufficiently distinguish between **concepts** and objects. According to Leibniz, for any individual object there will be a unique and complete concept of the individual that can be thought of as something like the concept of a lowest species. We are unable to grasp such concepts, although they can be thought by God, and so our grasp of the concepts of an individual is always confused and this is what our experience of physical objects consists in – a confused understanding of something that is fully understood by God. Kant rejects this position, arguing that all concepts are general and indeterminate, in the sense that they can always be further specified, and thus Kant denied the possibility of a lowest species or complete concept of an individual. Not even God possesses complete concepts of individuals, for concepts are always incomplete and are an aspect of imperfect human cognition. God, if he exists, does not have a discursive understanding like ours which can only think of objects by applying concepts to objects presented in intuition; instead God, if he exists, thinks of individuals immediately by an act of intellectual intuition. See: **Intuition; Leibniz; Amphiboly of the Concepts of Reflection.**

series

The notion of a series plays an important role in Kant's theoretical philosophy, for it plays a central role in his understanding of **space, time,** number and **causation.** The word 'series' comes from the Latin for a row or chain (the Latin verb '*serere*' means to join or connect). A series is an ordered set of elements, and Kant thinks that a line is an ordered set of elements (although the elements of a line are themselves lines and not extensionless points). So the notion of a series plays an important role in his understanding of **space** and of **time,** because Kant thinks that we can only represent time to ourselves through the drawing of a line and that the order of time is that of a series. The temporal states of a physical object in motion are also ordered as a series, as are numbers, and so understanding Kant's understanding of a series is important for understanding his account of **mathematics** and motion.

Kant thinks that in a series there must be some sort of **relation** between the members, for otherwise we would just have a random jumble of element rather than an ordered series, and because the notion of a series is a logical one he thinks that the relations between the elements in a series must be a logical one. Now, Kant thinks that there were only three basic types of logical relation which he enumerates under the heading of relation in the tables of **judgements** and **categories** in the *Critique of Pure Reason* (1781/1787). In a **categorical judgement,** which is a subject-predicate judgement such as 'the table is heavy', we have the relation of inherence. In a **hypothetical judgement** (or conditional judgement), such as 'if the table is heavy, then it will fall when dropped', we have the relation between ground and consequence and in a **disjunctive judgement,** such as 'the ball is either heavy or it is not heavy', we have the relation of logical exclusion, for a ball being heavy excludes its being not heavy. Now, Kant thinks that we cannot explain the notion of an ordered series in terms of the notions of inherence or exclusion, and so he concludes that the hypothetical form of judgement must be the principle of the series. Kant's thought here is that hypothetical judgements can be combined together to form a chain or series of arguments. So, for example, the judgements 'if *a* then *b*' and 'if *b* then *c*' and so on can be combined to form an ordered chain of reasoning. The hypothetical form of judgement involves the notions of ground and consequence, and so in claiming that the hypothetical form of judgement is the principle of the series Kant is committed to the view that earlier members of a series are grounds of the later members of the series and the later members are consequences of these earlier members. So for example, the fact that time constitutes a series means that later moments of time are dependent upon earlier moments of time for their existence. Similarly, he thinks that in the number series the smaller numbers are the grounds of the later numbers. According to his constructive account of numbers the number seven, for example, is constructed by adding one to six, and so the number six is the ground of the number seven and the number seven is the consequence of adding one to six.

Given the logic of Kant's time, his arguments are quite plausible. For the ground-consequence relation seems to be the only logical relation in Kant's logical toolbox that seems suitable for generating an ordered series, and it is clear that a chain of grounds and consequences is one type of ordered series. Developments in modern logic, however, have shown us how we can understand (and define) the logical relation between the members of a particular series without appealing to the ground-consequence relation, by providing an implicit definition of a relation by providing a set of axioms. For example, we can implicitly define the logical relation between points on an infinite line by appealing to the theory of dense linear order. Let us call this relation '<'. We can implicitly define '<' by stating that: the relation '<' is the relation governed by the following axiomatization.

(1) $\neg (a < a)$ (irreflexivity)
(2) $a < c \ \& \ c < b \rightarrow a < b$ (transitivity)
(3) $a < b \lor b < a \lor a = b$ (connectedness)
(4) $\forall a \exists b \ (a < b)$
(5) $\forall b \exists a \ (a < b)$ (no endpoints)
(6) $\forall a \forall b \exists c \ (a < b \rightarrow (a < c < b))$ (denseness)

These six axioms provide an implicit definition for the relation of 'less than' for a dense linear order without endpoints. Modern logic, then, shows how we can understand the relation between members of a series without appealing to the relation of ground and consequence, for using such a method we can define a great number of different types of relations that can be used to generate different types of series. Modern logic, then, suggests that Kant was wrong to think that there were only three types of logical relation and that the hypothetical form of judgement is the principle of all series, although a chain of grounds and consequences is at least one type of series. See: **hypothetical judgement; mathematics.**

silent decade

Between his *Inaugural Dissertation* (1770) and the publication of the first edition of the *Critique of Pure Reason* (1781), Kant published nothing of substance, and scholars often refer to this period of his life as his silent decade. Although Kant was not publishing, he was working solidly on the ideas that were to become the first Critique. We have some evidence of the development of his ideas in this period from his unpublished notes and student transcripts of his lectures, many of which have been published and translated in to English. The notes are generally referred to his 'reflections' and have been numbered and so are generally referred to in the secondary literature by a capital 'R' followed by the number they have been given.

singular judgement

In the table of **judgements** of the *Critique of Pure Reason* (1781/1787) Kant claims that, when it comes to their **quantity**, all judgements are either **universal, particular** or singular. Singular judgements are of the form 'this (or the) *A* is *B*' and so the subject concept in a singular judgement picks out a single particular object. From the perspective of general **logic**, which merely examines the relationship between concepts, it does not matter whether a judgement is singular or universal, for both singular and universal judgements apply to all the objects that fall under the subject concept, it is just that in a singular judgement the 'all' is a single object. Thus, Kant argues, the distinction between single and universal judgements is one that strictly speaking only occurs in what he calls transcendental logic, which is not purely formal and deals with the relationship between concepts and objects. Kant derives the **category** of totality from this form of judgement. Kant does not clearly explain the purported relationship between singular judgements and the concept of totality, but his thought seems to have to do with the fact that the subject of a singular judgement is a particular object, and objects, unlike concepts, are completely (or totally) determinate. To understand what is meant by this it is necessary to understand his account of the relationship and distinction between **concepts** and objects. For Kant, concepts are essentially general and as such are indeterminate in regard to what is not included in the concept. So, for example, if we take the concept bachelor, there is a determinate answer to the question of the relationship between the concept bachelor and the concept unmarried, but insofar as we are merely analysing concepts, there is no determinate relationship between the concept bachelor and the concept happy. We cannot judge analytically that bachelors are happy; nor can we judge that bachelors are not happy. The concept happiness is neither included in nor excluded from the concept bachelor. Concepts, then, are general in the sense that they are indeterminate. Objects, however, are entirely different in this respect, for Kant thinks that for any arbitrary concept there is a determinate answer to whether or not the object falls under the concept. Objects, as opposed to concepts, then are subject to what Kant calls 'the principle of thoroughgoing determination' according to which for any arbitrary concept either the concept or its opposite must be applicable to the thing. In a singular judgement, then, the subject concept picks out and directly refers to a single object and so the subject of such a judgement (unlike the subject of a universal or particular judgement) is completely, or totally, determinate. And Kant's thought is that this notion of complete determination involved the concept of totality, and this seems to be why he thinks that the category of totality is required for the making of singular judgements. See: **judgements, table of.**

skepticism

A skeptic is someone who denies or doubts the possibility of knowledge. In the Preface to the *Critique of Pure Reason* Kant gives a schematic history of **metaphysics**, which, he notes, used to be called the queen of all the sciences. In the beginning he claims, metaphysics was **dogmatic**. Dogmatic metaphysicians are those who claim to have knowledge about the nature of reality without sufficient justification. Clearly Kant is here thinking of **rationalist** philosophers, such as **Descartes, Leibniz** and **Wolff**, who claimed to have knowledge of the nature and existence of God, the soul, and the world as it is in itself. This metaphysical dogmatism was overturned by skeptics such as **Hume** who showed that the claims of dogmatic metaphysicians were unjustified. Kant believes that this skeptical undermining of metaphysical dogmatism was a step in the right direction, but was not a stable resting place for a thinker being a form of intellectual anarchy or nomadism. Although not content with skepticism as a final resting place for thought, Kant does not advocate a return to dogmatism. Instead he advocates what he calls **critique**, and this is why the three central works in his philosophical system are called Critiques. Critical philosophy rather than starting with an attempt to understand the nature of the world begins by examining our capacity of knowledge or cognition with the goal of understanding the scope and limit of human cognition and the *a priori* principles that govern our knowledge of objects.

Kant also discusses skepticism in the **Refutation of Idealism**, a section he added to the *Critique of Pure Reason* in the second edition. Here Kant criticizes the view that all we can know immediately are our subjective mental states and not physical objects, for he believes that such a position leads to skepticism about the existence of external physical objects. Here Kant attacks the doctrine which either denies or doubts the existence of material objects in space outside of us. Elsewhere he will call the position he opposes **empirical idealism**. The first type of idealism he calls dogmatic idealism and attributes such a position to George **Berkeley** (1685–1753). The second type of idealism he calls problematic idealism and attributes such a position to René **Descartes** (1596–1650), although such a position is also defended by many empiricists. This second form of idealism leads to a form of skepticism about the existence of physical objects, for it assumes that we do not immediately perceive material objects but are immediately aware only of our own mental states, and have to infer the existence of material objects as the cause of these mental states. The problem is that it is difficult to explain what justifies such an inference, for if we are only aware of our own mental states, or sense data, what sort of evidence could we ever have that these mental states are caused by external material objects, which according to the theory can never be immediate objects of perception. Kant solution is to advocate a form of perceptual direct realism, which he sometimes calls empirical realism. This is the position that we immediately perceive material objects and not just our subjective mental states. He argues, however, that empirical realism is only tenable if one also accepts what he calls **transcendental idealism**, the view that claims that space and time are merely forms of intuition and that we can only know things as they appear and not as they are in themselves; and he argues that if one is a **transcendental realist**, one must be an **empirical idealist**. In other words, Kant believes that transcendental idealism is the only way of avoiding skepticism about the existence of material objects. See: **dogmatism; critique; Refutation of Idealism; Hume.**

Space

In the **Transcendental Aesthetic** of the *Critique of Pure Reason* (1781/1787) Kant famously argues that space and time are merely our forms of intuition, and that things as they are in themselves are not in space and time. In this section Kant rejects both the Newtonian and Leibnizian theories of space and time. Isaac **Newton** (1643–1727) and his followers had defended an absolute conception of space and had argued that space and time are entities with objects existing within them. According to such a view space and time could exist independently of any objects in them and the position of an object is determined by its location in absolute space. Gottfried Wilhelm **Leibniz** (1646–1716), in contrast, advocated a relative conception of space and time arguing that space and time are constituted by the relations between point-like objects. According to this view the spatial and temporal position of an object can be understood completely in terms of its relations to other objects. Kant rejects both of these theories and instead argues that space is a form of intuition and is ideal. Existing in space is, for Kant, a necessary condition for outer experience, for we can only intuit objects that can exist in space and time. However, just because existing in space is a necessary condition for experience, this does not imply that it is a necessary condition for existence in general, and there is no logical contradiction in the idea of an object, for example the idea of God, that does not and cannot exist in space, and although we have no justification for believing that an object corresponding to such an idea exists, we also have no justification for believing that such objects do not exist. See: Transcendental Aesthetic; Newton; Leibniz; time.

Spinoza, Baruch (1632–77)

Baruch, later Benedict, Spinoza was a Dutch Jewish philosopher of Portuguese descent. In this most important work, the *Ethics* (1677), he argues that there can be only one substance, which he calls God or nature, and that particular finite physical bodies and minds are not themselves individual substances but merely modes of this one substance. In terms of the relationship between mind and body, Spinoza rejects the **dualism** of René **Descartes** (1596–1650) and argues that the mental and physical are merely two aspects or attributes of a single underlying reality. As a consequence of his commitment to the principle of **sufficient reason**, Spinoza also defends a strong form of determinism, and argues that the belief in free will is an illusion. In the eighteenth century, Spinozism was generally regarded as synonymous with atheism. The **pantheism controversy**, sparked by the publication of the correspondence between Friedrich Heinrich **Jacobi** (1743–1819) and Moses **Mendelssohn** (1729–86) in 1785, led to a renewed interest in Spinoza in late-eighteenth-century Germany, which grew in the nineteenth century, and had a strong influence of the development of philosophical naturalism. See: **pantheism controversy; Jacobi; Mendelssohn; sufficient reason, principle of; rationalists.**

sublime

Sublime literally means to be raised up or to be set on high. In **aesthetics** the experience of the sublime has to do with our response to objects that are great or overpowering. It is clear that such experiences can produce a feeling of pleasure, but it is difficult to explain why we enjoy such experiences, because they involve feeling that we ordinarily find unpleasant or painful. For example, many people enjoy watching huge spectacles, riding on rollercoasters and watching horror films, but it is difficult to explain why we enjoy such experiences. The question of why we enjoy such experiences can be traced back to Aristotle's (384–322 BCE) discussion of tragedy in his *Poetics*. Aristotle had argued that although the events depicted in a tragedy were disturbing, the experience of watching tragedy led to a pleasurable, and morally improving, *catharsis* (or purging) of our emotions. Discussions of the sublime in the eighteenth century were also concerned with the problem raised by Aristotle of how certain feelings that are normally unenjoyable can be the source of pleasure. In the eighteenth-century aesthetics the relationship between the beautiful and the sublime was also a major topic of debate. Edmund Burke (1729–97) in his *Philosophical Enquiry into the Origin of Our Ideas of the Sublime and Beautiful* (1757) had argued that the experience of beauty and the sublime were distinct and incompatible aesthetic reactions and that the source of the sublime is whatever is in any sort terrible or operates in a manner analogous to terror. Burke, however, did not offer a plausible account of why we find such experiences enjoyable. Kant's **pre-critical** essay *Observations on the Feeling of the Beautiful and Sublime* (1764) is a response to Burke's work.

In the **Critique of Judgment** (1790) Kant also distinguishes between the feelings of the beautiful and the sublime. He argues that although both experiences involve a feeling of pleasure, the pleasure we get from a beautiful object is a result of the form of the object, whereas in the experience of the sublime we receive pleasure from a certain formlessness in the experience of the object. Kant distinguishes between two types of sublime, which he names the mathematically sublime and the dynamically sublime.

The mathematically sublime is Kant's name for the aesthetic experience we have when we experience something huge or great, such as the experience one has when observing the pyramids or entering St Peter's Basilica in Rome. Kant explains that in such experiences there is a feeling of the inadequacy of one's imagination for presenting the object as a whole made of parts, and this feeling produces a particular sort of pleasure. Kant believes that this feeling is produced when we experience objects that we are unable to fully grasp as totalities in intuition. For example, when we see huge pyramids from the right distance we experience the object as a whole, but we can also see that it is built from individual blocks, but there are too many blocks for us to grasp the whole as constructed from the individual blocks. There are too many of them for us to comprehend the whole as made up of a determinate number of blocks. There are too many parts for us to take in and enumerate, and so it feels to us as if the object is made up of uncountably many parts. In such experiences our recognition of the inability to take in the magnitude of the object gives us a feeling of the infinitude of the object. And this feeling is, Kant argues, pleasurable. Now this feeling of infinity is really a recognition of the incapacity of our imagination, and one might think that recognition of an inability would be painful, not pleasurable. Normally when we recognize that we cannot do something, the feeling we experience is one of frustration, not one of pleasure. Kant thinks, however, that this recognition of the incapacity of imagination gives us the feeling that there is more than the world of sense, for in a way such experiences transport us, at least in terms of feeling, into the intelligible realm. The feeling of displeasure brought about by the recognition of the inadequacy of our imagination is outweighed by the feeling of pleasure we get from the recognition of the fact that our reason transcends our sensibility.

The dynamically sublime, on the other hand, involves experiencing the terrifying power of nature but feeling it as a power that has no dominion over us. In such cases we recognize the destructive power of nature but feel safe. Two of Kant's own examples are the pleasures we get from experiencing overhanging and seemingly threatening cliffs, or violent thunderstorms. Contemporary examples might be the pleasure we get from riding on rollercoasters and watching horror films. Kant argues that the dynamically sublime involves the feeling of fear. Normally fear is not pleasurable. But we get pleasure if we recognize something as fearful but are not afraid. A good way of having such an experience is through artistic representations of the threatening power of nature. In such cases we recognize the awesome and threatening power of nature, but know that we are safe. For example, in the cinema we may experience a terrifying storm, and recognize that if we were actually there we would probably die. We recognize the storm as threatening, but we are not threatened. Such experiences allow us to feel our moral **freedom** in the face of nature. Such experiences allow us to feel that however threatening nature may be to us, it is always possible for us to resist this power, to stand up to the force of the storm and do the right thing, and this feeling of our own moral freedom, the felt recognition of our capacity to do the right thing in the face of potential threats to our life is, Kant believes, immensely pleasurable. See: *Critique of Judgment*; beauty.

substance

The **category** of substance is the first category of relation presented in the table of **judgements** of the *Critique of Pure Reason* (1781/1787). Kant derives the concept of substance from the **categorical** (subject-predicate) form of judgement. In such judgements something is predicated of the subject of the judgements, and Kant's suggestion is that the concept of substance is to be thought of in terms of the notion of a subject of predication, and the relationship of inherence between a substance and its accidents (or properties) can be understood in terms of the relationship of predication in a subject-predicate judgement. In the First **Analogy** Kant argues for the **principle** that in all change of appearances substance persists. It is important to note, however, that Kant thinks that this is only a principle that applies to objects of experience, and he argues in the **Paralogisms** against rationalist metaphysicians who opine that we know that the soul is a simple persistent substance. See: categories, table of; categorical judgement; Analogies of Experience; Paralogisms.

sufficient reason, principle of

The principle of sufficient reason, which was defended as a general principle governing all beings by rationalist philosophers, such as Baruch **Spinoza** (1632–77), Gottfried Wilhelm **Leibniz** (1646–1716) and Christian **Wolff** (1679–1754), is the principle that everything must have a reason, cause or explanation. The German for this principle is '*Der Satz vom Grund*' and the word '*Grund*' (ground) here can be translated either as reason or cause. The critical Kant rejects the principle of sufficient reason as a general principle. He agrees with the rationalists that it is a principle that can be applied to all objects of experience that exist in space and time, arguing in the Second **Analogy** that all alteration of phenomenal objects occurs in accordance with the law of the connection of cause and effect. So he is committed to the principle that everything that can be an object of experience must have a cause. He argues, however, that we have no justification for assuming that the principle applies *generally* to objects beyond those that are possible objects of experience (if any such objects exist). And so he denies that it is a principle that must govern things as they are in themselves. Critics of the principle of sufficient reason, such as Friedrich Heinrich **Jacobi** (1743–1819), argued that the principle implied fatalism, and if it were true, then this would imply that human free will was impossible. In the Third **Antinomy**, Kant argues that if the principle of sufficient reason is only a principle that applies to objects of experience, then this still allows room for the possibility of human free will because it allows us to think without contradiction that things-in-themselves are undetermined and hence free. Although as I must regard myself as fully determined insofar as I regard myself as a phenomenal object in the world, there is no contradiction in thinking that as I am in myself, I am free and capable of real spontaneity. See: **causation; rationalists; Leibniz; Wolff; Spinoza; Jacobi; pantheism controversy.**

summum bonum

See: **highest good**

Swedenborg, Emanuel (1688–1772)

Swedenborg was, in his early life, a respected engineer, mathematician and scientist and an important figure in the Swedish enlightenment. In 1744, however, he had a major mystical experience; he believed that he had personally encountered God, face to face, who had opened up his soul and revealed the world of spirits to him and commissioned him to spread the word about the true nature of the spirit world. After this he gave up his official position and concentrated on his spiritual writings. From this period onwards he had frequent visions of both heaven and hell, and wrote many books about his experiences. According to Swedenborg, heaven is a community of individuals governed by laws and each one of us while living in the body is already a member of some spiritual, or in Kant's language **intelligible**, community although entirely unaware of it, although after death, to use the words of his follower the British poet William Blake (1757–1827), there will be a 'cleansing of the doors of perception', and we come to see which intelligible community we belong to. Swedenborg also thought that it is up to us, and not God, to choose which spiritual community (either heaven or hell) we belong to through the choice of our character. After his death, his followers founded a Swedenborgian Church, the church of the New Jerusalem, which exists to this day.

Kant's pre-critical *Dreams of a Spirit-seer elucidated by Dreams of Metaphysics* (1766) is an evaluation of Swedenborg's eight-volume *Heavenly Secrets*. In this work Swedenborg, among other things, recounts his visions of heaven and his experiences of the world of spirits. Although Kant thought that Swedenborg was probably insane, his reading of Swedenborg was important in his development. On the one hand, Kant's engagement with Swedenborg was a step on his road to the rejection of rationalist metaphysics, for Kant came to the conclusion that such metaphysical speculation about the nature of things-in-themselves was insane in a way analogous to Swedenborg's visions of heaven, being based on a type of hallucination. On the other hand, there are reasons to think that his reading of Swedenborg had a positive influence on Kant's ethical theory and played a role in the development of his idea of a **realm of ends**; indeed, Swedenborg himself sometimes calls heaven a kingdom of ends. Thus, Kant was quite congenial towards Swedenborg's modern conception of heaven as a spiritual community and the idea that the spiritual (or intelligible) world is not somewhere we are transported after death, but is an intelligible community of which we are already members, although without being able to intuit it. In addition Kant was also deeply struck by Swedenborg's suggestion that it is up to us to determine which type of spiritual community we belong to and that in choosing a particular moral character we are choosing to be members of a community of similar characters. See: *Dreams of a Spirit-Seer*; enthusiasm; metaphysics; realm of ends.

sympathy

Kant defines sympathy (or compassion) as our capacity to enjoy or be pained by the joy or pain of others. Philosophers such as Jean-Jacques **Rousseau** (1712–78) and **David Hume** (1711–76) had placed the feeling of sympathy at the heart of their moral theories. Hume, for example, argues that being moral involves being motivated by the feeling of sympathy. Kant rejects such a central role for the feeling of sympathy for he thinks that morality requires being motivated by respect for the moral law, and he points out that sympathy can be the source of bad as well as good actions. A naturally sympathetic person may by moved by sympathy to help a vicious person achieve their immoral goals. In addition, Kant thinks that an individual with a **good will** helps others in need even if their capacity to feel sympathy has been impaired. So the feeling of sympathy is neither sufficient nor necessary for moral action. However, although he does not give the feeling of sympathy a central motivation role in his moral theory, he does argue in the *Metaphysics of Morals* (1797) that we have a duty to cultivate our capacity to feel sympathy. See: **feelings**; **duty**; **love**; *Metaphysics of Morals*.

syllogism

A syllogism is a logical argument consisting of two premises and a conclusion which follows logically from the premises. One example of a syllogism is

Premise 1:   All men are mortal.
Premise 2:   Socrates is a man.
Conclusion: Socrates is Mortal.

The first premise here is called the major premise, the second the minor premise and taken together they imply the conclusion. Kant distinguishes between **reason,** which he understands to be the faculty of making syllogistic inferences (the German word for 'syllogism' is 'vernunftschluss' which literally means an 'inference of reason'), and the **understanding,** which he calls the faculty of **concepts.** Kant often claims that reason seeks the unconditioned. And this claim can be better understood if we remember that for Kant reason is the faculty of syllogistic thinking. In a syllogism the truth of the two premises is a condition for the truth of the conclusion, and so the conclusion is conditioned by the premises. In a valid syllogism the premises imply the conclusion. This is not enough, however, to establish the truth of the conclusion, for to do this, we must prove that the premises are also true, and to do this is to present the premises as the conclusions of yet prior premises, and so as themselves conditioned, and so on. Thus, in claiming that reason seeks the unconditioned, Kant means that reason seeks (although is never able to find) complete justification. Reason is not content to derive conclusions from premises, but also always demands that we prove the premises of any argument and restlessly seeks for foundations for our thought that do not themselves require justification. See: **reason.**

synthetic

See: **analytic**

synthetic *a priori*

Kant claims that the task of his theoretical philosophy was to explain the possibility of synthetic *a priori* knowledge. Examples of synthetic *a priori* knowledge are the truths of **mathematics** and certain general principles about the physical world. Thus, Kant argues that all mathematical knowledge is synthetic *a priori*. This includes statements of arithmetic, such as $7 + 5 = 12$, and truths of geometry, such as the judgement that the shortest distance between two points is a straight line. Kant believes that mathematical truths are universal and necessary and so *a priori*, but they are also applicable to the physical world, which, Kant believes, implies that they are also synthetic. He also argues that a part of our knowledge of the physical world, and in particular the most basic principles of natural science, is synthetic *a priori* knowledge. Some of the examples he gives of such knowledge are the fact that in all alterations the quantity of matter remains unaltered, that in all communication of motion effect and counter effect must always be equal and that all alterations occur in accordance with the law of the connection of cause and effect. In claiming that such knowledge is *a priori*, Kant is claiming that this knowledge is not empirical, and these judgements are both necessary and strictly universal. In claiming that such knowledge is **synthetic**, Kant is claiming that these judgements do not just provide us with knowledge of our concepts, but provide us with insight into the object our concepts refer to.

To help understand what Kant means by this, it is helpful to compare Kant's position with that of **David Hume** (1711–76). In his *Enquiry Concerning Human Understanding* (1748) Hume had argued that all beliefs are either about matters of fact or about relations of ideas, and he argues that knowledge of matters of fact is always contingent, whereas when it comes to relations of ideas we can provide demonstrations or proofs. Knowledge of relations of ideas can provide us with no knowledge of the world. To use Kant's terminology we could say that knowledge of matters of fact is always **synthetic** and *a posteriori*, whereas knowledge of relations of ideas is **analytic** and *a priori*. Hume then denies the possibility of synthetic *a priori* knowledge. Hume agrees with Kant that mathematical knowledge is *a priori*, but he argues that it is **analytic** rather than **synthetic**, and Hume denies that we can have any *a priori* knowledge about the physical world. Instead Hume argues that there are certain beliefs that we naturally form about the physical world, such as the belief that events are causally related, but that such beliefs are not justified, but arise naturally because of habit. As such, these beliefs do not constitute knowledge.

Kant has two problems with Hume's position. First, with regard to mathematics, Kant argues that if mathematical truths were analytic, then we would have no way of explaining the application of mathematical knowledge to the world. **Mathematics** does not just tell us about the relationships between our mathematical concepts but also tells us something about the relationships between things. If I have 5 coins and am given another 7 coins then I know that I have 12 coins. My ability to count allows me to learn about the world. And Kant thought that the case of geometry was even clearer, for our knowledge of geometry allows us to build bridges and cut oddly shaped cakes into equal-sized slices. If mathematical knowledge only concerned the relationship between ideas, how could mathematical knowledge tell us anything about the world? Concerning physics, Kant believes that Hume is too much of a **skeptic**, for Kant believes that the possibility of natural science requires some sort of *a priori* knowledge about the structure of the world. If Hume were right, then modern science does not really provide us with any real knowledge. So Kant felt he had to provide some sort of answer to Hume's challenge, and an explanation of how synthetic *a priori* knowledge is possible would be to provide such an answer.

Since the time of Kant, debates about the possibility of synthetic *a priori* knowledge have been a central topic of philosophical debate. For example, the axiomatization of arithmetic and geometry in the late nineteenth century led many philosophers to argue that the truths of mathematics are known *a priori*, but are **analytic**. For in an axiomatic system true statements are logically derived from the axioms. If an analytic truth is one that can be derived merely using definitions and the laws of logic, then the axiomatization of arithmetic and geometry would suggest that mathematical truths are analytic, although some defenders of Kant argue that many of the truths of modern quantificational logic are in fact synthetic. But the discovery of non-Euclidian geometry and the use of this geometry in relativity theory suggested another alternative. Euclidian and non-Euclidean geometry are both consistent geometries but they contain different axioms, and some philosophers have argued that the question of which geometry is true is ultimately an empirical matter, and the fact that the most successful physics now uses non-Euclidean geometry provides some evidence for the belief that physical space is non-Euclidean. If this is right then, for example, the claim that the shortest distance between two points is a straight line, a claim that Kant presented as a paradigm case of a synthetic *a priori* judgement, is actually false! Developments in physics and geometry, then, suggest that even if geometrical judgements are synthetic, they are known *a posteriori* not *a priori*.

There have been similar debates about the possibility of synthetic *a priori* knowledge in physics. The principles that Kant himself thought were synthetic *a priori* were intended to play a role in the justification of Newtonian physics, and the development of relativity theory and quantum physics have shown that Newtonian physics only provides us with, at most, an approximation of the laws of the physical universe. Many of Kant's claims, then, seem to have been undermined by developments in modern physics. However, some philosophers of science have not totally rejected the notion of synthetic *a priori* judgements in physics. Kant's claims may have been too specific, but perhaps there are more general claims that really do have the status of synthetic *a priori* principles. Kant, for example, thought that the judgement that 'in all alterations the quantity of matter remains unaltered' was synthetic *a priori*, but developments in physics suggests that this specific claim is false, for mass can be converted into energy. However, modern mathematical physics, insofar as it provides mathematical equations to explain and predict change in the universe, seems to be committed to the presupposition that something is preserved in change. So perhaps the more general judgement 'in all alteration something is preserved' has something like the status of a synthetic *a priori* principle in mathematical physics. See: *Critique of Pure Reason*; *Metaphysical Foundations of Natural Science*; *Critique of Practical Reason*; *Critique of Judgment*; *a priori*; analytic/synthetic; mathematics.

synthetic method

Kant distinguishes between what he calls the analytic and synthetic methods in philosophy, and claims to be following the synthetic method in the *Critique of Pure Reason* (1781/1787) and chapter three of the *Groundwork of the Metaphysics of Morals* (1785). However, he claims to be following the **analytic method** in chapters one and two of the *Groundwork* and in the *Prolegomena to Any Future Metaphysics* (1783). The synthetic method starts with an examination of the elements of a particular sphere and proceeds to give an account of how these elements must be combined. See: **analytic method**.

systematicity

Reason is the faculty of making inferences, but is also a type of desire. For reason seeks systematicity and has as its goal the **idea** of the systematic unity of the **concepts** of the **understanding**. The idea of such a system of our concepts is the ideal of a complete tree of concepts, with the highest genus at the top. This highest genus would be divided into lower species and these lower species into still lower species until no further specification was possible, and then the system of our concepts would be complete. So, for example, we might think that highest genus as being the concept of an object. This concept could be divided into the concepts of living and non-living objects, living objects into animals and plants, etc. In a completely organized conceptual scheme all our concepts would be related in such a systematic way. Now, in order to organize our concepts in such a way, reason seeks for a set of principles that can serve as the foundation for such specification. Now, this idea of a set of principles that can be used to produce a completely specified conceptual scheme can only serve as a regulative ideal, for what it seeks is impossible, for Kant is committed to the view that all concepts are essentially specifiable and so believes that the idea of a lowest species, that is, the complete concept of an individual that cannot be divided into distinct species, is impossible. However, although such an ideal set of principles cannot be found, the search for such principles plays an essential role in the organization of our conceptual scheme and the development of our understanding of the world. Kant also argues that this ideal of reason is the source of our idea of God, and he says that, through what he calls transcendental illusion, we mistake the ideal of such a set of principles which could function to bring complete unity to our conceptual scheme, and in a sense be the source of all our concepts, for the cognition of an individual being that is the source of all essences. That is, we mistake the regulative ideal of such a set of principles for a cognition of **God**. See: **reason; ideal.**

thing-in-itself

At the heart of Kant's doctrine of **transcendental idealism** is the distinction between **appearances** (**phenomena**) and things-in-themselves, together with the claims that although we can have *a priori* knowledge of appearances, we can have no knowledge of things as they are in themselves. Although central to his whole philosophy, there is no consensus among commentators on how to interpret this distinction. Some commentators offer a metaphysical interpretation of the distinction, according to which appearances and things-in-themselves are distinct kinds of objects. Such commentators often claim to be offering a 'two worlds' or 'two object' interpretation of Kant's **transcendental idealism**. On this view there is a causal relationship between things-in-themselves and appearances, and commentators who offer such an interpretation are often extremely critical of transcendental idealism, arguing that although Kant claims that we can know nothing about things-in-themselves, the doctrine of transcendental idealism presupposes a significant amount of knowledge of the nature of things-in-themselves, for example, that such objects exist and that they are the causes of appearances. Other commentators, often aiming to provide a more attractive interpretation of Kant's position, argue for a non-metaphysical, epistemic interpretation of the distinction, and defenders of such an interpretation often also claim to be offering a two-aspect, rather than two worlds, reading of the distinction. According to this view there is only one world or set of objects, but there are two ways of regarding this one world. The distinction is not between two types of object, but between two types of concepts of an object. The phenomenal concept of an object includes reference to the necessary conditions of experience, and so is the concept of a spatio-temporal object, whereas the concept of an object as thing-in-itself abstracts from all human cognitive capacities. See: **transcendental idealism**; **phenomena**; *Critique of Pure Reason*; Transcendental Aesthetic; Paralogisms of Pure Reason; Antinomies of Pure Reason.

transcendent

To 'transcend' literally means to climb over a limit or obstacle. So something is 'transcendent' if it is beyond some sort of limit. Kant usually uses this word to signal his criticism or disapproval of a particular position. In particular, he believes that the **rationalist** philosophers often make claims that illegitimately transcend the limits of experience, and so Kant normally uses this word in a negative sense to signal that he believes that a position is making unjustified claims to knowledge of objects that are beyond the possibility of experience. The rationalists believed that we can have knowledge of objects, such as God and the soul, that are beyond the limits of human experience, and they thought it was the task of **metaphysics** to discover truths about such objects. Kant, in contrast, argues that our knowledge is limited to what we can experience. A transcendent claim is one that goes beyond the limit of our knowledge and a transcendent object is one that is in principle inaccessible to us because it could never be a possible object of experience. Philosophers who claim to know things that cannot be known are engaged in transcendent philosophy and this is a bad thing. Kant sometimes calls his own type of philosophy **transcendental**, as opposed to transcendent. See: **metaphysics**, **transcendental**.

transcendental

Although Kant rejects the possibility of **transcendent** knowledge, he does allow for the possibility of transcendental knowledge and sometimes calls his type of philosophy 'transcendental philosophy'. In the Introduction to the *Critique of Pure Reason* he explains that transcendental philosophy is not concerned with our knowledge of objects but with our *a priori* concepts of objects. In particular Kant believes that there are certain concepts and principles that are necessary conditions for the possibility of experience and transcendental philosophy aims at discovering these concepts and principles. In traditional rationalist **metaphysics** it was assumed that we could have knowledge of certain objects, such as **God** and the soul that could not possibly be objects of experience. Kant denies the possibility of such **transcendent** knowledge. Transcendental philosophy, in contrast, is not concerned with the nature of such objects, but with our capacity to know objects, and Kant's project is to examine how human knowledge is possible. He argues that human cognition of objects is governed by certain *a priori* principles and subject to certain limitations, and the task of the *Critique of Pure Reason* (1781/1787) is to map these principles and concepts and ascertain the limits of human knowledge. Although he thinks that such an examination cannot provide us with knowledge of things as they are in themselves, it can tell us something about what objects must be like if they are to be knowable by us, and so can provide us with *a priori* knowledge of possible objects of experience. See: *Critique of Pure Reason*; transcendent; metaphysics.

Transcendental Analytic

Following the fairly short **Transcendental Aesthetic**, most of the *Critique of Pure Reason* (1781/1787) is taken up by a very long section called the Transcendental Logic, and this itself is divided into two main sections: the Transcendental Analytic and the **Transcendental Dialectic**. The Transcendental Analytic is the positive part of the work, where Kant tries to prove that there are certain *a priori* principles that govern the world as it appears to us. The Transcendental Analytic is itself divided into two mains sections. First, in the Analytic of Concepts, Kant introduces his table of **judgements** and table of **categories**, and then in the **Transcendental Deduction** tries to argue that these categories have **objective validity**, that is to say that we are justified in applying these *a priori* logical concepts to objects in the world. Second, in the Analytic of Principles, Kant attempts to prove the existence of specific *a priori* principles that govern the application of the categories. The most influential section of the Analytic of Principles is the **Analogies of Experience**, where Kant tries to justify principles governing the application of the categories of relation to the world. So, for example, in the Second Analogy, which concerns the concept of **causation**, Kant attempts to justify the principle that all alterations in the world must have some cause. See: **metaphysics; Critique of Pure Reason; categories, table of; judgements, table of; Transcendental Deduction; Analogies of Experience; causation.**

Transcendental Aesthetic

The Transcendental Aesthetic is the first major section of the *Critique of Pure Reason*. In this section Kant rejects both the Newtonian and Leibnizian theories of space and time. Isaac **Newton** (1643–1727) and his followers had defended an absolute conception of space and had argued that space and time are entities with objects existing within them. According to such a view, space and time could exist independently of any objects in them, and the position of an object is determined by its location in absolute space. Gottfried Wilhelm **Leibniz** (1646–1716), in contrast, advocated a relative conception of space and time and argued that space and time are constituted by the relations between point-like objects. According to this view, space and time could not exist independently of any objects and the spatial and temporal position of an object can be understood completely in terms of its relations to other objects. For example the plate on the table is to the right of the fork and to the left of the knife; and all that is involved in having a spatial position is to stand in such relations (such as, 'to the left of' and 'to the right of') to other objects. Kant rejects both these theories. His main objection to the Newtonian theory is that if space and time are mind-independent entities, it is impossible to explain our knowledge of them. His main objection to the Leibnizian theory is that it assumes that the parts of space are prior to the whole, whereas Kant is convinced that the whole is, at least in some sense, prior to the parts. The **critical** Kant also, and relatedly, rejects the Leibnizian position that the basic constituents or parts of space are extensionless points and instead argues that the parts of a particular space are themselves spaces. Thus, for Kant a line is not made of points, but the parts of a line are themselves lines (and so on *ad infinitum*) and points are not parts but limits of a line.

Kant's alternative to the positions of both Leibniz and Newton is that our representations of space and time are *a priori* **intuitions**. Kant believes that Space and Time are *a priori* representations because he believes that they are conditions for the possibility of experience and so could not have been abstracted from experience as empirical concepts are. In saying this Kant rejects the notion that we could have acquired the concept of 'space' in the same way as we acquire an empirical concept such as 'dog'. Kant's thought is that although we do not need to possess the concept 'dog' to experience dogs, our ability to experience spaces presupposes a prior representation of 'space'. It is a fact that people can experience dogs without having the concept 'dog'; one can experience a dog without experiencing it as a dog; and it is this fact that explains the fact that the concept 'dog' can be acquired empirically. We experience many different objects and over time we notice similarities and differences between them and we group together objects that are similar and create names, such as 'dog', for them. This story of empirical concept acquisition presupposes that we can experience the objects prior to the possession of the concept and Kant's argument is that we cannot tell a similar story about the concept of 'space'. If 'space' were an empirical concept like 'dog', we would have to be able to experience spaces without experiencing them *as* spaces. To be able to abstract the concept of 'space' from our experience of spaces, we would have to experience these spaces not merely as different, but in difference places; but to experience two things as in different places is to experience them *as* in space, and so presupposes a representation of space. So, Kant concludes, our representation of space cannot be an empirical concept and hence must be *a priori*.

Kant's second main claim is that our representations of space and time are not concepts but intuitions. In claiming this Kant is rejecting the Leibnizian theory that space and time are reducible to logical relations. Kant's main argument for this rests on his understanding of the relationship between space and spaces. His claim is that particular spaces must be thought of as parts of space as a whole, and that space is prior to its parts. The relations between space and spaces is very different from that between a concept and its instances. Individual dogs are not part of the concept dog, instead they are instances of the concept – they fall under the concept. Particular spaces, in contrast, are not essentially *instances* of the concept 'space', but are *parts* of space.

From the fact that space and time are *a priori* intuitions Kant concludes that they are forms of intuition and as such are merely subjective conditions of human experience and that things-in-themselves are not spatio-temporal. For us to experience objects, we must experience them as in space and time. Kant names objects that can be experienced phenomena and he argues that because space and time are our *a priori* forms of intuition, we can know *a priori* that **phenomena** must be spatio-temporal. This is the positive conclusion he draws from the Transcendental Aesthetic. He also draws a negative conclusion, arguing that because space and time are merely our subjective forms of intuition, **things-in-themselves**, if such things exist, are necessarily non-spatio-temporal. He names this doctrine **transcendental idealism**. Although we can have no knowledge of things that cannot exist in space and time, we can, however, have the ideas of things that cannot exist in space and time, for example God or angels. Now a materialist will argue that space and time are not merely conditions for the possibility of experience but also conditions for the possibility of existence and so will argue the fact that God cannot exist in space and time implies that God does not exist. Kant rejects such materialism as dogmatic. And he calls this position **transcendental idealism.** See also: Thing-in-itself, Phenomena, intuition; Newton; Leibniz; space.

Transcendental Deduction

Kant claims that the Transcendental Deduction of the *Critique of Pure Reason* (1781/1787) was the section of the first *Critique* that he found most difficult to write and he completely rewrote it for the Second Edition, and so there are two different versions of which are commonly referred to by commentators as the 'A' and 'B' Deductions. The goal of the **Transcendental Deduction** is to prove the **objective validity** of the **categories,** which is to justify our application of these logical concepts to objects of experience. The categories are logical categories derived from the forms of logical judgement enumerated in the **table of judgements.** So, for example, Kant argues that the ground-consequence relation is a logical relation that holds between our judgements. He also thinks, however, that we apply this notion of ground and consequence to objects in the world when we make causal judgements, for a cause is a ground and an effect is its consequence, and the question he asks is: What right do we have to assume that a relation that holds between thoughts also holds between objects in the world? What justifies our taking a subjective relation that holds between judgements as an objective relation that holds between objects? This is the question of the **objective validity** or reality of the categories. So Kant is asking: What right do we have to assume that concepts that necessarily structure our thinking must also structure the external world of objects? Thus, Kant himself famously distinguishes between what he calls the *quid facti* (the 'what' or question of fact) and the *quid juris* (the 'what' or question of right) and claims that the main aim of the Transcendental Deduction is to establish the *quid juris*, explaining our entitlement to apply the logical categories to objects of experience. His general strategy will be to argue that the application of the categories to experience is a necessary condition for the possibility of experience of spatio-temporal objects.

In the 'A' Deduction Kant presents his famous account of the threefold synthesis. According to this account, experience involves three forms of what Kant calls synthesis. The best way of thinking of these three forms of synthesis is as three capacities that the mind requires in order to experience objects in space and time. The *first* form of synthesis is what Kant calls the synthesis of apprehension in the imagination, and involves our capacity to grasp the modifications of our mind as existing in time. Our subjective experience is necessarily experienced as a flow and so this capacity has to do with our ability to grasp a plurality of distinct experiences as part of a unified temporal flow of experiences. The *second* form of synthesis is what Kant calls the synthesis of reproduction in imagination. This involves our capacity to make associations between experiences, and empiricist philosophers who defended a form of associationist psychology thought that our experience of the world could be explained purely in such associationist terms. It is this capacity that lies at the heart of David **Hume**'s (1711–76) account of the functioning of the human mind, according to which we come to associate experiences through the operation of habit. The third form of synthesis is what Kant calls the synthesis of recognition in the concept. This form of synthesis involves our capacity to recognize bits of the world as falling under *a priori* concepts, and Kant argues that this capacity requires a form of self-consciousness, which is the consciousness of the numerical unity of the self, which Kant calls the **transcendental unity of apperception**. He argues that the transcendental unity of apperception is a necessary condition for the cognition of objects. And so, any condition for the possibility of the unity of apperception will also be a condition for the cognition of objects. And Kant seems to want to show that using the categories is a necessary condition for the unity of consciousness, and because of this categories are somehow necessary in experience of the world. It is not clear, however, exactly how this argument is supposed to work. Kant's discussion of **apperception** is developed further in the 'B' Deduction.

Now, many readers of Kant assume that Kant, in providing his account of the threefold synthesis, is basically offering a sausage factory theory of experience. According to such a misreading, the mind is like a sausage factory. In goes the messy raw material, it goes through a three-stage process and out pops a nice, clean sausage. According to such a reading, the raw data is our immediate awareness of our own subjective states, perhaps thought of as something like sense data, and this raw material is processed by the mind which first becomes aware of its own inner sensations, then associates this raw data. Once enough associations have been made, it is then finally able to apply concepts – a process that transforms our experience of our own subjective states into the experience of an objective world. But such an interpretation gets Kant's story back to front. Kant is not trying to give an account of the way in which the mind processes information but is instead offering a transcendental argument. He is not attempting to explain how the mind transforms subjective experiences into the experience of an objective world, but instead is offering an argument to show that our experience of our subjective states as in time is only possible on the assumption that we are immediately aware of a world of objects subject to the categories. His goal here is the same as in the **Refutation of Idealism** and is to show that that the experience of objects of **outer sense** is a necessary condition for the experience of our own mental states as objects of **inner sense**. Kant's strategy, then, is to argue that the capacity to recognize our own mental states through inner sense (the first form of synthesis) presupposes our capacity to associate our representations (the second form of synthesis) and that this capacity in turn presupposes that we can recognize objects as subject to the categories (the third form of synthesis).

The relationship between the A and B editions of the Transcendental Deduction is not clear. Early reviewers of the first edition had attacked Kant for defending a form of subjective idealism akin to **Berkeley**'s, and the changes between the two editions may have been intended to block such a misreading of his position. It seems that in his rewriting of the text he attempted to cut down on his psychological and phenomenological language, and in the B Deduction he stresses the logical and methodological aspects of his arguments. For this reason, those commentators who advocate a more metaphysical reading of Kant's argument tend to prefer the A Deduction, while those who advocate a more epistemological interpretation prefer the 'B' Deduction.

One of the biggest controversies among commentators regarding the 'B' edition has to do with whether the text is supposed to offer a single long argument or whether it offers a number of distinct arguments for the same conclusion. The reason for these disagreements is that Kant seems to reach identical conclusions about the necessary role of the categories in experience both at the end of section 20 and at the end of section 26. Some commentators have taken this to mean that Kant offers two quite distinct arguments for this conclusion. Most commentators, however, believe that these two parts are intended to offer two stages in a single proof. It is not exactly clear, however, how the two parts of the argument are supposed to work together. One influential suggestion is that the first part of the argument (up until section 20) is designed to show that the application of the categories is necessary for any *unified* experience, whereas the second part (from sections 21 to 26) is designed to show that our sensible spatio-temporal experience is necessarily unified. If Kant succeeded in proving both of these steps, he would have proved that the application of the categories is a necessary condition for our sensible spatio-temporal experience.

Transcendental Dialectic

The longest portion of the *Critique of Pure Reason* (1781/1787) by far is the Transcendental Logic and this consists of two main sections: the **Transcendental Analytic** and the Transcendental Dialectic. In the Transcendental Dialect Kant criticizes the arguments of traditional rationalist metaphysicians claiming to provide *a priori* knowledge of the soul, the world and of God. Kant lectured on metaphysics for over 20 years and used Alexander Gottlieb **Baumgarten**'s (1714–62) *Metaphysics* as his textbook. Following the rationalist Christian **Wolff** (1679–1754), Baumgarten divided metaphysics into general metaphysics (ontology) and special metaphysics. Ontology (general metaphysics) was understood to be the study of being as being in general and examined the categories and principles that had to be applied to objects in general, irrespective of the type of object involved. Special metaphysics was concerned with our *a priori* knowledge of particular objects or types of object and was divided into three special sciences corresponding to the three objects of rational cognition: the soul, the world and God. Rational psychology was concerned with *a priori* knowledge of the *soul*; rational cosmology dealt with *a priori* knowledge of the *world*; and rational theology dealt with *a priori* knowledge of *God*. The structure of the *Critique of Pure Reason* is based on this structure.

The Transcendental Analytic replaces Baumgarten's ontology, and the Transcendental Dialectic covers the topics of Baumgarten's special metaphysics, although Kant rejects the possibility of rational psychology, cosmology and theology. His reason for this is that although we have the ideas of the soul, the world and of God, we do not have any experience of objects corresponding to these ideas and so can have no cognition involving these matters. The Transcendental Dialectic is divided into three main sections: The **Paralogisms of Pure Reason** examines our idea of the soul and criticizes the arguments found in rational psychology; the **Antinomies of Pure Reason** examines our idea of the world, and criticizes the arguments found in rational cosmology; and the Ideal of Pure Reason examines our idea of God, and criticizes the arguments of rational theology. See: **reason; idea; metaphysics; Paralogisms of Pure Reason; Antinomies of Pure Reason; ontological argument.**

transcendental illusion

In the Transcendental Dialectic of the *Critique of Pure Reason* (1781/1787) Kant explains that the errors of rationalist metaphysicians such as René **Descartes** (1596–1650), Gottfried Wilhelm **Leibniz** (1646–1716) and Christian **Wolff** (1679–1754) are due to a natural illusion that has its source in the nature of human **reason**. Human reason constructs **ideas** of the soul, the **world** as a whole and of **God**, and these three ideas are the source of a natural illusion, because although they are merely subjective ideas, we naturally mistake knowledge of these ideas for *a priori* knowledge of **transcendent** objects corresponding to these ideas. Kant names this mistaking of knowledge of these three ideas for knowledge of three objects transcendental illusion. Kant thinks that such illusion arises naturally and unavoidably, and involves mistaking a subjective condition of thought for the cognition of an object. And he argues that this illusion of reason is unavoidable in the same way a visual illusion is. Just as we cannot help but see a stick in water as looking bent, Kant thinks that the subjective principles of reason *seem* objective to us. Although this illusion is in a sense inevitable, as in the case of visual illusion, once we recognize it for what it is, we can avoid being led into making false judgements as a result of it. Although we cannot avoid seeing a straight stick in water as bent, if we know that a straight stick looks bent in water, the fact that it looks bent does not lead us to judge that it actually is bent. Similarly, although we cannot avoid the illusion of thinking of the ideas of the soul, the world as whole, and God as providing us with access to objects that transcend our experience, once we recognize this fact we can avoid drawing false conclusions from these illusions. See: **Paralogisms of Pure Reason; Antinomies of Pure Reason; reason; metaphysics.**

transcendental idealism

Transcendental idealism is the name Kant gives to his own philosophical position. According to this doctrine, space and time are merely forms of **intuition** and we can only have knowledge of things as they appear in space and time, or what Kant calls the phenomenal world. We can have no knowledge of **things-in-themselves**, which are not in space and time. How exactly to interpret this doctrine has been a major topic of debate among Kant scholars. Some interpreters, who defend what is known as a two-world interpretation, think that the distinction between the world of phenomena and things as they are in themselves is a distinction between two types of objects, with things-in-themselves being the cause of appearances. Other commentators, defending what is known as a two-aspect interpretation, argue that the distinction between phenomena and things-in-themselves is a distinction between two aspects of the world. According to this interpretation, there is only one world or set of objects, but there are two ways of regarding this one world. The distinction is not between two sets of objects, but between different ways of thinking about objects. The phenomenal concept of an object includes reference to the necessary conditions of experience, and so is the concept of a spatio-temporal object, whereas the concept of an object as a thing-in-itself abstracts from all human cognitive capacities and limitations. And, because Kant thinks that space and time are our forms of intuition, the concept of a thing-in-itself is the concept of a thing insofar as it is not considered in spatio-temporal terms.

Kant argues that only a transcendental idealist can be an empirical **realist** as she believes that matter, as phenomena, has a reality that can be immediately perceived, and does not need to be inferred. Kant's thought here is that if we want to be direct realists about perception, believing that we immediately perceive physical objects in space and time rather than inferring their existence from the content of our sense data, then we need to assume that space and time are forms of intuition and not things-in-themselves. See: thing-in-itself; intelligible; phenomena; realism; Transcendental Aesthetic; *Critique of Pure Reason*.

transcendental realism

Kant himself claims to be a **transcendental idealist,** and so Transcendental realism is the name Kant gives the philosophical position he rejects. According to Kant Transcendental Realism is the doctrine that says space and time exist independently of our mental capacities, and that material objects that exist in space and time are things-in-themselves. Kant argues that a transcendental realist has to be an empirical idealist. What he seems to mean by this is that a transcendental realist has no way of explaining our knowledge of the material world. According to the transcendental realist, all we are aware of are our sensations, and we have to infer the existence of material objects in space and time that are the cause of these subjective sensations. The problem is that if we start with a picture of our relationship to the material worlds that is like this, it is impossible to explain how our inferences from our subjective sense data to the existence of a world of material objects in space and time can be justified. See: **transcendental idealism.**

transcendental unity of apperception

Kant claims in the **Transcendental Deduction** of the *Critique of Pure Reason* (1781/1787) that the transcendental unity of consciousness is a necessary condition for the cognition of objects. Apperception means reflective consciousness, and so what this means is that cognition of objects requires some sort of self-consciousness or, as Kant puts it, a representation of the 'I think'.

The representation 'I think', however, is a purely formal condition of thought that plays the role of unifying our thought and is not the experience or awareness of ourselves as an object. Kant is insistent that we should not confuse the representation 'I think', that is a necessary condition of thought and judgement, with the intuition of ourselves as objects; the transcendental unity of apperception is not a form of self-knowledge or self-cognition, for, as Kant argues in the **Paralogisms of Pure Reason,** we only know ourselves as we appear to ourselves and do not know ourselves as we are in ourselves.

Some commentators think that Kant's discussion of the transcendental unity of apperception is designed to form the basis of an anti-skeptical argument against a form of solipsism. The solipsist claims to know that he exists, but doubts the existence of a mind-independent world of objects. For an anti-skeptical argument to be successful, it must be based on premises that the skeptic can accept. Now the skeptic does not doubt his own existence as a unified subject of consciousness. So, if Kant can show that consciousness of oneself as a unified subject of consciousness presupposes knowledge of the existence of a world of independent objects, he would be able to offer an argument that might convince such a skeptic. Thus, those commentators who think that Kant, in the Transcendental Deduction, is trying to offer an anti-skeptical argument think that he is not just trying to prove that the unity of self-consciousness is a necessary condition for the cognition of objects, but the much stronger claims that the cognition of mind-independent objects is a necessary cognition for the transcendental unity of apperception. If he could prove this stronger claim, he should be able to convince the skeptic that knowledge of objects is a necessary condition for self-knowledge. See: **apperception; Transcendental Deduction; Paralogisms of Pure Reason; dualism.**

truth

Kant seems to accept a correspondence theory of truth because he argues that truth involves the agreement of cognition with its object. He is, however, more interested in giving an account of our criteria for truth rather than the nature of truth. Such an account would provide necessary and sufficient conditions for the truth of a judgement. Kant, however, believes that a general account of such conditions is impossible, and this lies behind his claim that we can have no knowledge of **things-in-themselves.** He argues, against some rationalists, that the principle of **non-contradiction** can only provide us with a negative criterion of truth. Kant calls that part of philosophy that deals with this negative criterion of truth **general logic**, and the fact that he thinks that the principle of non-contradiction only provides us with a negative criterion of truth means that Kant thinks, unlike the **rationalists**, that general **logic** can never provide us with any knowledge of objects. A judgement that contradicts itself cannot be true. As such, the principle of non-contradiction provides us with a necessary criterion of truth but not a sufficient one. The principle can be put to positive use in the case of **analytic** judgements, for we can establish the truth of an analytic judgement by demonstrating that its negation implies a contradiction. In the case of **synthetic** judgements, however, we need to go beyond the subject and predicate concepts and appeal to some 'third thing' to justify the combination of the concepts and the truth of the judgement, and Kant argues that there cannot be a sufficient criterion of truth here. In the case of *a posteriori* (empirical) synthetic judgements, the 'third thing' will be objects in the physical world. For example, to establish the truth of the judgement 'tables exist', we have to go out and find some tables. In the case of synthetic *a priori* judgements about the phenomenal world, the 'third thing' are the conditions for the possibility of experience. So, for example, Kant thinks we can prove the truth of a judgement such as 'every (phenomenal) event must have a cause' by showing that spatio-temporal experience would not be possible if this were not true. And Kant names that part of philosophy that deals with establishing the truth of such judgements transcendental **logic**. In the case of things-in-themselves, however, Kant thinks that we have no positive criterion of truth. There is, for example, no contradiction involved in the concept of **God**, and so the concept is logically possible. God, however, could not be a possible object of experience, for no object corresponding to the concept 'God' could be experienced in space and time. So we have no way of determining the truth of synthetic judgements about 'God', including the judgement 'God exists'. See: **synthetic** *a priori*; **analytic/synthetic**; *Critique of Pure Reason*.

unconditionally good/unconditional value

At the beginning of the *Groundwork of the Metaphysics of Morals* (1785) Kant claims that the only thing that has unconditional value is a **good will**. To understand what he means by this, it is important to distinguish between something having unconditional value and something having intrinsic value. If something has intrinsic value, it is valued for its own sake. If we value something for the sake of something else, then it has extrinsic as opposed to intrinsic value. Money, for example, has only extrinsic value, for we value money because we value what we are able to use if for. Now, if something has merely extrinsic value, then its value will be conditioned. So, for example, the value of money is conditioned by the fact that other people are willing to accept it for goods and services. However there are things that have conditional but intrinsic value, that is, things that we value for their own sakes, but the value of which is conditioned. Examples of such things would be **happiness** and the **pleasure** we get from satisfying desires. We value pleasure for its own sake, so the value of pleasure is intrinsic. However, Kant believes that the value of pleasure is conditioned by the value of the desire, for he believes that the value of pleasure that arises from satisfying a desire is conditioned by the moral character of the agent. Although the pleasure and happiness a virtuous person experiences is intrinsically good and desirable for its own sake, the pleasure that a serial killer gets from satisfying her desire to kill is not. For Kant, then, the value of pleasure and happiness is intrinsic but conditioned. See: **happiness**.

understanding

Kant distinguishes between three cognitive faculties: **sensibility**, understanding and **reason**. Sensibility is the faculty through which objects are immediately given to us in **intuition**. Understanding is the faculty of judging by means of **concepts**, and it is only through such judgements, which involve the subsumption of objects under the concepts of the understanding, that the objects given in sensibility can be thought. Reason is the faculty of principles and inferences, and it strives to unify the conceptual scheme of the understanding by attempting to systematize the concepts of the understanding through the use of principles. For Kant, experience and cognition of objects requires both understanding and sensibility, for experience involves the cognition of objects which involves subsuming the objects presented to the mind by sensibility under concepts. Thus, although Kant claims that without sensibility no objects would be given to us, without the understanding no objects would be thought. See: concepts; reason; sensibility; intuition.

universal judgement

In the table of judgements of the *Critique of Pure Reason* (1781/1787) Kant claims that, when it comes to their quantity, all judgements are either universal, particular or singular. Universal judgements are of the form 'all *a*s are *b*s', and Kant derives the category of unity from this form of judgement. Kant's thought here is that in a universal judgement we judge a particular domain to be unified; for we apply a single concept to all objects in the domain and in this way think of the domain as one. For example, in the judgement 'all even numbers are divisible by two', we think of all the even numbers as falling under one concept, and so think of the domain of even numbers in a unified way. See: judgements, table of.

universalizability, formula of

The formula of universalizability is the first formulation of the categorical imperative given in the *Groundwork of the Metaphysics of Morals* (1785). This formula states: act only according to that maxim through which you can at the same time will that it should become universal law. Kant explains that there are two ways in which a maxim can fail to be universalizable. Some maxims are such that it is impossible to conceive of a world in which they were a universal law. So, for example, Kant thinks that it is impossible to conceive of a world in which the maxim to make a lying promise when in need in order to alleviate one's need were a universal law, for in such a world no one would trust the word of anyone else. Therefore, the institution of promise-making would not be able to exist, and so a maxim to make a lying promise would be impossible because promises would not exist. There are other maxims, however, where, although it would be possible to conceive of a world in which such maxims were universal laws, it would not be possible to rationally will the existence of such a world. An example of such a maxim would be the maxim that when others are in need, always ignore their needs in order to focus on satisfying one's own desires. Although a world in which everyone adopted this as a maxim is conceivable, it is not possible to rationally will such a world, because willing such a world involves willing that no one would help anyone when they are in need, and this includes willing that no one would help me when I am in need. However, assuming that there will be times when the only way for me to achieve my ends is with the help of others, willing such a world would violate the **hypothetical imperative** which demands that if we will an end, we will the necessary means to that end. For insofar as one is rational, one must will the necessary means to one's ends, and so it would be irrational for me to will a world in which others do not help me when I am in need. The only way I can achieve my ends is with their help.

Critics of Kant, such as Georg Wilhelm Friedrich Hegel (1770–1831) have argued that the categorical imperative, and particularly the formula of universalizability, is empty formalism, and we cannot generate any positive moral content from it. Kant himself, however, is quite explicit that this formulation of the categorical imperative is supposed to be a purely formal principle, and it is only in the second formulation, the formula of **humanity**, that we are provided with a matter. Kant himself compares the formula of universalizability with the **principle of non-contradiction** in logic, which is also a purely formal principle and only provides us with a negative criterion of **truth**. For, Kant thinks that truth involves the correspondence of a concept with an object, and the mere fact that a concept is non-contradictory does not imply that there actually is or even could be an object corresponding to it. Similarly, the formula of universalizability does not, by itself, provide us with a positive criterion of what maxims we should have, but merely a negative criterion of which maxims are impermissible. The actual content of maxims comes from outside the will in the form of our actual needs, inclinations, feelings and contingent desires as well as from our recognition and respect for the humanity of others. And in the absence of particular content, reason does not demand that we adopt any particular maxim. Some commentators, however, think that positive duties to perform particular actions can be derived from the purely negative formula of universalizability, and there are some texts that support this as an interpretation of Kant's own position. But if it was Kant's own position, then it looks as if it is not consistent with his account of universalizability. For example, one might think that when what is impermissible is not doing something, then this implies a positive duty to do something. For example, if it were impermissible to not pay one's taxes, then this would suggest that we have a positive duty to pay our taxes. However, what the categorical imperatives rule out as impermissible are not specific actions but maxims. So, for example, one might think that the maxim never to pay taxes in order to keep more money to satisfy one's desire is a maxim that could not be universalized. But this does not imply that we must pay our taxes, for the maxim of not paying one's taxes in order to help force a repressive administration out of power might be fine. A more plausible and charitable reading of Kant's position is that he thinks that the formula of universalizability can only lead to positive duties when combined with the other formulations, which introduces the idea of ends which are also duties. It is only if there are specific ends that we have a duty to adopt that the formula of universalizability can be used to specify particular positive duties. See: *Groundwork of the Metaphysics of Morals*; categorical imperative; hypothetical imperative; non-contradiction, principle of; law; humanity, formula of; *Critique of Practical Reason*.

unsocial sociability

The central aim of Kant's works on **history** is to justify the reasonableness of our hope that human history is, or at least could be, progressive. To provide such a justification he tries to show that there are aspects of human nature, understood naturalistically and in purely descriptive terms, that tend to promote the development of civilization and legitimate political institutions. Like Adam Smith (1723–90), who had argued that social progress emerges as the unintended result of the self-interested behaviour of individuals, Kant argues in his *Idea for a Universal History with a Cosmopolitan Aim* (1784) that what he calls the unsocial sociability of human beings tends to promote social progress. On the one hand, human beings are, according to Kant, by nature social beings who need to live together in communities in order to thrive. On the other hand, when we live together with others, we are also competitive.

As a result of these two tendencies, the natural condition of human beings is to live in society but in a state of conflict with one another. It is in our nature to live together, but our social relations are not naturally peaceful and harmonious but full of conflict. And Kant argues that it is this competitive and unsociable element in human nature that is, paradoxically, the driving force of human progress, and which leads to the development of culture, science and political institutions. Thus, for example, in his *Conjectural Beginning of Human History* (1786), Kant argues that war is an indispensable means of driving human history forward. Some support for this claim is provided by the history of the twentieth century if we consider that major technological, cultural and political advances resulted from the two world wars. Kant himself is particularly concerned with the development of legitimate political institutions and how human conflict can result in the slow development of the rule of law. He would have been particularly interested in how the events of World War II led to the creation of the United Nations, the charter of which is strongly influenced by his arguments in *Perpetual Peace* (1785), and by the gradual development of international law.

In appealing to the way in which it is the competitive, antisocial elements in human nature that tend to drive progress, Kant is drawing on the work of Thomas Hobbes (1588–1679), who had argued in his *Leviathan* (1651) that although it is our self-interested nature that leads to conflict and implies that the state of nature (i.e. a condition in which there were no political institutions) would be a state of war, the same element that leads to conflict also produces the solution to this conflict, which is the development of political institutions and the rule of law. Kant agrees that those features of human nature that push us into conflict and wars, also push us towards creating institutions that could, and hopefully will, guarantee a lasting, perpetual peace. See: *Idea for a Universal History*; history; *Perpetual Peace*.

utilitarianism

Utilitarianism is a form of **consequentialism**. Utilitarians, such as Jeremy Bentham (1748–1832) and John Stuart Mill (1806–73), argue that the moral worth of an action is determined by its consequences: a good action is one that maximizes the total amount of happiness in society. Although classical utilitarianism was developed after Kant's death, the utilitarians were influenced by the thought of Epicurus (341–270 BC), and Kant's criticisms of **epicureanism** are often relevant for understanding his attitude towards utilitarianism. See: **consequentialism; happiness.**

virtue, duties of

Kant's most sustained discussion of the duties of virtue is to be found in the *Metaphysics of Morals* (1797), although the notion of virtue is at the heart of his ethical system, for although he is often regarded as an ethicist who is concerned principally with the rightness of actions and downplays the notion of virtue, Kant's ethics is actually primarily concerned with the character of agents. He believes that a virtuous agent is one who cultivates their virtues. Duties of virtue, unlike duties of right, do not primarily have to do with our external actions but with our motivation, and as such they cannot be externally coerced by the state. Kant argues that duties of virtue involve ends that are duties. As such, duties of virtue are what Kant calls wide or **imperfect duties**, for they do not require or forbid particular actions, but merely require that we adopt certain ends. And he argues that virtue demands that we promote two particular ends: our own **perfection** and the **happiness** of others. Although morality requires that we promote these two ends, it does not specify when or how we are to promote these, and so it is up to us to freely decide individually how to promote these ends.

Kant divides duties of virtue into two main classes: duties towards ourselves and duties towards others. Our primary duty towards ourselves is to seek our own perfection, which involves developing our natural talents and moral capacities. Our principal duty towards others is what Kant calls practical love, which has as its end or goal the happiness of others. And he names the duty to promote the happiness of others beneficence, but he also argues that in order to do this effectively we need to cultivate certain feelings, such as the **feeling** of **sympathy**. See: **duty; feelings;** *Metaphysics of Morals.*

What does it Mean to Orient Oneself in Thinking? (1786)

This short piece was Kant's contribution to the so-called **pantheism controversy**, sparked by the publication in 1785 of the correspondence between **Friedrich Heinrich Jacobi** (1743–1819) and **Moses Mendelssohn** (1729–86) concerning the alleged Spinozism of their mutual friend Gotthold Ephraim Lessing (1729–81). Jacobi defended a type of fideism that rejected the authority of reason in matters of faith and that Mendelssohn regarded as a form of irrationalism and **enthusiasm**. Both Jacobi and Mendelssohn hoped that Kant would join the debate on their side. In the essay Kant rejects what he takes to be Jacobi's irrationalism and denies the possibility of an immediate intuition of the divine, the sort of intuition that mystics often seem to presume is possible, and urges Jacobi and his followers to not abandon reason. See: **Jacobi, Mendelssohn; Spinoza; pantheism controversy.**

What is Enlightenment? (1784)

This short and extremely influential text was Kant's contribution to an ongoing debate among German intellectuals about the nature of and prospects for enlightenment. In this essay, Kant famously defines enlightenment as a human being's emergence from self-incurred minority, with minority being the legal state of a child. Lack of enlightenment, then, is an inability to make use of one's own understanding, and to rely on others' doing one's thinking, and deciding, for you. To be enlightened, by contrast, involves thinking for oneself, and so the process of enlightenment is like the emergence from a form of childhood to adulthood and maturity. Although Kant begins the essay by discussing individual enlightenment, he is primarily interested in what is necessary for a society to become enlightened.

The eighteenth-century enlightenment had advocated a form of top-down social progress, according to which the uneducated masses were not yet capable of thinking for themselves, and so the transformation of society required the establishment of a small, enlightened elite who could think for, and perhaps slowly educate, the public. Such thinkers implicitly advocated a form of paternalism, regarding the great mass of people as children who were not capable of thinking for themselves, and thought of the role of the enlightened elite as analogous to that of wise parents. Kant, influenced by his reading of Jean-Jacques **Rousseau** (1712–78), which he claimed had convinced him of the moral capacities of common people, rejects this paternalistic conception of enlightenment arguing that waiting until the public are ready for enlightenment will result in them never becoming enlightened. Such a situation is like that of parents who wait until their children become adults before they start treating them like adults. Such children are likely to remain immature, because we learn to become adults when we are treated like adults and are given adult responsibilities. Kant argues that the only way that a society can become enlightened is when people are given freedom in the **public use** of their reason, for if they are given such freedom, they will naturally come to enlighten themselves. In the course of this discussion Kant makes a distinction between what he calls the public and **private use of one's reason**. His point here is quite simple, but because he uses these terms in a way that is different from our contemporary usage, it is liable to be misunderstood. The public use of our reason is our ability to communicate as a member of the public to (all) other members of the public, as for example in writing a scholarly paper. And Kant argues that enlightenment requires that such communication should be free and not subject to state control or interference. But not all speech to a large group of people counts as the public use of one's reason. For example, one might speak as a representative of a particular group or as a holder of a particular office. In such situations one is not making public use of one's reason, but what Kant calls private use of one's reason, and Kant argues that such speech can legitimately be subject to state control. Kant's point here is that if an individual is speaking *as*, say, a priest or as a member of the government, then he has an obligation to express the doctrine of the church or of the government. The same individual, however, perhaps writing an article for an academic journal *as* a scholar, has a right to criticize the doctrines of the church or the government. If his disagreement with the church or government is so strong that he cannot honestly defend or teach their doctrines, then he should resign his office. Insofar as he is speaking as an officeholder, he has an obligation to not contradict the official doctrine, and if he is speaking as a state officeholder, as were pastors in eighteenth-century Prussia, the state has the right to regulate his speech. See: **public use of reason; private use of reason; Rousseau; history.**

Wolff, Christian (1679–1754)

Wolff, who was a follower of Gottfried Wilhelm **Leibniz** (1646–1716), was probably the most important German philosopher of the eighteenth century prior to Kant. He was an extreme **rationalist** who attempted to systematize the philosophy of Leibniz and was one of the first philosophers to write in German and so had an important role in the development of philosophical German.

In his theoretical philosophy he was an extreme rationalist, believing that pure reason, guided by the principles of **logic**, was the source of metaphysical knowledge. He divided **metaphysics** into general metaphysics, or ontology, which examined principles that apply to all types of beings, such as the principle of sufficient reason, and special metaphysics, which dealt with our *a priori* knowledge of particular objects or types of object. Special metaphysics was divided into three special sciences: rational psychology, which dealt with our *a priori* knowledge of the soul; rational cosmology, which dealt with our *a priori* knowledge of the world; and rational theology, which dealt with our *a priori* knowledge of **God**. One of his most controversial claims in ontology, which was rejected by Kant, was that the metaphysical principle of **sufficient reason,** which claims that everything that exists must have a reason or cause, could be derived from the logical principle of **non-contradiction.** Although Kant rejects the possibility of rationalist metaphysics, for he thinks that pure logic can only provide us with a criterion of thinkability, not real **possibility,** the structure of the *Critique of Pure Reason* (1781/1787) is based upon Wolff's division of metaphysics into these four sciences. Wolff's commitment to the principle of sufficient reason led him to endorse a strong form of determinism that his **Pietist** enemies claimed implied a rejection of human free will and moral responsibility, and these attacks led, in 1723, to his removal from his post of professor at the University of Halle. In terms of his ethics Wolff was a perfectionist and an intellectualist. As a perfectionist, he thought that the good was to be understood in terms of perfection, and so thought that the principle of morality was to seek perfection. As an intellectualist, he thought that every individual desired what they believed was good, and so he thought that immoral behaviour was always the result of false beliefs as to what was truly good. As a result of this, he believed that the role of the moral philosopher was to acquire knowledge of what was truly good, which could then be communicated to the common people. Kant rejected both perfectionism and intellectualism. He agreed that morality involves striving for perfection, but he thought that Wolff's account of what constituted perfection was empty and purely formal, and would suggest that a serial killer should strive to be a perfect serial killer. Kant rejected intellectualism as he thought that the common human understanding had adequate knowledge of what was good, and immorality was not a matter of lack of knowledge but of choosing to subordinate the demands of morality to self-interest. See: **Baumgarten; metaphysics; perfectionism; sufficient reason, principle of; non-contradiction, principle of; rationalists.**

world, noumenal

The word 'noumenal' is the adjectival form of the noun 'noumenon' which is derived from the Greek word 'nous' which is normally translated as 'intellect'; a noumenal individual then is one that can be known only by the intellect not the senses. A noumenal individual then is an intelligible individual, and Kant often uses the expressions 'noumenal world' and 'intelligible world' interchangeably. Kant often contrasts the noumenal world with the phenomenal world. The noumenal world is the idea of a community of individuals that are not in space and time. The idea of such a noumenal individual is **problematic**. We can have the idea of a being that is not in space and time, such as **God** or an angel is thinkable as there is no contradiction involved in the idea of such a being. However, as we can only experience beings that exist in space and time we have no way of knowing whether individuals corresponding to such ideas do actually exist. Now, although Kant thinks that we have no theoretical justification for believing in the existence of such noumenal individual, he thinks that from the practical, moral perspective we are committed to the existence of such individuals. For insofar as we believe in the possibility of morality, we have to regard ourselves and others as free, and Kant thinks that anything that can exist in space and time must be determined and so cannot be free. And so the idea of a community of free individuals, or what Kant calls in his moral writings the idea of a **realm of ends**, is an intelligible idea, the idea of an intelligible world. Even though such a world cannot be a possible object of **cognition**, morality demands that we strive to be a member of such an intelligible world. See: world, phenomenal; intelligible; metaphysics; thing-in-itself.

world, phenomenal

The word 'phenomenal' derives from the Greek and literally means that which appears or can be seen. A phenomenal object, then, for Kant is an object of possible experience. Now, Kant thinks there are two basic species of experience, which he calls **inner sense** and **outer sense**. Through outer sense we experience physical objects in space-time, and through inner sense we experience our own states. Thus for Kant both physical objects in space and time, and our own inner states, insofar as they are possible objects of experience, are phenomenal. Thus, although the phenomenal world is the world as it appears to us, we should not confuse Kant's account of the phenomenal with Berkeley's idealism. The relationship between phenomena and things as they are in themselves is a major topic of disagreement between Kant scholars. Some interpreters, who defend what is known as a two-world interpretation, think that the distinction between the world of phenomena and things as they are in themselves is a distinction between two types of objects, with things-in-themselves being the cause of appearances. Other commentators, defending what is known as a two-aspect interpretation, argue that the distinction between phenomena and things-in-themselves is a distinction between two aspects of the world. According to this interpretation, there is only one world or set of objects, but there are two ways of regarding this one world. The distinction is not between two sets of objects, but between different ways of thinking about objects. The phenomenal concept of an object includes reference to the necessary conditions of experience, and so is the concept of a spatio-temporal object, whereas the concept of an object as a thing-in-itself abstracts from all human cognitive capacities and limitations. And, because Kant thinks that space and time are our form of intuition, the concept of a thing-in-itself is the concept of a thing insofar as it is not considered in spatio-temporal terms. See: **world, noumenal; Refutation of Idealism; appearances; inner sense; outer sense**

BIBLIOGRAPHY

Published works by Kant referred to in the dictionary

Physical Monadology (1756) in Immanuel Kant, *Theoretical Philosophy: 1755-1770*, translated and edited by David Walford, in collaboration with Ralf Meerbote, Cambridge University Press, 1992.

Dreams of a Spirit-Seer Elucidated by Dreams of Metaphysics (1766) in Immanuel Kant, *Theoretical Philosophy: 1755-1770*, translated and edited by David Walford, in collaboration with Ralf Meerbote, Cambridge University Press, 1992.

Inaugural Dissertation (1770) in Immanuel Kant, *Theoretical Philosophy: 1755-1770*, translated and edited by David Walford, in collaboration with Ralf Meerbote, Cambridge University Press, 1992.

Critique of Pure Reason (1781/1787), translated and edited by Paul Guyer and Allen W. Wood, Cambridge Unviersity Press, 1998.

Prolegomena to Any Future Metaphysics (1783) in Immanuel Kant, *Theoretical Philosophy after 1781*, edited by Henry Allison and Peter Heath, Cambridge University Press, 2002.

Idea for a Universal History with a Cosmopolitan Aim (1784) in Immanuel Kant, *Anthropology, History, and Education*, edited by Günter Zöller and Robert B. Louden, Cambridge University Press, 2007.

An Answer to the Question: 'What is Enlightenment? (1784) in Immanuel Kant, *Practical Philosophy*, translated and edited by Mary J. Gregor, Cambridge University Press, 1996.

Groundwork of the Metaphysics of Morals (1785) in Immanuel Kant, *Practical Philosophy*, translated and edited by Mary J. Gregor, Cambridge University Press, 1996.

Conjectural Beginning of Human History (1786) in Immanuel Kant, *Anthropology, History, and Education*, edited by Günter Zöller and Robert B. Louden, Cambridge University Press, 2007.

Metaphysical Foundations of Natural Science (1786) in Immanuel Kant, *Theoretical Philosophy after 1781*, edited by Henry Allison and Peter Heath, Cambridge University Press, 2002.

What Does it Mean to Orient oneself in Thinking? (1786) in Immanuel
   Kant, *Religion and Rational Theology*, edited by Allen W. Wood,
   Cambridge University Press, 1996.
Critique of Practical Reason (1788) in Immanuel Kant, *Practical
   Philosophy*, translated and edited by Mary J. Gregor, Cambridge
   University Press, 1996.
Critique of the Power of Judgment (1790), edited by Paul Guyer and
   translated by Paul Guyer and Eric Matthews, Cambridge University
   Press, 2000.
Religion within the Boundaries of Mere Reason (1792) in Immanuel
   Kant, *Religion and Rational Theology*, edited by Allen W. Wood,
   Cambridge University Press, 1996.
Toward Perpetual Peace (1795) in Immanuel Kant, *Practical Philosophy*,
   translated and edited by Mary J. Gregor, Cambridge University
   Press, 1996.
Metaphysis of Morals (1797) in Immanuel Kant, *Practical Philosophy*,
   translated and edited by Mary J. Gregor, Cambridge University
   Press, 1996.
Anthropology from a Pragmatic Point of View (1798) in Immanuel Kant,
   Anthropology, History, and Education, edited by Günter Zöller
   and Robert B. Louden, Cambridge University Press, 2007.

Unpublished works by Kant referred to in the dictionary

Immanuel Kant, *Correspondence*, translated and edited by Arnulf Zweig,
   Cambridge University Press, 1999.
—, *Lectures on Anthropology*, edited by Allen W. Wood and Robert B.
   Louden, translated by Robert R. Clewis, Robert B. Louden, G. Felicitas
   Munzel and Allen W. Wood, Cambridge University Press, 2012.
—, *Lectures on Ethics*, edited by Peter Heath and J. B. Schneewind,
   translated by Peter Heath, Cambridge University Press, 1997.
—, *Lectures on Logic*, edited and translated by J. Michael Young,
   Cambridge University Press, 1992.
—, *Lectures on Metaphysics*, translated and edited by Karl Ameriks and
   Steve Naragon, Cambridge University Press, 1997.
—, *Notes and Fragments*, edited by Paul Guyer, translated by Curtis Bowman,
   Paul Guyer and Fredrick Rauscher, Cambridge University Press, 2005.
—, *Opus Postumum*, edited by Eckart Förster, translated by Eckart
   Förster and Michael Rosen, Cambridge University Press, 1993.

Books about Kant

General

Introductory:

Guyer, Paul. *Kant*, Routledge, 2006.
—. *The Cambridge Companion to Kant*, Cambridge University Press, 1992.
Seung, T. K., *Kant: A Guide for the Perplexed*, Continuum, 2007.
Ward, Andrew. *Starting with Kant*, Continuum, 2012.
Wood, Allen W. *Kant*, Blackwell, 2005.

More advanced:

Allison, Henry E. *Essays on Kant*, Oxford University Press, 2012.
—. *Idealism and Freedom: Essays on Kant's Theoretical and Practical Philosophy*, Cambridge University Press, 1996.
Ameriks, Karl. *Interpreting Kant's Critiques*, Oxford University Press, 2003.
Banham, Gary and Schulting, Dennis (eds). *The Continuum Companion to Kant*, Continuum, 2012.
Guyer, Paul (ed.). *The Cambridge Companion to Kant and Modern Philosophy*, Cambridge University Press, 2006.

Theoretical Philosophy, including the Critique of Pure Reason

Introductory:

Buroker, Jill Vance. *Kant's Critique of Pure Reason: An Introduction*, Cambridge University Press, 2006.
Gardner, Sebastian. *Routledge Philosophy Guidebook to Kant and the Critique of Pure Reason*, Routledge, 1999.
Guyer, Paul (ed.). *The Cambridge Companion to Kant's Critique of Pure Reason*, Cambridge University Press, 2010.
Rosenberg, Jay F. *Accessing Kant: A Relaxed Introduction to the Critique of Pure Reason*, Oxford University Press, 2005.

More advanced:

Allison, Henry E. *Kant's Transcendental Idealism: an Interpretation and Defence*, 2nd edn, Yale University Press, 2004.

Ameriks, Karl. *Kant's Elliptical Path*, Clarendon Press, 2012.

—. *Kant's Theory of Mind: An Analysis of the Paralogisms of Pure Reason*, Oxford University Press, 2000.

Guyer, Paul. *Kant and the Claims of Knowledge*, Cambridge University Press, 1987.

Hanna, Robert. *Kant and the Foundations of Analytic Philosophy*, Oxford University Press, 2001.

Kitcher, Patricia. *Kant's Thinker*, Oxford University Press, 2011.

—. *Kant's Transcendental Psychology*, Oxford University Press, 1994.

Langton, Rae. *Kantian Humility: Our Ignorance of Things in Themselves*, Oxford University Press, 1998.

Longuenesse, Beatrice. *Kant and the Capacity to Judge*, Princeton University Press, 1998.

Schulting, Dennis and Verburgt, Jacco (eds). *Kant's Idealism: New Interpretations of a Controversial Doctrine*, Springer, 2010.

Van Cleve, James. *Problems From Kant*, Oxford University Press, 1999.

Watkins, Eric. *Kant and the Metaphysics of Causality*, Cambridge University Press, 2005.

Westphal, Kenneth R. *Kant's Transcendental Proof of Realism*, Cambridge University Press, 2004.

Ethics

Introductory:

Allison, Henry E. *Kant's Groundwork for the Metaphysics of Morals: A Commentary*, Oxford University Press, 2011.

Guyer, Paul. *Kant's Groundwork for the Metaphysics of Morals: A Reader's Guide*, Continuum, 2007.

Reath, Andrews and Timmermann, Jens (eds). *Kant's Critique of Practical Reason: A Critical Guide*, Cambridge University Press, 2010.

Sedgwick, Sally S. *Kant's Groundwork of the Metaphysics of Morals: An Introduction*, Cambridge University Press, 2008.

Timmermann, Jens (ed.). *Kant's Groundwork of the Metaphysics of Morals: A Critical Guide*, Cambridge University Press, 2009.

—. *Kants' Groundwork of the Metaphysics of Morals: A Commentary*, Cambridge University Press, 2007.

Uleman, Jennifer K. *An Introduction to Kant's Moral Philosophy*, Cambridge University Press, 2010.

More advanced:

Guyer, Paul. *Kant and the Experience of Freedom: Essays on Aesthetics and Morality*, Cambridge University Press, 1993.

—. *Kant on Freedom, Law, and Happiness*, Cambridge University Press, 2000.

Herman, Barbara. *The Practice of Moral Judgment*, Harvard University Press, 1996.

Korsgaard, Christine M. *Creating the Kingdom of Ends*, Cambridge University Press, 1996.

O'Neill, Onora. *Constructions of Reason: Explorations of Kant's Practical Philosophy*, Cambridge University Press, 1989.

Rawls, John. *Lectures on the History of Moral Philosophy*, Harvard University Press, 2000.

Wood, Allen W. *Kantian Ethics*, Cambridge University Press, 2008.

—. *Kant's Ethical Thought*, Cambridge University Press, 1999.

Political Philosophy

Byrd, B. Sharon and Hruschka, Joachim. *Kant's Doctrine of Right: A Commentary*, Cambridge University Press, 2010.

Ellis, Elisabeth (ed.). *Kant's Political Theory: Interpretations and Applications*, Pennsylvania State University Press, 2012.

Ripstein, Arthur. *Force and Freedom: Kant's Legal and Political Philosophy*, Harvard University Press, 2009.

Williams, Howard. *Kant and the End of War: A Critique of Just War Theory*, Palgrave Macmillan, 2012.

—. *Kant's Political Philosophy*, St. Martin's Press, 1983.

Williams, Howard, Baiasu, Sorin and Pihlstrom, Sami (eds). *Politics and Metaphysics in Kant*, Political Philosophy Now, University of Wales Press, 2011.

Aesthetics, Anthropology, History and Biology

Introductory:

Hughes, Fiona. *Kant's Critique of Judgment: A Reader's Guide*, Continuum, 2009.

More advanced:

Allison, Henry E. *Kant's Theory of Taste: A Reading of the Critique of Aesthetic Judgment*, Cambridge University Press, 2001.

Cohen, Alix. *Kant and the Human Sciences: Biology, Anthropology and History*, Palgrave Macmillan, 2009.

Guyer, Paul. *Kant and the Claims of Taste*, 2nd edn, Cambridge University Press, 1997.

—. *Kant and the Experience of Freedom: Essays on Aesthetics and Morality*, Cambridge University Press, 1993.

—. *Values of Beauty: Historical Essays in Aesthetics*, Cambridge University Press, 2005.

Louden, Robert B. *Kant's Human Being: Essays on His Theory of Human Nature*, Oxford University Press, 2011.

—. *Kant's Impure Ethics: From Rational Beings to Human Beings*, Oxford University Press, 2000.

Wicks, Robert. *Routledge Philosophy Guidebook to Kant on Judgment*, Routledge, 2007.

Zuckert, Rachel. *Kant on Beauty and Biology: An Interpretation of the Critique of Judgment*, Cambridge University Press, 2007.

INDEX